NEW 895

246-2115

94 hikes

IN THE CANADIAN ROCKIES
Yoho, Jasper, Mt. Robson and Willmore Wilderness Parks

Text by Dee Urbick
Photos by Vicky Spring
Maps by Helen Sherman

The Mountaineers • Seattle

Mt. Robson from viewpoint on Toboggan Falls Trail (Hike 83).

THE MOUNTAINEERS: Organized in 1906
"...to explore, study, preserve and enjoy the natural beauty of the Northwest."

© 1983 by Dee Urbick and Vicky Spring
All rights reserved

Published by The Mountaineers
715 Pike Street, Seattle, Washington 98101

Published simultaneously in Canada by Douglas & McIntyre, Ltd.
1615 Venables Street, Vancouver, British Columbia V5L 2H1

Printed in United States of America

Cover photo: *Terminal lake at toe of Angel Glacier, base of Mt. Edith Cavell (Hike 44).*

Photo on page 205 courtesy of the Park Service

Book layout by Tom Kirkendall
Book series design by Marge Mueller
Maps by Helen Sherman

Library of Congress Cataloging in Publication Data
Urbick, Dee.
  94 hikes in the Canadian Rockies.
  "Only the parks in the northern regions of the Divide are covered in this volume; southern parks are described in a companion book, 95 hikes in the Canadian Rockies"--Introd.
  Includes index.
  1. Hiking--Canadian Rockies (B.C. and Alta.)--Guide-books. 2. Canadian Rockies (B.C. and Alta.)--Description and travel--Guide-books. I. Spring, Vicky, 1953- . II. Title. III. Title: Ninety-four hikes in the Canadian Rockies.

GV199.44.C2U73 1983   917.11'044   82-24667
ISBN 0-89886-056-3 (pbk.)

CONTENTS

INTRODUCTION 9

YOHO NATIONAL PARK 18

1. Wapta Falls 20
2. Mt. Hunter Lookout 22
3. The Hoodoos 24
4. Ice River Trail 26
5. Ottertail River 28
6. Emerald River Trail 30
7. Otterhead River Trail 32
8. Amiskwi River Trail 34
9. Hamilton Lake 36
10. Emerald Lake Shoreline Loop .. 38
11. Emerald Lake—High Circuit ... 40
12. Emerald Basin Trail 42
13. Burgess Pass Trail 44
14. Yoho Lake Loop 46
15. Glacier View Loop 48
16. Presidential High Route 50
17. Paget Lookout 52
18. Sherbrooke Lake 54
19. Cataract Brook 56
20. Linda Lake Loop 58
21. Lake McArthur Circuit 60
22. McArthur Creek 62
23. Odaray/Grand View Prospect ... 64
24. Lake Oesa 66
25. Opabin Lake 68
26. Ross Lake 70

JASPER NATIONAL PARK 72

27. Nigel Pass 74
28. Wilcox Pass 76
29. Beauty Creek 78
30. Poboktan Creek Trail 80
31. Poboktan Pass Trail 82
32. Brazeau River Trail 84
33. Jonas Pass Trail 86
34. Maligne Pass Trail 88
35. Lower Sunwapta Falls 92
36. Fortress Lake Trail 94
37. Wabasso Lake 96
38. Valley of the Five Lakes 98
39. Wabasso Lake to
    Big Shovel Pass 100
40. Fryatt Creek 102

41. Geraldine Lakes 104
42. Geraldine Lookout 106
43. Athabasca Pass 108
44. Angel Glacier 110
45. Tonquin Valley via Astoria River 112
46. Tonquin Valley via
    Maccarib Pass 114
47. Outpost Lake 116
48. Moat Lake 118
49. The Whistlers 120
50. Sulphur Skyline Trail 122
51. Mystery Lake 124
52. Fiddle River 126
53. Merlin Creek 128
54. Overlander Trail 130
55. Devona Lookout 132
56. North Boundary Trail 134
57. Moosehorn Creek Trail 138
58. Vine Creek 140
59. Signal Mountain Lookout 142
60. Maligne Canyon 144
61. Watchtower Basin 146
62. Jacques Lake 148
63. South Boundary Trail 150
64. Maligne Lake Shoreline Trail .. 154
65. Opal Hills Loop 156
66. Skyline Trail 158
67. Bald Hills Lookout 162
68. Moose Lake 164
69. Marjorie and Caledonia Lakes . 166
70. Saturday Night Lake Loop 168
71. Mina and Riley Lakes Loop ... 170
72. Patricia Lake Trail 172
73. Pyramid Lake Trails 174
74. Palisade Lookout 176
75. Old Fort Point 178
76. Virl, Dorothy and
    Christine Lakes 180
77. Miette River Trail 182

MT. ROBSON PROVINCIAL PARK 184

78. Mt. Fitzwilliam Trail 186
79. Yellowhead Mountain Trail ... 188
80. Moose River 190
81. Overlander Falls 192
82. Berg Lake 194

83. Toboggan Falls 196	89. Eagles Nest Pass 210
84. Snowbird Pass 198	90. Indian Trail 212
	91. Berland Trail 214
WILLMORE WILDERNESS	92. Persimmon Creek Trail 216
PROVINCIAL PARK 200	93. Adams Creek Trail 218
	94. Adams Lookout 220
85. Wildhay River Trail 202	
86. Willow Creek Trail 204	
87. Rock Lake Lookout 206	
88. Pope-Thoreau Trail 208	**INDEX** 222

Mt. Lefroy and Lake O'Hara from Odaray Prospect, Hike 23

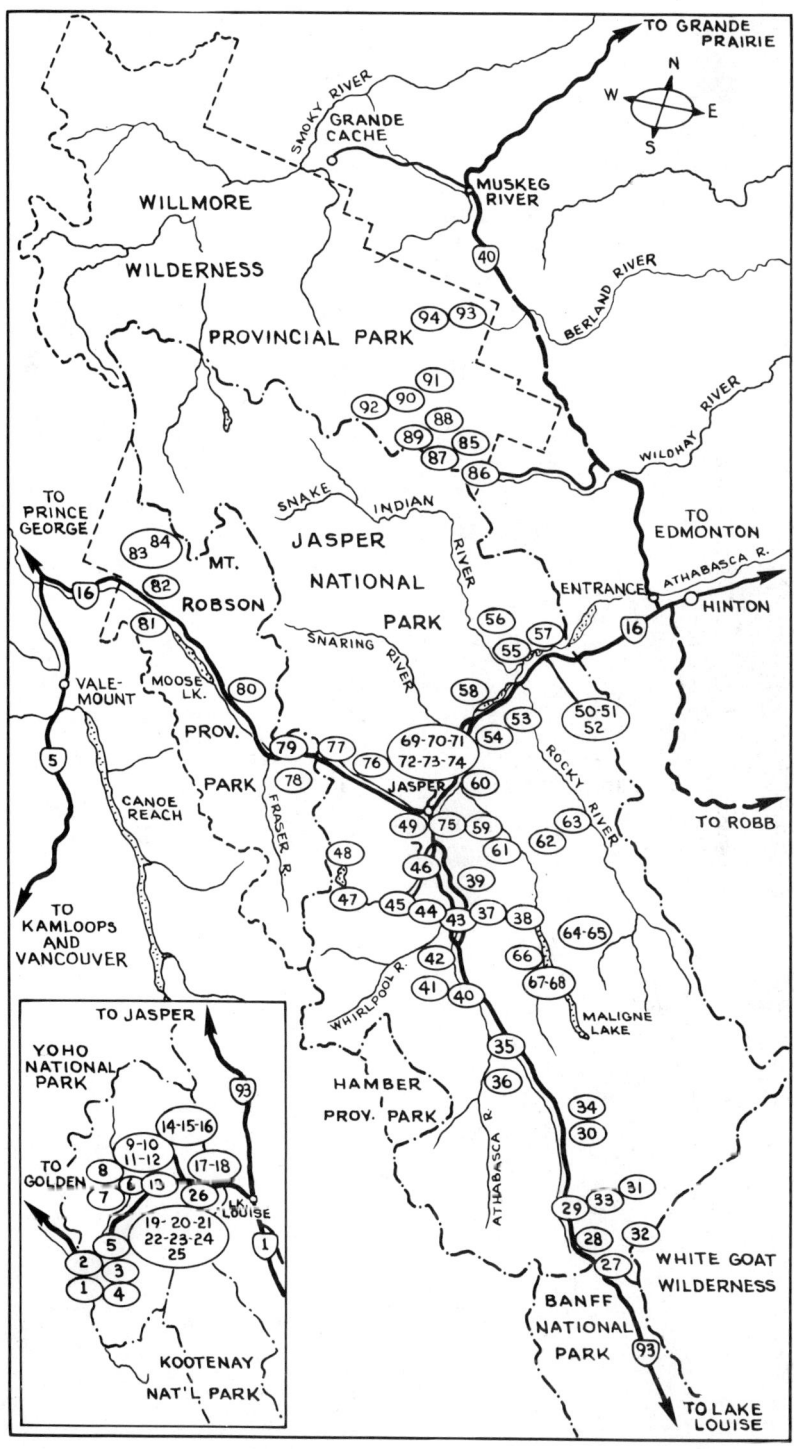

INTRODUCTION

Born of the oceans and fashioned by the forces of glaciers, weather and time, the Canadian Rockies are nothing short of awesome. Here are the highest of Canada's Rockies, towering above verdant valleys and leaning their reflections into icy lakes, their flanks a tapestry of forest and meadow. Here are unrestrained rivers and immense falls, a full range of life zones with abundant wildlife and huge glacial fingers that stretch down from rocky heights and windswept passes.

Those enticed by long backpacks into wild, unspoiled territory will find seldom visited regions to explore for days or weeks at a time. There are also shorter, gentler trails to viewpoints of glaciers, waterfalls and wide, rolling valleys. Possibilities extend even into winter when ski-touring enthusiasts make thier way into the otherwise impenetrable valleys. Indeed, there are trails to fit most expectations, as well as campsites ranging from fully equipped, roadside campgrounds to remote and primitive backpacker sites.

Well-maintained campsites are located in most of the major hiking areas, though they reach capacity long before all visitors can be accommodated. As have many other parks in the Canadian mountains, Jasper and Yoho parks have adopted a permit-quota system to regulate numbers of people in an area. Park use permits and quota information are available at information centres in Jasper townsite and the Icefields Centre, in Yoho, at the information centre at the west entrance to the park and in Field. For those planning cross-country or climbing excursions, it is advisable to register plans with the Warden Service. Be sure to advise them when you return as well, to prevent the initiation of a search. Permits or quotas have not been established in Mt. Robson or Willmore Wilderness Park. However, you might wish to check with the Robson Ranger Service for availability of campsites in the area you plan to visit.

The regions described in this book border the Continental Divide: Mt. Robson Provicial Park and Yoho National Park on the west, Jasper National Park and Willmore Wilderness Provincial Park on the east. They encompass a fair range of climate, weather and landscape. Differences are dramatized as one goes from the lush, western rainforest-like environments of Mt Robson to the dier, lodgepole forests and rain shadow locations on the eastern Divide. Only the parks in the northern regions of the Divide are covered in this volume; southern parks are described in a companion book, *95 Hikes in the Canadian Rockies—Banff, Kootenay and Assiniboine Parks.*

We feel we have captured a representative sample of the joys, challenges and special characteristics of the Canadian Rockies in the trails we have chosen for this book. As vast and complex as the Rockies are, the choices did not come easily, though hiking the trails and exploring the parks was certainly a delight.

Left: *Wapta Falls, Hike 1.* Below: *Bighorn sheep*

Maps

Topographic maps of the parks are useful both for navigation and for identifying natural features. They should be carried by anyone planning extensive backpacks or cross-country routes. The appropriate maps for trails in this guidebook are listed in the heading block of each trail description. In most cases, maps are available at convenient locations within the parks, such as visitor information centres and park headquarters, and from authorized map dealers in towns, including Jasper and Field.

For Willmore Wilderness Park, whose managing agency is the Alberta Forest Service, distribution offices are not always convenient to park access points and you may want to order maps in advance through the mail. Order topographic maps of all Canada's Rocky Mountain parks through the Canada Map Office. Write first for ordering information and a current price list:

Canada Map Office
615 Booth Street
Ottawa, Ontario K1A 0E9

In addition to the geographic survey maps that most dealers and parks carry, single-sheet maps of the parks and convenient hiker maps of specific areas are also available at the park offices.

For Mt. Robson Park a contoured map (scale 1:125,000) of the park is available for a nominal fee at Park Headquarters or the Visitor Centre. Or order it in advance from:

Map and Air Photo Sales
Ministry of Environment
Parliament Buildings
Victoria, British Columbia V8V 117

Marmot sunbathing at Lake Oesa, Hike 24

Tonquin Valley, Hikes 45 and 46

Clothing and Equipment

For anything more than a short nature hike or casual stroll, hikers in the Rocky Mountain parks should be equipped for sudden and drastic changes in the weather. Mountain weather can be deceiving: A warm, sunny morning may give no hint of a midday squall that can quickly drench an unsuspecting party. Trails that gain and lose elevation as they wind through the mountains will involve corresponding changes in temperature and precipitation. No matter how sunny the skies, a warm set of clothing should always be carried. Include a wool shirt or sweater, long wool pants, and a wind-and-rain-proof parka, coat or poncho.

For rough, rocky or wet terrain, long epic journeys or cross-country routes, sturdy lug-soled boots are usually the accepted footgear. However, tennis shoes or soft-soled, lightweight boots will often suffice for most of the shorter, well-graded trails and nature hikes, and they are much kinder to sensitive terrain. Many seasoned mountaineers carry them no matter what the route, for wearing in camp and on certain portions of the trails. They are certainly less wearying than stiff and heavy hiking boots, on long, fire road trails.

Finally, don't venture far down the trail without these minimum "Ten Essentials" in your rucksack.

1. Extra clothing—enough to spend a night out; keep it dry
2. Extra food—more than you need for your trip
3. Knife—for first aid uses and making kindling for emergency fires
4. First aid kit
5. Sunglasses—necessary on most alpine routes, and essential on snow
6. Firestarter—a candle or chemical fuel for starting fires with wet wood
7. Matches—in a waterproof container
8. Flashlight—include extra bulb and batteries
9. Map—of the area you're travelling in
10. Compass—know how to use it!

Bunchberry

Walk Softly and Carry a Garbage Bag

Hikers and backpackers, skiers and climbers—it's time to make a commitment! In the face of shrinking budgets and ever-increasing visitor numbers, the quality and integrity of parklands are more than ever in the hands of the users. So let's make that extra effort to minimize all impacts. Strive to leave no sign of where you walk or camp.

Soft soils and fragile meadows are easily disturbed, so stay on the established trails whenever possible. If you should leave the trails in a sensitive environment, try to step on rocks instead of fragile plants. Carry tennis shoes to wear around camp—they are much kinder to delicate plants and sensitive terrain, not to mention sore feet.

Much enjoyment of wilderness comes from experiencing the land and its ecology in the natural state, so leave wildflowers, edible plants and other elements of the environment in place. Moving them disturbs the natural order and the habitats of wildland residents. The campfire, so beloved in the past, has lost favor among backcountry users who recognize the impact fires can have. Carefully consider the necessity before deciding to burn up components of the environment. Except in emergencies, never build fires in alpine areas. Natural fuels here are scarce and should not be counted on anyway. In lodgepole forests, where trees tend to drop lots of debris each year, the problem of fuels may not be as critical; however, even these can be quickly used up if everyone depends on them. Why not get in the habit of using a stove? Lightweight and inexpensive backpacker models are easy and efficient to operate. They do not require a saw or dry kindling, and some even have built-in flints that eliminate the need for a match! Best of all, they leave no ugly scars of charred rocks, burned logs and bits of unburned garbage that tend to accumulate in and around fire rings.

Garbage can no longer be buried. It disturbs the soil and introduces potential pollutants. Cans, foil, glass and plastics must be carried out. Leftover food should not be buried or cached for other hikers. It's an unnatural and dangerous food source to wildlife. They will dig it up anyway and scatter it around. Leaving it near campsites is an open invitation to a visit from a bear or other wild animal. Candy wrappers and orange peels are an eyesore to the next traveller. If you should forget to include a garbage bag when packing for your trip, pick up one (usually available without charge) at park offices when you stop for your park use permit.

Help protect the water purity. Do not swim or bathe in small lakes used for drinking water. Carry water away from the shore to wash dishes or socks, and use only biodegradable soaps. Better yet, wait until you get home if at all practical. Except for high-use areas, the water sources in Canada's parks are still reasonably pure. But, the consequences of drinking contaminated water far outweigh the extra effort required to boil or otherwise purify it, if its quality is suspect.

Don't neglect sanitation. Where privies or rest rooms are not available, go at least 50 to 75 m from any water source, campsite or trail. Scratch a small hole in the duff (about 6 to 10 cm deep), and then cover the evidence with soil or humus to expedite its decay.

Finally, adopt a low-impact attitude towards other park users. Recall how a noisy or messy camper can detract from your own enjoyment of the parks and try to give others the same consideration you would appreciate. Respect their rights when sharing trails, campsites or shelters.

The hike-light/camp-light doctrine has become the law of the land—an ethic that will determine the future of parks and wilderness areas as places where nature prevails.

Pets

Taking pets into the parks and especially into the backcountry is emphatically discouraged, although, providing they are leashed, they are permitted on these trails. Even the most "well-behaved" pets present a danger and leave an impact. Their very presence is a threat to small, wild creatures and might provoke the curiosity or anger of bears, thereby creating a serious hazard to both pet and owner.

Other hikers who have made the trip to escape the everyday world do not wish to find a wilderness of domesticated animals. Nor do they appreciate finding the mementos pets leave behind. If at all possible, plan to leave your pet at home.

Hoary marmot

The Hoodoos, Hike 3

Horses

The use of horses as pack and saddle animals holds a historically significant spot in the Canadian Rockies. Most way trails and long routes were initially established by and for horses. Consequently, the trails reflect this use in their construction and placement. Not only do trail conditions often differ from hiker expectations, but routes themselves do not always accoos the most convenient or scenic course.

The remarkable influx of foot travellers during this last decade has given rise to the need for hiker-oriented trails. The parks should be commended for their sensitive response to these changes in use patterns. Many trails have been upgraded and horse and hiker routes separated, while other specifically hiker-oriented trails have been developed in new locations. In some of the more fragile alpine environments, horse traffic has been banned altogether.

Horses, however, are likely to remain an integral part of travelling in the Rockies. If you hold a particular objection to sharing the trail with them, consult with the park staff for advice on which trails do not permit horse use.

Early season hikers on the Berg Lake Trail, Hike 82

Bears

The word "bears" often closely follows mention of the Rocky Mountain parks. It's true, the parks have bears; and there have been some unfortunate consequences of hikers' taking their presence too lightly. Recently, park-initiated education progams have made excellent progress in minimizing disastrous visitor/bear encounters, but the danger can never be eliminated as long as we want to preserve the parks as safe and healthy habitats for otherwise dwindling bear populations. One should never assume that these "park" bears are tame. We all have a responsibility to help maintain an attitude of respect for bears.

Some excellent pamphlets and interpretive displays are available at facilities throughout the parks. Take a few minutes to read through these materials. Check at trail information centres for bear-warning notices. Park staff can advise of areas where bears have been feeding or have harassed hikers, and help you choose an alternative route.

Whether you are in the backcountry or at a roadside campground, the same principles apply: If food, garbage and toiletries cannot be locked out of sight in a car, suspend them on a line between 2 trees, at least 3 m off the ground and 2 m from the trees. Do not prepare or keep food in or around your tent. Keep your campsite clean and tidy.

When hiking, don't allow a bear to be surprised by your sudden appearance on the trail. If it hears you coming, the bear is more likely to move off the trail and into the forest. Chat or sing as you walk along, or rattle a bell or a pebble in a can. If you should encounter a bear in the park, give it a wide berth. Never approach or try to feed it. Just move quietly, calmly, away from the area.

Huts and Cabins

A number of huts exist throughout the backcountry and are usually indicated on the park maps. Some are managed by the parks, others are privately owned and operated by clubs. In either case, prior arrangements must be made before arrival at the hut. There is no charge for use of park-managed huts, although reservations are required for overnight stays, and visitors are expected to maintain the firewood supply and cleanliness of the facility. Further information on specific huts can be acquired from the park information services when you pick up a park use permit.

Privately owned huts can usually be rented for a fee. Contact the Alpine Club of Canada (ACC) or the park information centres for additional information.

Warden's cabins are also located throughout the parks. However, they are intended for park staff use and are not available for visitor accommodations. Do not plan to stay in a warden's cabin.

Conversions

Since most distances and elevations in this book, as well as signs within the parks, are given in metric form, here's how to make the conversion:

kilometres x 0.621 = miles
metres x 3.281 = feet

Acknowledgements

It would be impossible to name all of the people who played a role in the gathering and sifting of material that went into this book. We are grateful to both park visitors and park staff who provided us with valuable insights and information. Specifically, we'd like to mention those who lent a hand on some perhaps less glamorous and often tedious, but very critical, aspects of producing the finished book. To Gordon King, Spencer Garrett and Jerry Baillie—our sincere thanks.

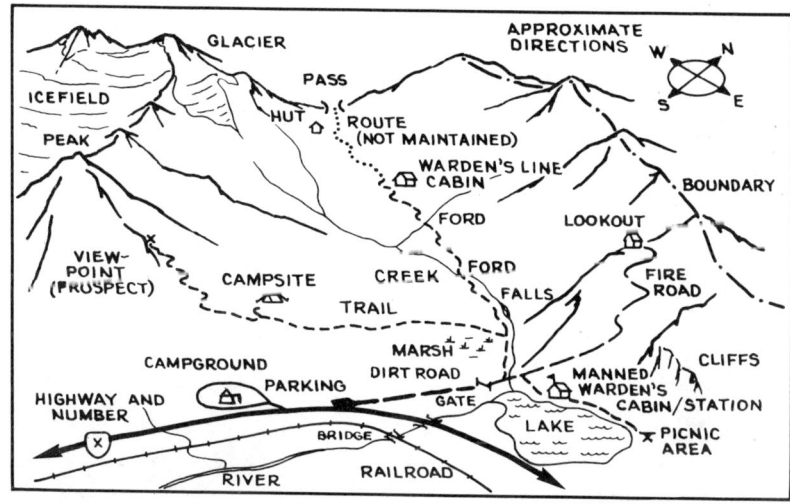

YOHO NATIONAL PARK

Yoho Park, though only about one-eighth the size of Jasper, experiences a very high visitor rate. Within its 1313 square kilometres of rugged high-country are intricate networks of hiker trails that penetrate nearly every river valley and connect through numerous alpine passes. As in Jasper Park, the potential here for extended trips is remarkable, though most visitor and hiker activity is centered around 2 major and particularly dramatic locations: the Yoho Valley near the President Range and the Lake O'Hara region near the Bow Range. Both are spectacular regions and draw large numbers of hikers each year. Between these 2 areas lies the Emerald Lake region—a magnificent and less remote centre of hiker activity.

The park staff at Yoho is faced with the difficult task of protecting a beautiful and fragile resource from exceptionally large numbers of admiring, if sometime unaware, visitors. This task is made more difficult by the concentration of hikers in a few compact and particularly sensitive alpine regions. Through their program of visitor education and backcountry use monitoring, much unnecessary and perhaps irreparable damage will be avoided. Park use permits are required for overnight trips into the backcountry and are available through information centres in Field and near the west entrance. Due to the high visitor count, backcountry sites tend to fill up fast in peak season, and it's strongly recommended that visitors write or phone ahead for reservations and trip planning information. Call (604) 343-6324 or write c/o Chief, Visitor Services, Yoho National Park, Box 99, Field, British Columbia, V0A 1G0.

Left: *Twin Falls*
Above: *Clark's nutcracker*

YOHO

1 Wapta Falls

Distance: 4 km/2.5 mi round trip
Hiking time: 1.5 hours
Elevation loss: 30 m/100 ft
High point: 1120 m/3674 ft
Type: short hike/nature walk
Best time: May through September
Map: McMurdo 82 N/2

Witness the usually placid Kicking Horse River being transformed as it leaps over Wapta Falls. Tumbling 30 m to the riverbed below, it becomes a wall of mist, foam and rainbows for a few moments before reverting to its quiet demeanor. It was near this site that the river acquired its descriptive name—the result of an incident in 1858 when Sir James Hector, geologist and surgeon of the Palliser Expedition, was kicked by his horse.

The trail to the falls is an easy one—less than 2 nearly level kilometres to the overlook. A designated picnic area is located at the trailhead.

Drive 3.5 km east of the Yoho National Park west entrance and turn south off Highway 1 (Trans-Canada Highway) onto a gravel road. Then drive 1.6 km to the trailhead and picnic site (no water available here).

The hike begins on the old gravel access road which soon narrows to a single footpath. Travelling through a typical Rocky Mountain blend of lodgepole pine, spruce and aspen poplar, reach the overlook in 1.6 km. An interpretive sign describes the formation of 2 unusual islands just below the falls.

For a head-on look at the falls, descend the rough trail to the river's edge, where the ample "beach" makes a pleasant stop.

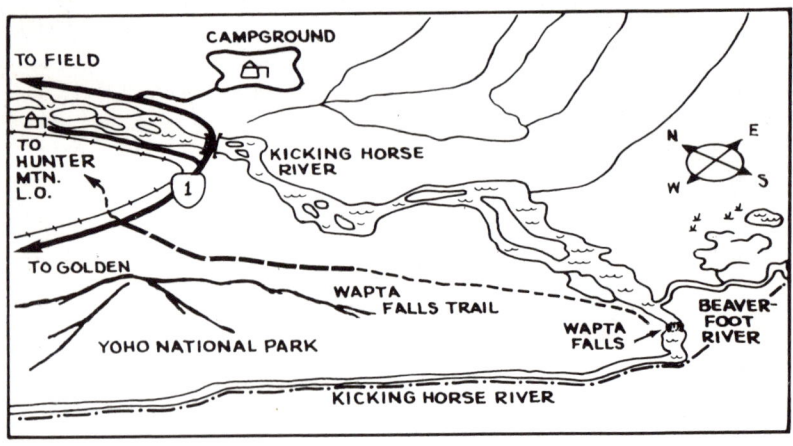

Wapta Falls

YOHO

2 Mt. Hunter Lookout

Distance: 7 km/4.3 mi round trip
Hiking time: 3 hours
Elevation loss: 396 m/1300 ft
High point: 1524 m/5000 ft
Type: half-day hike
Best time: May through September
Map: McMurdo 82 N/2

Climb steadily along the narrow southeast rib of Mt. Hunter for over 3 km of dry, hot trail to the lofty lookout tower that will make you forget the toil. From this airy vantage, scan impressive peaks in the Ottertail Range and look over the sprawling Kicking Horse and Beaverfoot valleys. Obviously a well-chosen lookout site, for the vistas are superb.

Mt. Hunter Lookout station and the Beaverfoot Range

Porcupine

Drive east on Highway 1 (Trans-Canada Highway) for 3.5 km from the information centre at the western entrance to Yoho National Park. Find a parking spot along the Wapta Falls Road on the southern side of the highway. Then walk back across the highway to the trailhead, located directly opposite the Wapta Falls road. Scramble down the road embankment and up the other side; then enter a cool, dense forest and walk beside bunchberry, columbine and lady's-slipper. Continue hiking upward through forest and flowers for a few hundred metres and cross the railroad tracks, taking care to look both ways; it's a busy track.

The trail then begins its steady ascent of the rib, where openings in the trees and scrub afford fine views of the Beaverfoot Valley and Range. Look up to see the fire tower above sheer cliffs on Mt. Hunter's southwest flank.

For the last kilometre, the trail climbs more steeply as it ranges to the east side of the ridge. Through the sparse trees are good views of the Kicking Horse Valley and the President Range to the north. Round the last corner to find the lookout site and the end of the trail. Take plenty of water; there is none along the trail.

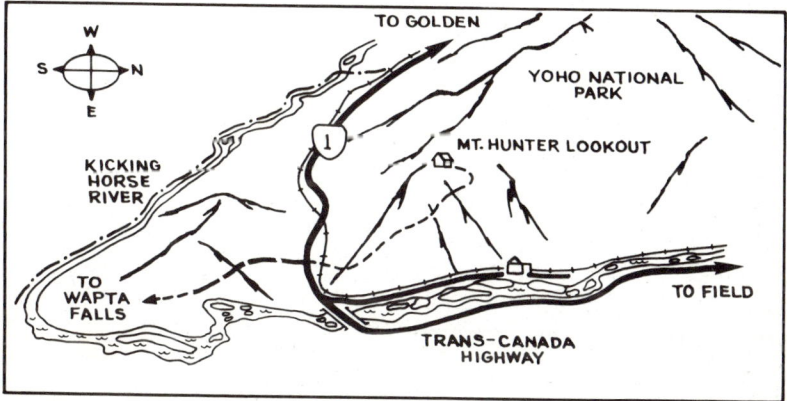

YOHO

3 The Hoodoos

Distance: 6 km/3.8 mi round trip
Hiking time: 2.5 hours
Elevation gain: 228 m/750 ft
High point: 1372 m/4500 ft
Type: nature hike
Best time: May through October
Map: McMurdo 82 N/2

This weirdly unique assortment of erosion-sculpted oddities, known as The Hoodoos, is an intriguing climax to the half-day hike required to visit them. The well-graded trail makes relatively easy work of the hike, in spite of the steady climb. A short nature trail, a pleasant picnic site and several viewpoints along the way make this an ideal family trip.

From the West Yoho Visitor Information Centre, drive Highway 1 (Trans-Canada Highway) east for 5.8 km and turn left at Hoodoo Creek Campground. At 0.6 km, go right at the fork (away from the camping area) and continue another 0.3 km on gravel road to the parking area (1143 m).

Following the signs for the Beaver Dam Nature Trail, stay to the left at the first trail fork (0.2 km). Fifteen metres beyond is a second fork. Again, keep left here. (The right branch makes an interesting side trip to the restored Deerlodge Cabin about 30 m off the main trail—recommended if time permits.)

Continue through dense forest, yellow violets and bunchberry, skirting the campground and reaching Hoodoo Creek at 1.7 km. Cross the creek on a sturdy bridge, and find an interpretive sign just beyond. The sign details the formation of the stone-capped pillars of gravel, known as hoodoos.

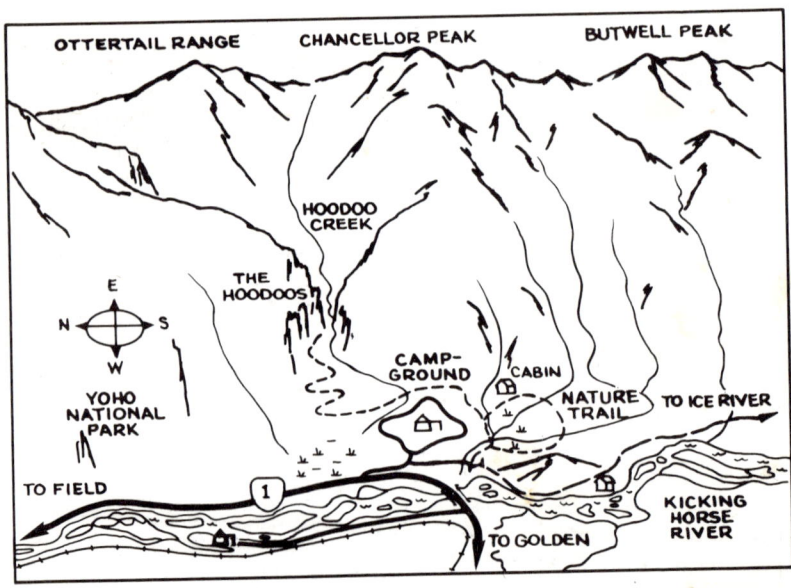

Now the trail begins to climb, switchbacking up the timbered hillside. At 2.4 km it levels off for a brief respite and an opportunity to view the Beaverfoot Range, visible beyond the plains and swamps of the Kicking Horse River. In a short 0.5 km, the trail forks; the lower fork passes beneath The Hoodoos to a pleasant spot along the creek while the upper fork continues for a closer look at these geologic curiosities. Go a short distance farther (0.2 km) for additional views of the pillars. Above, the towering peaks of the Ottertail Range provide a beautiful backdrop to the scene.

The Hoodoos

YOHO

4 Ice River Trail

Distance: 4.5 km/2.8 mi round trip
Hiking time: 2-4 days
Elevation gain: 457 m/1500 ft
High point: 1600 m/5250 ft
Type: backpack
Best time: mid-June through mid-October
Maps: McMurdo 82 N/2, Mount Goodsir 82 N/1

The keynote of this little-used area beneath the western slopes of the Ottertail Range is solitude. Sixteen kilometres on a fire road followed by 6.4 km of rarely travelled trail discourages most would-be visitors. But wilderness lovers will find much to enjoy, from abundant signs of moose, deer, elk, fox and bear to the views of the upper Ice River Valley.

Unlike more populous areas of the park where designated campsites often predetermine routes and progress, here the freedom to make such decisions is left to the hiker. The upper Ice River Valley offers trail-less exploring below open slopes of Mt. Goodsir and Zinc Mountain. For the technical climber, this trail serves as an access to the 3562-m Mt. Goodsir, highest peak in Yoho National Park.

Begin the hike at the parking lot for The Hoodoos Trail (Hike 3), and follow the gated fire road to the right of the nature trail. Trail signs or markers are not provided

Mt. Goodsir from Ice River Valley

here, though the trail itself is well marked and easily followed in spite of early season deadfall. The road climbs briefly, then descends and follows the Kicking Horse River to the old Leanchoil Warden's Cabin. Gradually move away from the river and continue through dense forest at the edge of the valley.

Reaching the Tallon Creek Warden's Cabin at 8 km, the hiker finds comfortable camping with abundant water. Beyond, water may be extremely scarce until the lower Ice River Warden's Cabin some 8 km up the trail. Here, the soft, grassy fields make a natural campsite.

Leaving the cabin, cross the Ice River into British Columbia provincial parkland. Keep left when the trail forks about 6 m beyond the river. (The right fork follows the Beaverfoot River through the tangle and confusion of logging operations towards Kootenay National Park.) The trail remains in British Columbia for about 2.5 km.

At 18 km a large bridge recrosses the river. Do not cross. This bridge is part of an old, abandoned trail. The only problem encountered on the Ice River Trail is a potentially difficult ford of Mollison Creek at 19 km.

Views begin around 21 km, with glimpses of 3132-m Mt. Ennis. At trail's end, 22.5 km, find the upper Ice River Warden's Cabin and inviting campsites. Views here are minimal, however. For the truly enchanting scenery, continue along the footpath to the right of the valley. Early season visitors may be able to go only a km or so before finding the way blocked by deadfall and avalanche debris. Later, when the river is not so unruly, bypass this debris by dropping to the river and climbing back up to find a trail continuing for several kilometres up-valley, where peaks and glaciers of the Ottertail Range crowd the horizons.

An alternative approach may be possible from the maze of logging roads southwest of the park. Beginning about 0.5 km west of the western park boundary on Highway 1 (Trans-Canada Highway), turn south onto a logging road. Follow the Kicking Horse River, then the Beaverfoot River, for about 27 km, staying left at a major Y at 24 km. Continue 5 km to another junction, where a side road branches left. Take this spur for 3 km, to the crossing of the Beaverfoot River and an intersection with another trail. Go left at the trail to meet the Ice River Trail in 7.5 km.

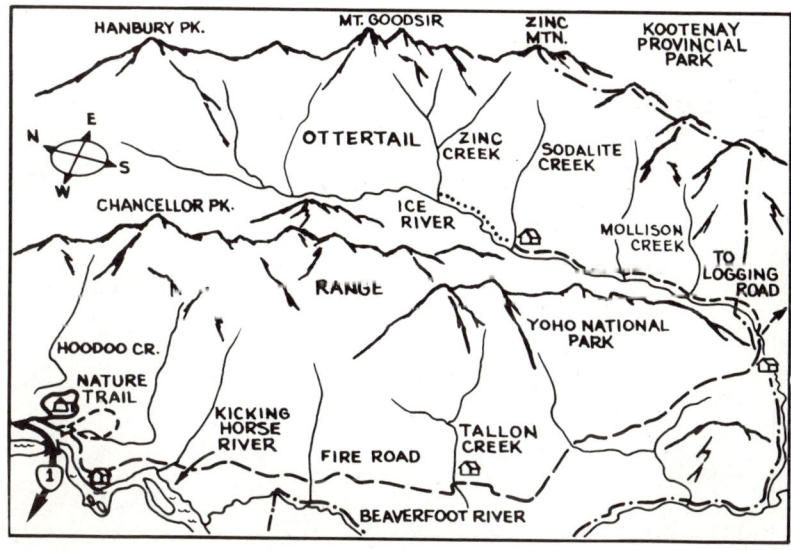

27

YOHO

5 Ottertail River

Distance: 26 km/16 mi round trip
  to road end
Hiking time: 2-3 days
Elevation gain: 305 m/1000 ft
High point: 1463 m/4800 ft
Type: long day hike or backpack
Best time: July through mid-October
Maps: Golden 82 N/7, Lake Louise 82 N/8

The Ottertail River provides both overnight trips or half-day hikes, with an easy-to-follow trail throughout and numerous viewpoints from which to admire the glaciered peaks of the Ottertail Range.

The trail is actually a 16-km fire road, which provides quick access to the Great Divide Trail at the confluence of McArthur and Goodsir creeks with the Ottertail River. The river valley has been designated by Yoho National Park as one of its natural areas, indicating that camping is restricted to designated sites at Float Creek and at McArthur Creek at the end of the trail. To further minimize impact along this route, park wardens discourage off-trail wandering.

The trail starts from Highway 1 (Trans-Canada Highway), 8 km southwest of Field. Shortly before the highway crosses the Ottertail River, a gated fire road merging on the left marks the beginning of the trail. Park at the edge of the fire road on the east side of the highway (3930 m).

From the highway, walk up towards the old warden's cabin, following the fire road as it bends and climbs behind the buildings. The first 2 km of trail concentrate on passing the north flank of Mt. Hurd while entering the first scenic area. Several viewpoints provide panoramas of the Ottertail Range, featuring Mts. Vaux (3319 m) and Ennis (3132 m). At 3 km, a small stream, Giddie Creek, (1341 m) marks a convenient turnaround for day hikers. Beyond, the road enters thick timber, which obscures views for awhile. But scenery improves after 6 km, with the appearance of glaciated Hanbury Peak and Mt. Goodsir.

The road descends again towards the river, reaching it near the Ottertail River/Float Creek confluence (approximately 1371 m). For the next 3 km, the road stays close to the forested valley floor. But Mt. Owen to the north and Allen and Hanbury peaks to the south are visible above the trees. Around 10 km the

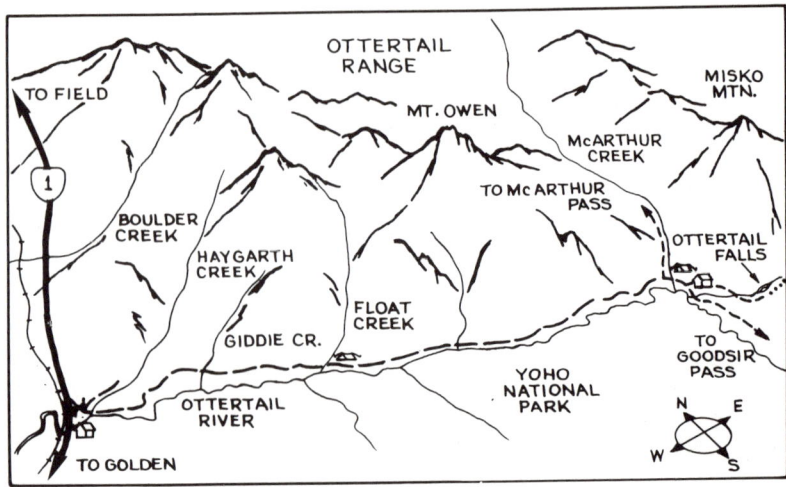

28

Ottertail Range

valley opens somewhat for the final stretch to McArthur Creek (1478 m). A bridge crosses the creek to the camp area and a warden's line cabin.

Several options are easily accessible from camp. A 2-km trail along the river makes an easy trip to the beautiful Ottertail Falls (1547 m). Though inviting, the riverbanks are fragile and susceptible to severe impact, so avoid the temptation to wander along them. Beyond the falls, the trail continues to the Kootenay National Park boundary; however, this trail is not maintained and is reported to be a difficult undertaking through rough and boggy terrain.

To the north, the McArthur Creek Trail (Hike 22) leads to the splendid scenery of the Lake O'Hara area in 11 km. To the south, the Great Divide Trail winds along Goodsir Creek to Goodsir Pass (2209 m) in Kootenay National Park (see a companion book, *95 Hikes in the Canadian Rockies—Banff, Kootenay and Assiniboine Parks*).

YOHO

6 Emerald River Trail

Distance: 15 km/9.6 mi round trip
Hiking time: 5 hours
Elevation gain: 122 m/400 ft
High point: 1302 m/4272 ft
Type: day hike
Best time: June through mid-November
Map: Golden 82 N/7

A cool, protected forest walk along the Emerald River, linking the Animal Salt Lick/Natural Bridge vicinity with the Emerald Lake area. Although the Emerald Lake Road lies just across the river, the path offers a more natural setting for a trip to the lake area. Since the trail is frequented quite often by wildlife, the early morning or late afternoon hiker can expect to interrupt some local elk, moose or deer. At midday, numerous attractive picnic spots invite walkers to linger along the river.

Take Highway 1 (Trans-Canada Highway) 2.5 km southwest of Field to the Emerald Lake turnoff. Turn right and drive 1.5 km to the Natural Bridge parking area. Continue straight onto a dirt roadway, as the paved Emerald Lake Road swings right. Continue for 1.5 km and park on the roadside between the bridges of the Emerald and Amiskwi rivers. Find the well-marked trailhead on the right side of the road.

Climb a steep but short hill to more level terrain along the river, where the trailside is verdant with patches of bunchberry, Labrador tea and wild strawberry. At 2 km, the trail intersects an abandoned branch of the Amiskwi River Trail (Hike 9).

The first 5 km follow the river course closely, then veer west to climb an old moraine and ramble along on generally flat, occasionally muddy terrain. Pass a small marsh at 6 km and descend slightly towards Emerald Lake. Cross a horse trail at 7 km and meet the Hamilton Lake Trail (Hike 9) about 150 m beyond. Make a right turn here and reach the parking lot in 7.7 km.

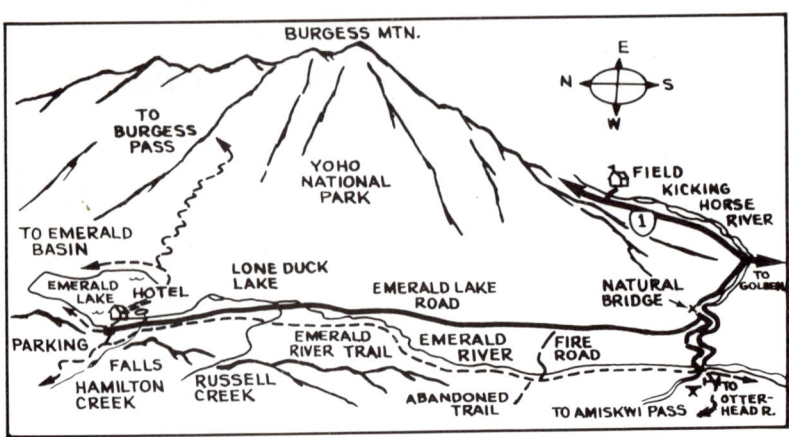

Emerald River

Bunchberry

YOHO

7 Otterhead River Trail

Distance: 23 km/14 mi round trip to road end
Hiking time: 1-2 days
Elevation gain: 335 m/1100 ft
High point: 1494 m/4900 ft
Type: long day hike or backpack
Best time: late May through September
Map: Golden 82 N/7

Seclusion and fine wildlife viewing await you on this seldom-used access to the remote northwest corner of Yoho National Park. The Otterhead River Trail also provides access to a pair of abandoned lookouts, both with magnificent views.

At 2.5 km southwest of Field, take the Emerald Lake turnoff from Highway 1 and drive 1.5 km to the Natural Bridge parking area. Proceed through the parking area and follow the dirt road for 1.5 km to the picnic ground at the road's end.

Ottertail Range rising above Kicking Horse River Valley

Two gated fire roads originate from the picnic grounds; the left-hand road is the Otterhead River Trail, while the right-hand leads up the Amiskwi River (Hike 8).

Walking along the road-turned-trail, follow the Kicking Horse River for 1.5 km before swinging west to enter the Otterhead Valley. Just over 3 km from the trailhead the road splits; the left fork returns to meander along the Kicking Horse, and the right continues up the Otterhead River.

At the 9-km point, the abandoned trail to the Mt. King Lookout departs from an old campsite. Resting on an alpine flank of the 2892-m peak, the lookout promises superb views. But there is one hitch—the bridge spanning the swiftly flowing Otterhead River has long since washed out, necessitating a ford. Once across the river, the trail is well-defined, though progress is hampered by fallen trees.

The Otterhead Trail continues its upward journey beyond the Mt. King Trail junction, still following the old road. At 9.5 km an old road branches right to the Tocher Lookout. It's a steep climb with no water available along the 6.4-km trail. But, for the sturdy of lungs and legs, the abandoned but still-standing lookout provides outstanding views of the Kicking Horse Valley. The Otterhead Trail ends 2 km beyond the Tocher Lookout road.

Numerous streams flowing into the Otterhead River provide abundant water along the way. There are also several fine campsites located near the trail. The valley has been designated a primitive area by the the Yoho National Park Administration, and as such, the existing roads are being allowed to grow over into footpaths, receiving minimum maintenance. This policy will ensure that the Otterhead Trail continues as a fine place to see wildlife.

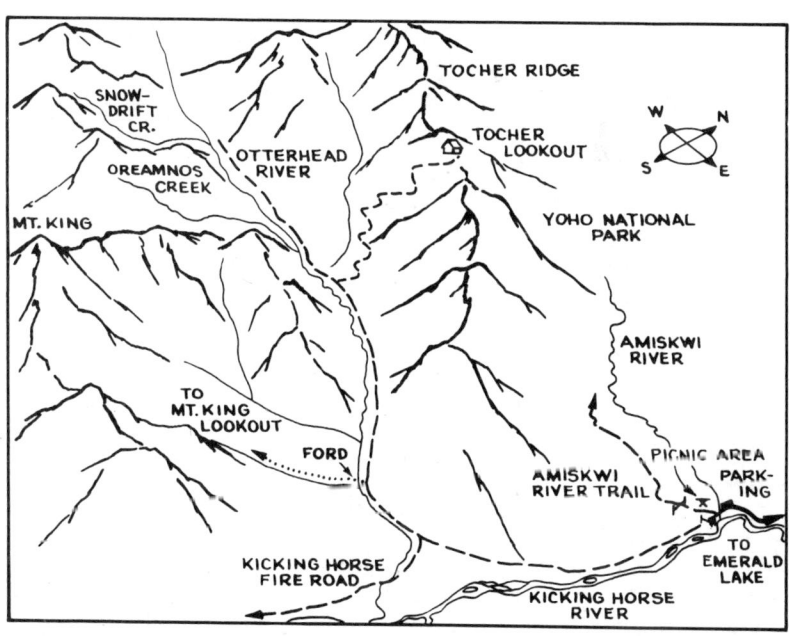

Milled boards, remnants of a logging industry in the Amiskwi River Valley

YOHO

8 Amiskwi River Trail

Distance: 64 km/40 mi round trip to park boundary
Hiking time: 4-6 days
Elevation gain: 837 m/2745 ft
High point: 1995 m/6545 ft
Type: backpack
Best time: July through October
Maps: Golden 82 N/7, Blaeberry River 82 N/10

Enormous glaciers and rugged mountain ranges, viewed from a peaceful, uncrowded setting, reward the persevering hiker of this long river route. The trail is actually a well-maintained fire road for all but the last 6 km, ensuring excellent trail conditions albeit some tedium and probably sore feet.

The long approach discourages many, so the trip is ideal for those seeking solitude. Because the area lacks many pack-toting visitors, it has abundant wildlife. Deer, elk, moose and bear frequent the area in large numbers and can often be sighted by the observant hiker.

Drive Highway 1 (Trans-Canada Highway) 2.5 km southwest of Field and turn right at the Emerald Lake turnoff. At 1.5 km, pass the Natural Bridge parking area and continue straight onto a dirt road. At 6.4 km reach the road's end and picnic area. The Amiskwi River Trail is the fire road on the right.

Begin the walk, passing a gate around the first shallow bend. The fire road then climbs high above the river and travels northwest up the valley. Frequent reminders of the Amiskwi's past importance to the logging industry are encountered during the first 5 km. Old two-by-fours, dilapidated buildings and remnants of the old corduroy are still evident. But the appearance of the President Range at 5 km hints of the views ahead.

The 5 campsites are located at convenient intervals, allowing hikers to set a comfortable pace. Slowly gaining elevation, the road persists up the river valley, crossing the river twice before ending some 2.5 km below the falls. A well-developed footpath continues to Amiskwi Falls and beyond, 4 km to Amiskwi Pass on the park boundary.

Though views from the pass are superb, a climb of 300 m to the left or right will reveal even better sights of vast icefields and chilling heights.

Beyond the park boundary, the trail continues into the provincial forest, where hikers choose their own campsites. Proceeding north from the pass, the trail eventually meets a logging road (alternative access to the area) that starts near Golden and follows the Blaeberry River for over 64 km. From the end of the road, there are 11 km of trail to Amiskwi Pass. Hikers who are interested in entering this way may want to obtain map 82 N/6 showing the road.

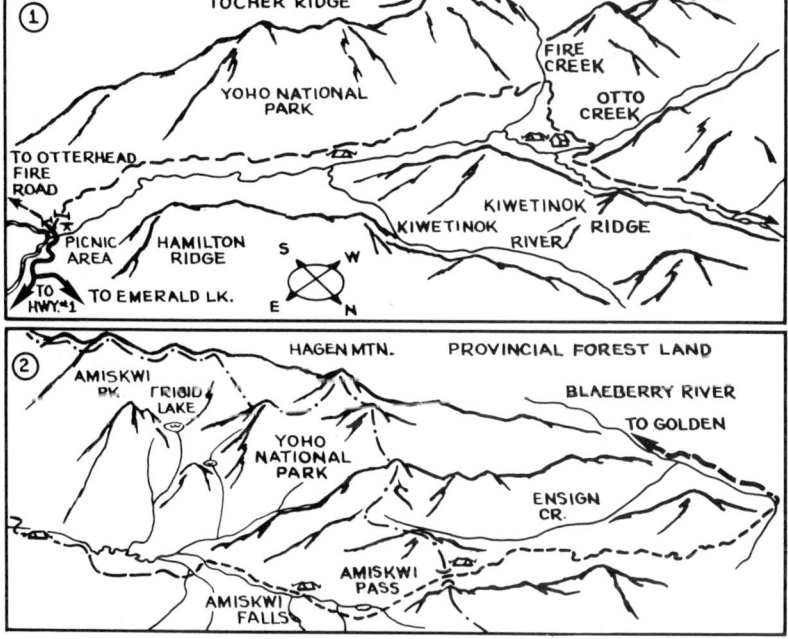

YOHO

9 Hamilton Lake

Distance: 11 km/6.8 mi round trip to lake
Hiking time: 4 hours
Elevation gain: 855 m/2804 ft
High point: 2135 m/7003 ft
Type: day hike
Best time: July through October
Map: Golden 82 N/7

Resting elegantly in a mounting of sculpted stone, this jade jewel, known as Hamilton Lake, surprises you with its beauty. Though the glacier-designed surroundings at the lake are certainly a treat, don't neglect views above of the highest peaks in the park.

Find the trailhead at the end of the Emerald Lake Road, 27 km southwest of Field, 8 km from Highway 1 (Trans-Canada Highway). The trail starts 30 m from the southwest end of the Emerald Lake parking lot. Drinking water is available here.

About 150 m beyond the trailhead, cross the swath cut by the combined Emerald River Trail (Hike 6) and the Emerald Lake horse trail. Continue upwards a kilometre more to a viewpoint of the lower portion of Hamilton Falls, where the 45-m waterfall sluices through a narrow rock chute.

Fifty metres past the viewpoint, a side trail leads left 30 m for another view of the lower falls. The well-defined Hamilton Lake Trail continues upwards another 0.5 km to a vantage point of the upper section of the falls. From this lookout, switchback steadily and steeply up through a forest of spruce and Douglas fir. Bunchberries flank the trail in June and July. As you gain elevation, notice the subtle transition from bunchberry to avalanche lillies.

At 4.8 km reach a viewpoint: Emerald Lake lies at your feet, Mt. Burgess directly across the valley. To the left are Burgess Pass and Mt. Wapta.

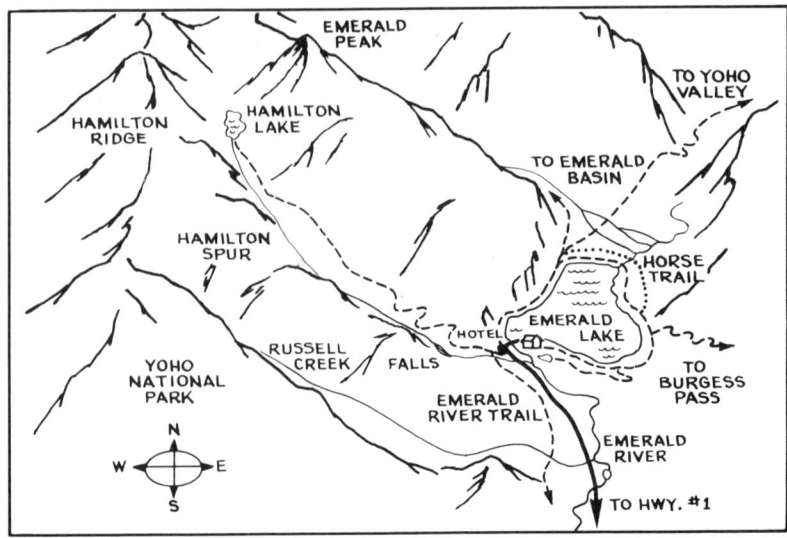

From the viewpoint, the grade moderates a bit as it continues up the slope. Cross a rocky avalanche gully, and exchange dense forest for sparsely vegetated subalpine terrain. The lake, usually frozen until mid-July, appears as you enter the mountainous bowl. Look for mountain goats on the crags above. From the foot of Hamilton Lake there are excellent views of Mts. Vaux and Goodsir. Find more view spots by continuing on around the shore. No camping allowed here.

Hamilton Lakes and a shoulder of Mt. Carnarvon

YOHO

10 Emerald Lake Shoreline Loop

Distance: 5.6 km/3.5 mi loop
Hiking time: 2 hours
Elevation gain: 40 m/130 ft
High point: 1341 m/4400 ft
Type: nature hike
Best time: May through October
Map: Golden 82 N/7

Left in the wake of the last small ice age, Emerald Lake remains to tell the story of this scenic spot: the story of monstrous sheets of flowing ice that receded in jerky retreat, of rock and gravel and soil scooped up and abandoned in a mound of debris and of waters confined by the terminal moraine, to become this enchanting lake.

A circuit around the lake takes hikers through widely varied terrain ranging from forest to barren glacial waste. Signs offer interpretive remarks on the trail and its surroundings. Views of encircling heights are superb, but best of all, the trail is nearly level—a perfect find for a family outing.

From Highway 1, take the Emerald Lake cutoff, 2.5 km southwest of Field. Then, follow the paved road 8 km, to the parking lot (1302 m).

Walk towards the lake from the parking area, following a paved path 100 m to its end. The trail then continues as a dirt path, through open forest where views are of the dark massif of Mt. Burgess across the lake. From time to time, the horse trail merges briefly or crosses the hiker route; remain on the obvious footpath whenever the two separate.

At about 1.5 km, reach an intersection; keep right to continue around the lake. The left fork climbs to the Emerald Basin, giving access to more trails (see Hikes 11 and 12) and the Yoho Lake area (see Hike 14).

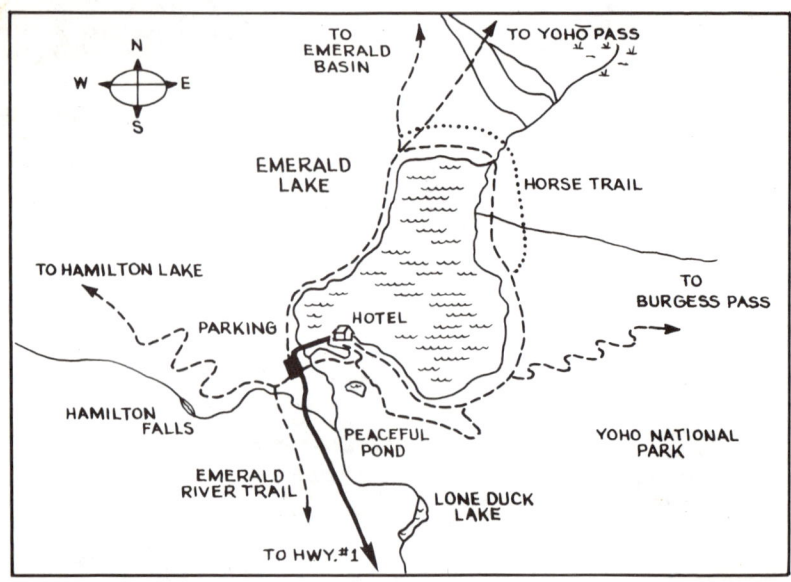

Emerald Lake

Following the right fork as it crosses a large alluvial wasteland, feast your eyes on the President Range and recall that all that gravel underfoot was once a part of the mountains above. As hiker and horse trails diverge again, keep right and enjoy long views of Emerald Lake and the Van Horne Range beyond.

At 4 km, the Burgess Pass Trail (Hike 13) and the Emerald Lake—High Circuit (Hike 11) intersect the shoreline trail. The next kilometre is enlivened by views of the upper Emerald Basin across the lake and of a hanging glacier flowing from Michael Peak.

A negligible rise to the top of the terminal moraine is the trail's only climb. At the top, an unmarked intersection may cause some confusion. The left-hand trail meanders down to a small catch basin known as Peaceful Pond. This trail then rejoins the main trail at the Emerald Lake Resort. Complete the circuit by following the paved road down to a small bridge and back to the parking area.

President Range from the High Circuit Trail above Yoho Pass

YOHO

11 Emerald Lake High Circuit

Distance: 19 km/12 mi loop
Hiking time: 7 hours
Elevation gain: 880 m/2888 ft
High point: 2182 m/7160 ft
Type: day hike
Best time: July through September
Maps: Golden 82 N/7, Lake Louise 82 N/8

Go in early summer and be prepared to ford a stream; go in late season and you'll have to carry water. Either way, mountain views and alpine meadows are the rewards of this fine trip. Be prepared to make the trip in one day, as camping is not permitted along the route.

Follow directions to Emerald Lake (see Hike 10) and leave cars at the parking area (1301 m). Start the circuit from either side of the lake; the directions here will begin on the north side to take advantage of the gentler climb and better views from the lake.

The first 1.5 km follow the Emerald Lake Shoreline Loop (Hike 10). Go left at the intersection, towards Yoho Lake. Keep right when the Emerald Basin Trail (Hike 12) branches off in 150 m. The trail then beelines across the wide alluvial fan from the Emerald Basin. This is the spot where early season hikers should be prepared to wade.

At 2 km begin the ascent to Yoho Pass (1838 m). At first the climb is enhanced by views over Emerald Lake and beyond, but the upper section becomes forested, thus obscuring the sights. Cross the pass at 4.8 km. Just beyond is a major trail junction (an excellent trail continues on to Yoho Lake). Take the sharp right towards Burgess Pass and get ready for the most exciting part of the trip. Cross open, rocky slopes beneath impressive, vertical cliffs of Mt. Wapta while views open up to the Waputik Icefield above Yoho Valley and range west to Mt. Deville.

At 9.6 km, the trail crosses over to a long ridge between Mts. Field and Burgess, bringing the Ottertail Range into view. The high point of the trip (2182 m) is Burgess Pass. Here, a trail descends left to Field (see Hike 13). The right-hand branch returns to Emerald Lake after 7.2 km of dry, forested switchbacks.

Go left at the lake trail to complete the circuit, passing through the resort area and crossing the bridge to the parking lot.

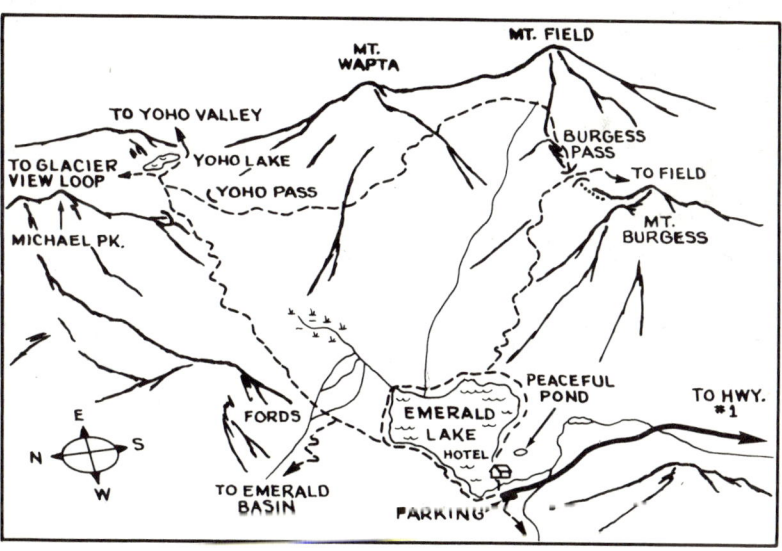

YOHO

12 Emerald Basin Trail

Distance: 10 km/6 mi round trip
Hiking time: 4 hours
Elevation gain: 274 m/900 ft
High point: 1600 m/5250 ft
Type: day hike
Best time: mid-July through September
Map: Golden 82 N/7

Tucked against the southeast base of Mt. Marpole, the rock-strewn Emerald Basin gives a close-up view of the eastern portion of the President Range. Peaks tower on 3 sides, dwarfing hikers venturing into the basin.

Begin at the Emerald Lake parking lot, where drinking water is available for filling canteens. Walk north along the Emerald Lake Shoreline Loop (Hike 10) to the junction at 1.5 km. About 150 m beyond, the Emerald Basin Trail strikes out to the left to climb westward into the basin. Passing the horse trail, continue to bear left, climbing steeply up a rocky, root-entwined trail.

Fine views of Yoho Pass and Mt. Niles become visible near the 3-km point. A kilometre farther, the rough pathway crosses an avalanche slope. Here you get your first good view of the peaks around Emerald Basin. Look above Mt. Hector (the central peak in the area) for a view of The President (3138 m), the highest peak in the President Range. Venturing across the slide path, find bunchberries, false Solomon's seal and alder lining the trail, while above, the Emerald Basin slowly comes into view. Look behind you now, for the panorama of Mt. Wapta, Burgess Pass and Burgess Peak. Return by retracing steps to the Emerald Lake Shoreline Loop and the parking area.

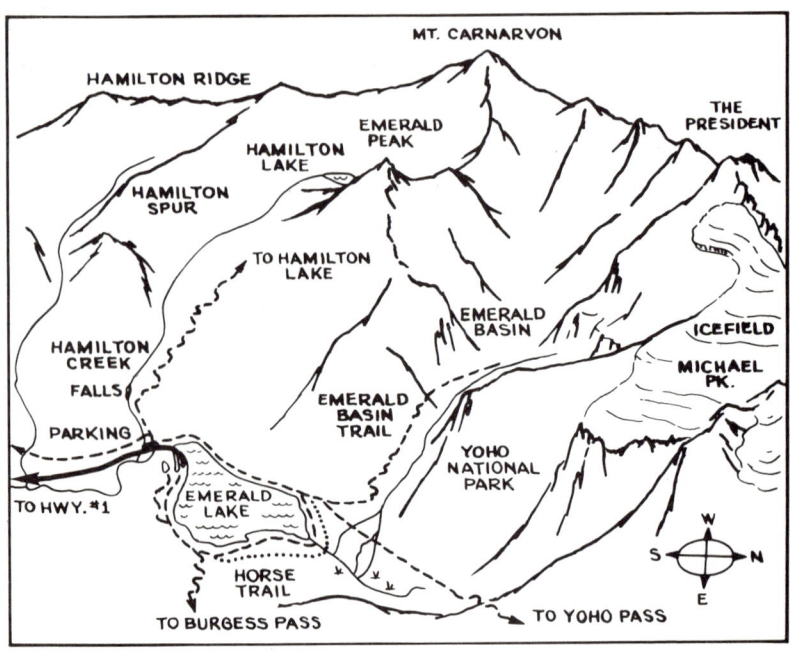

Emerald Basin

YOHO

13 Burgess Pass Trail

Distance: 16 km/9.7 mi round trip
Hiking time: 6 hours
Elevation gain: 931 m/3056 ft
High point: 2182 m/7156 ft
Type: day hike
Best time: mid-June through September
Map: Lake Louise 82 N/8

As seen from Field, Burgess Pass appears to be a rather uninteresting, forested gap between Mts. Burgess and Field. However, the curious and energetic hiker will find quite the opposite. Along the way to the pass and from Burgess Pass itself are superb views of the Kicking Horse Valley and surrounding peaks and of the Emerald Lake area. Take along a good supply of water; the slopes above are open and dry.

Begin at 1 km east of the Field turnoff on Highway 1 (Trans-Canada Highway). A trail sign on the north side of the highway marks the trailhead.

Ascend steadily along the densely forested slope. About 1 km from the trailhead, there may be a small stream to cross depending upon the season.

Switchback steadily up the mountainside, skirting and occasionally crossing slide paths. A little over 3 km from the start, emerge upon a large avalanche slope reaching down Mt. Burgess. Burgess Pass appears tantalizingly close, but don't be fooled; there are still 3 km to go before reaching it.

Alternate between open slopes and the bordering forest. At 4 km cross a split-log bridge spanning a dry creekbed. Continue upward across sparsely treed slopes, reaching the pass at 8 km.

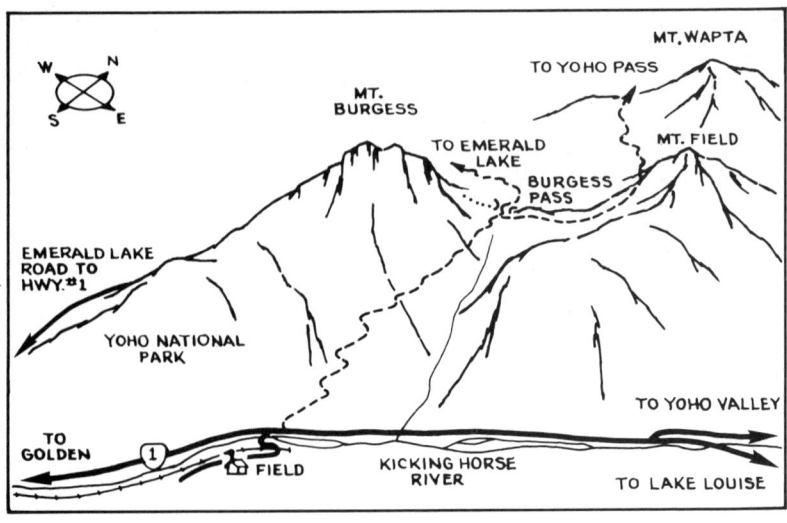

Trail near Burgess Pass

There are no signs marking the pass, but there is no mistaking the spot upon reaching the crest of the ridge separating Mts. Burgess and Field. A left-hand trail leads about 200 m east to join with the Emerald Lake—High Circuit and Yoho Lake Loop trails (Hikes 11 and 14). Hikers can plan a scenic return using these trails, if transportation back to Field can be arranged.

Though a strenuous uphill trek (but an easy downhill return), the Burgess Pass hike is a fine day trip. Take a lunch, lots of water and time to sample the mountainous grandeur of Yoho National Park from Burgess Pass.

YOHO

14 Yoho Lake Loop

Distance: 8.8 km/5.5 mi loop
Hiking time: 3 hours
Elevation gain: 518 m/1700 ft
High point: 1981 m/6500 ft
Type: half-day or backpack
Best time: July through September
Map: Lake Louise 82 N/8

With an alpine lake and views of glaciers, mountains and waterfalls, this trip offers a sampling of the Yoho Valley, packed into a reasonably short loop trail. Complete the trip in a few short hours, or make it an overnight or longer by reserving a spot at the Yoho Lake campsite.

The Yoho Valley is an extremely popular hiking area and consequently is crisscrossed with numerous, well-maintained trails. The loop trip suggested here includes a full sampling of the area, though longer loops and side trips are options.

Drive northeast from Field on Highway 1, and turn left (north) at 3.7 km towards Yoho Valley and Takakkaw Falls. At 12.2 km, pass the Whiskey Jack Youth Hostel on the left. As there is no parking here except for hostel users, continue on for 0.6 km to the parking area at the end of the road, or go back 0.2 km to the wide gravel turnouts. (The road to the hostel and trailhead is very steep and narrow, with exceptionally sharp turns—not recommended for trailers or motor homes.)

Return to the hostel by foot and climb the avalanche slope on a broad, well-marked trail. At 1.2 km, a small trail branches left, leading to Hidden Lakes. These are 2 small lakes nestled in the trees, a short 0.8 km from the main trail. Another 100 m along the main route is a second trail, branching to the right this time and leading to a viewpoint overlooking Takakkaw Falls and Yoho Valley.

Reach a major intersection shortly after the viewpoint trail. The left fork continues on to Yoho Lake; the right fork connects with the descent trail. Continue along the route (left fork) to arrive at the lake after 4-km total distance. Set in an airy forest below the 2696-m Michael Peak, the lake offers camping near the far (southwest) shore.

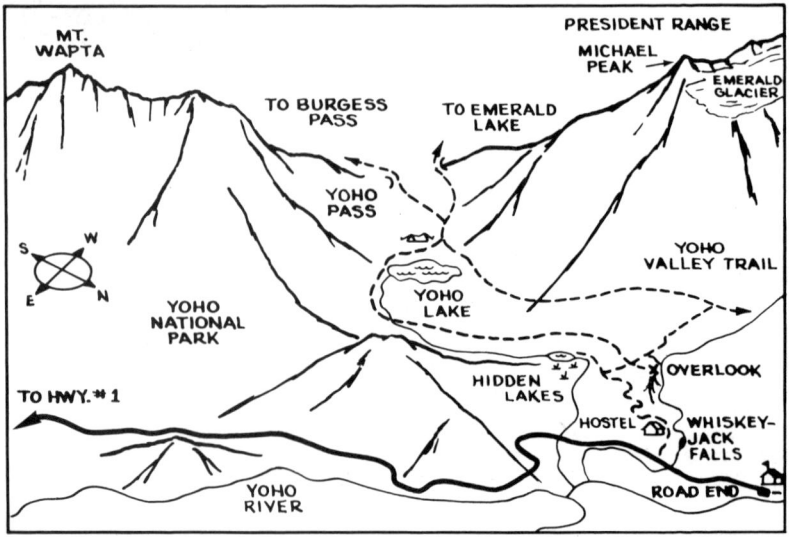

From Yoho Lake, side trip options include a 0.6-km jaunt to the 1838-m Yoho Pass and perhaps on to Emerald Lake (see Hike 12). Awaiting those who continue around the loop is the most scenic part of the trip. Follow the trail north from the campsite, towards Twin Falls. Climb steeply for 1 km, passing through more open forest, then richly flowered meadows.

At 6 km, make a right turn at the trail junction and head steeply downhill to meet with familiar trail for the last 1.5 km to the hostel.

Takakkaw Falls

YOHO

15 Glacier View Loop

Distance: 19 km/12 mi loop
Hiking time: 8 hours
Elevation gain: 686 m/2250 ft
High point: 2210 m/7250 ft
Type: day hike or backpack
Best time: mid-July through mid-October
Maps: Lake Louise 82 N/8,
  Hector Lake 82 N/9,
  Blaeberry River 82 N/10

Here are all the ingredients for an alpinist's paradise: spirited rivers and waterfalls, grand peaks and icefields, flowered meadows and a chance to design your own type of trip. An ambitious hiker may do it all in one day, but leisurely types might prefer to savor these delights in smaller bits, camping along the way. Just one hint: The area is extremely popular and campsites must be reserved through the park in advance.

Take the Yoho Valley-Takakkaw Falls turnoff on the north side of Highway 1, at 3.7 km east of Field. Pass the east park information centre and follow the road 13.2 km to its end. Make the parking lot tour and pick the appropriate one for day or overnight visitors.

This route is a logical loop that includes all or part of 3 separate trails—the Yoho Valley, Whaleback and Little Yoho Valley trails. Begin hiking at the last parking lot (1515 m). After 60 m, turn left onto an old, narrow road that passes through the Takakkaw Falls walk-in campground. A glance back down the valley gives a good view of Takakkaw Falls. At 2.4 km the road ends and the trail forks. To the right a path leads 200 m to Angel's Staircase Falls; the main trail continues to the left. Just beyond, another trail branches right for a short walk to the base of Point Lace Falls. In another 0.8 km a third trail departs to the left for a 0.4-km walk to the forested Lake Duchesnay.

Yoho Glacier from the Whaleback

At 4 km the trail crosses the Little Yoho River, just below Laughing Falls. Beyond, the trail makes a major fork, marking the beginning of the loop. The trip may be done in either direction, but will be described here in the less steep counterclockwise fashion for the convenience of those carrying overnight packs.

The trail forks again at 6.5 km. A 2.4-km trail (signed Yoho Glacier Trail) continues straight, climbing 100 m to an observation area of the glacier-scoured, rock terminus of the Yoho and Trolltinder glaciers.

Take the trail going left and descend slightly to the Twin Falls campsite. Enter the forest and climb 1.6 km to a major junction (1801 m). To the left is the Twin Falls Chalet where lunch and hot drinks may be purchased. Beyond the chalet a trail makes a lowland circuit back to Laughing Falls via Marpole Lake. Walk along this trail for about 35 m, to a creek crossing and splendid views of Twin Falls.

Back at the junction, go left to continue toward Whaleback Mountain. The climb is steep, with several switchbacks ascending a series of benches. The best views of the loop start at the first of these benches. Here the trail goes downhill slightly to a campsite near the top of the falls. Views are unparallelled, but this is not a place for sleepwalkers or anyone who suffers from vertigo.

Continue by crossing the bridged Twin Falls Creek (1905 m) and begin the final climb through open meadow. The trail crosses over a shoulder of Whaleback Mountain, reaching an elevation of 2210 m. Broad icefields and glaciers, the President Range and alpine grandeur in all directions make this the high point of the trip.

Leaving Whaleback Mountain, the trail descends in a series of switchbacks, losing 300 m in 1.5 km. Meet the Presidential High Route (Hike 16) and turn left, following it down the valley for about 2 km to close the loop at Laughing Falls.

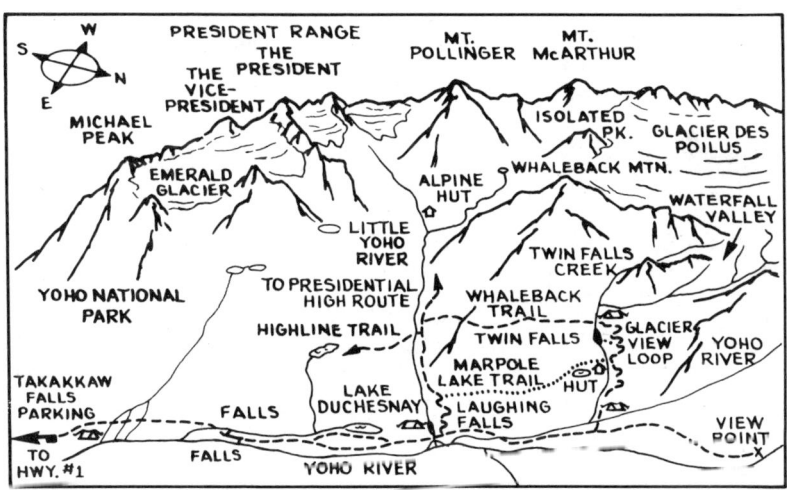

YOHO

16 Presidential High Route

Distance: 22 km/13.6 mi loop
Hiking time: 9 hours
Elevation gain: 212 m/695 ft
High point: 2121 m/6957 ft
Type: long day hike or backpack
Best time: mid-July through September
Maps: Lake Louise 82 N/8,
　Hector Lake 82 N/9,
　Blaeberry River 82 N/10

Watch your step on this route; the scenery is so magnificent you'll probably be looking everywhere but where you put your feet. From start to finish the skylines are filled with rock, snow and ice. The trail makes a long, narrow loop up the Little Yoho River Valley, using a combination of several shorter trails—the Yoho Valley, Little Yoho Valley, Skyline and Highline trails as they are named by the park. Hike the trail in a counterclockwise direction to get head-on views of the Emerald Glacier and President Range for most of the walk.

Drive Highway 1 for 3.7 km east of Field and turn left on the Yoho Valley/Takakkaw Falls turnoff. Follow this road for 13.2 km to the parking lots at the end of the road. Then walk the 4 km along the Glacier View Loop (Hike 15) to Laughing Falls.

Turn left (west) at the trail junction to follow the Little Yoho Valley, climbing via switchbacks for nearly 1 km along an often-muddy trail. On the right, pass a trail that runs past Marpole Lake and connects with the Glacier View Loop to Twin Falls (Hike 15). In another kilometre, meet the Lake Celeste Trail on the left. It climbs about 200 m, passing a small tarn and joining the descending leg of the Presidential High Route in 2.5 km.

Just beyond the last trail junction, encounter the Whaleback portion of the Glacier View Loop merging on the right. Continue straight ahead, passing all junctions and following the well-beaten path. To the left looms the President Range, dominating the western skyline.

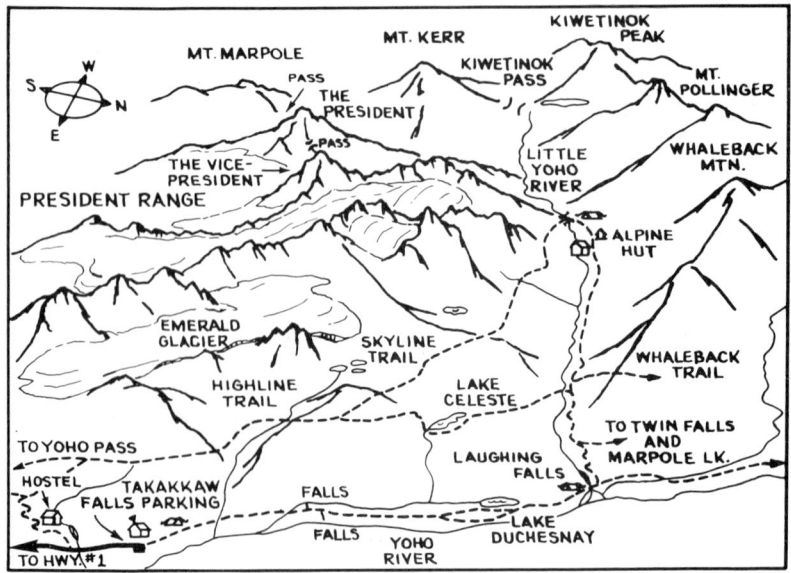

Along the High Route

Twelve kilometres from the Takakkaw Falls parking lot, arrive at the Alpine Club of Canada (ACC) Stanley Mitchell Hut and the park warden's cabin, both nestled on the fringes of a lush meadow. On the western side of the meadow, just beyond the hut, find the Little Yoho campsite. The trail passes through the campsite, angling towards the river. Cross the river just west of the camp on a log bridge, and turn left going back along the river.

At the bridge crossing is an unsigned junction. On the right is a climbers' path leading up towards the glacial moraines beneath the President Range. Walk south (left) along the river a short way, then veer right to climb through forest and emerge shortly at the moraines of the Emerald Glacier. For 3 km wander along through moraines and meadows, crossing numerous meltwater streams, while surrounded by unparallelled alpine grandeur.

Beyond the meadows, at about 17 km, meet the Celeste Lake Trail again. Turn right (a left turn would rejoin the Presidential Route, 2.5 km above Laughing Falls) and descend below the President Range to a junction with the Yoho Lake Loop (Hike 14). Take the left fork heading downhill to the Whiskey Jack Youth Hostel. Return to your car by walking 1 km back up the paved road to the Takakkaw Falls parking area.

By combining the Presidential High Route with the Glacier View Loop (Hike 15) you can, in 2 or 3 days, make a grand tour of Yoho's finest alpine country. Remember to make reservations for a backcountry campsite before starting out.

YOHO

17 Paget Lookout

Distance: 7.2 km/4.5 mi round trip
Hiking time: 3 hours
Elevation gain: 777 m/2550 ft
High point: 2393 m/7850 ft
Type: half-day hike
Best time: mid-June through October
Map: Lake Louise 82 N/8

Before the advent of fire patrol planes in the national parks, some lucky lookout spent whole summers contemplating the view from the top of a vertical cliff. From his perch on a shoulder of Paget Peak, the lookout's daily fare consisted of snow-and-ice-capped mountains above and lush, green valleys below.

The lookout is an appealing place, even without the view. Behind the building, a small alp, dotted with blossoms and stunted trees, offers a sharp contrast to the crumbly slopes above.

Follow Highway 1 east of Field for 10.8 km and park at the Wapta Lake picnic area (1586 m). The hike starts just above the picnic shelter.

The first section of trail follows the Sherbrooke Lake Trail (Hike 18). At approximately 1.5 km (1829 m), the trails diverge, the lookout route striking off to the right. Traverse an old clearing where views of the lookout appear for the first time. Then begin the serious climbing at about 2.4 km. The trail is rough and demands careful footing, particularly on the descent.

As the forest thins, look out to views of the broad valley of the Kicking Horse River. Below, Sherbrooke Lake adds a splash of blue to the mountainous scenery.

The white walls of the lookout come into view as you top the last rise. The last few metres are on level ground. All around are exceptional sights. The Slate Range of Banff National Park dominates the eastern horizon, but the long valley of Cataract Brook steals the show. Stretching north from Lake O'Hara, steep

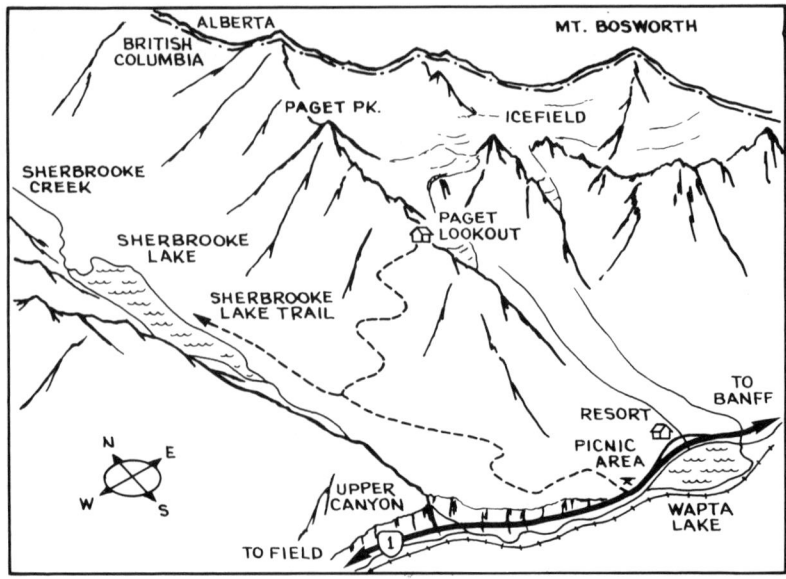

Cataract Brook Valley from Paget Lookout

mountains rise on either side: Narao Peak, Mts. Victoria, Huber and Hungabee and Cathedral Mountain to name a few.

Spend some time exploring the scenic environs. Follow a short footpath that climbs through pleasant, though fragile meadows behind the lookout (please stay on the trail). The path continues in a sketchy manner up the crumbly slopes of Paget Peak (2560 m). Views from the summit are worth the effort for experienced alpine scramblers.

Sherbrooke Lake

YOHO

18 Sherbrooke Lake

Distance: 9 km/5.5 mi round trip to upper end of lake
Hiking time: 2.5 hours
Elevation gain: 185 m/607 ft
High point: 1804 m/5917 ft
Type: half-day hike
Best time: mid-June through September
Map: Lake Louise 82 N/8 W

Contained in a narrow valley between Mt. Ogden and Paget Peak and flanked by forested hillsides and stunning peaks in the distance, Sherbrooke Lake is an appealing objective just a short hike from the highway. Beyond the lake, more trail treats hikers to a day full of scenic walking.

Drive to the Wapta Lake picnic area 10.8 km east of Field on Highway 1 (Trans-Canada Highway). The trail departs from the uphill side of the picnic shelter. The trails to Sherbrooke Lake and Paget Lookout (Hike 17) are one and the same for the first 1.5 km.

Ascend steadily along forested slopes to reach the junction with the Paget Lookout Trail. Keep left here. At 0.5 km beyond the intersection, the trail levels off and enters a series of small clearings along the way. Look to your left across the valley for views of Cathedral Crags, Cathedral Mountain and Vanguard Peak.

Milky green from glacier-ground rock flour, the rippling waters of Sherbrooke Lake appear to the left, about 3 km from the trailhead. Just beyond is an access trail down to the boggy shore. Camping is not permitted at the lake.

The trail continues another 1.5 km along the shore to the upper end of the tarn, which is shallow and partially filled with fallen timber. From here, get glimpses (on a clear day) of the snow-shrouded ramparts of Mt. Victoria (3444 m) in Banff National Park.

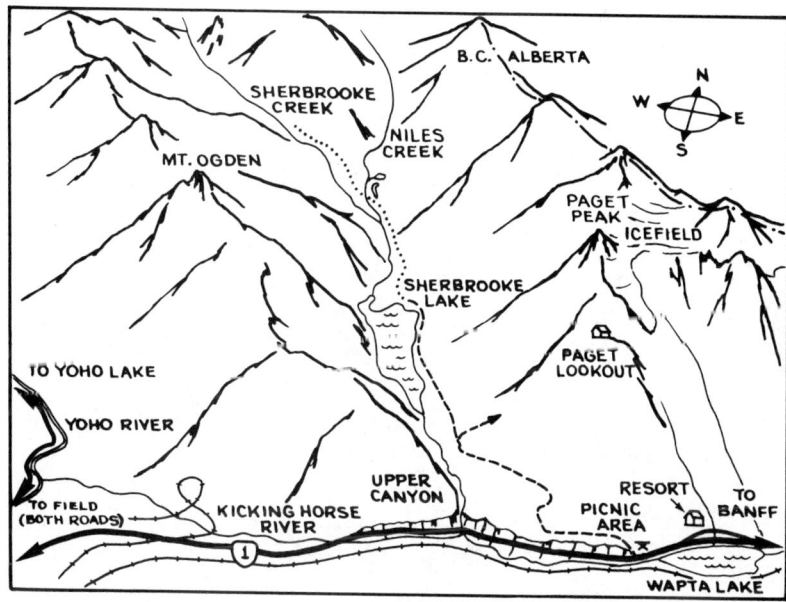

YOHO

19 Cataract Brook

Distance: 24 km/15 mi round trip to
  Lake O'Hara Campground
Hiking time: 6 hours
Elevation gain: 381 m/1250 ft
High point: 1981 m/6500 ft
Type: day hike or backpack
Best time: mid-June through October
Maps: Lake Louise 82 N/8,
  Yoho Hiker's Map—Cataract Brook

Hike to one of Yoho's most well-known and popular areas. Camp near a mountain lake, where images of tall trees, rock and ice skitter across the water. Though Lake O'Hara has long been a favored destination, the real joy comes from the network of trails radiating out from the lake, to more lakes, viewpoints and meadows.

The wide valley of Cataract Brook is the major access to the Lake O'Hara area. The trail, however, is lightly used in comparison with the access road, which parallels it on the opposite side of the creek. The result: a pleasantly wooded walk, with few fellow hikers.

Lake O'Hara

The road is closed to private vehicles, but the lodge at Lake O'Hara operates a bus service, which will carry day hikers and campers for a fee. Reservations are needed for both camping and the bus, and they can be arranged at the east information centre, 3.2 km east of Field.

Those preferring to walk to the lake will find an excellent trail, with bridged creek crossings and a total elevation gain under 400 m. The trail departs from the Lake O'Hara bus parking lot about 15.5 km northeast of Field. Drive Highway 1 (Trans-Canada Highway) to the Lake Louise turnoff. Turn right, cross the railroad track and make another right turn into the parking lot (1631 m).

Heading southwest from the upper parking area, walk along flat trail. Reach the first of 3 bridged creek crossings at 1.2 km. Two more quick crossings across the scenic gorge occur in another short kilometre. The trail then abandons the brook to climb a hillside and continue through woods.

Occasional views of Narao Peak and snow-clad Mt. Victoria appear through openings in the forest. Cross Duchesnay Creek (1950 m) at 8.8 km. Pass the Linda Lake Loop (Hike 20) and continue across valley flats to cross Morning Glory Creek (1981 m). Turn right at the next junction (several metres beyond the creek) and walk on relatively level trail for the final 1.5 km to the campground.

Campsites are available by reservation only, so don't forget to call or write ahead to the Yoho Park Information Centre. Then plan to spend 2 to 3 full days in the area to take in the numerous trails (Hikes 20 through 25.)

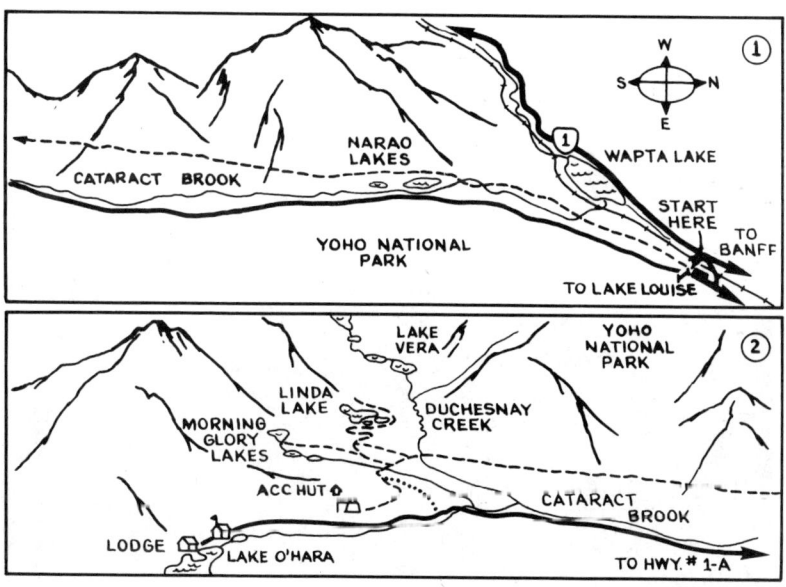

YOHO

20 Linda Lake Loop

To Linda Lake
Distance: 9.6 km/6 mi round trip
Hiking time: 4 hours
Elevation gain: 244 m/800 ft
High point: 2278 m/7474 ft
Type: day hike
Best time: July through September
Maps: Lake Louise 82 N/8 or Yoho Hiker's Map—Linda Lake (some of the trails and lakes are not shown on the topographic map)

To Cathedral Basin
Distance: 16 km/10 mi round trip
Hiking time: 6.5 hours
Elevation gain: 457 m/1500 ft
High point: 2491 m/8174 ft

A forest of tall trees with a carpet of moss, small meadows, great views and a series of sparkling lakes with the clearest blue water one could ever find, all on a trip from Lake O'Hara. As this is a loop, it can be done in either direction. Here the trip is described counterclockwise so the hiker will start in the mossy forest and climb to heather and flowers.

Linda Lake and a shoulder of Odaray Mountain

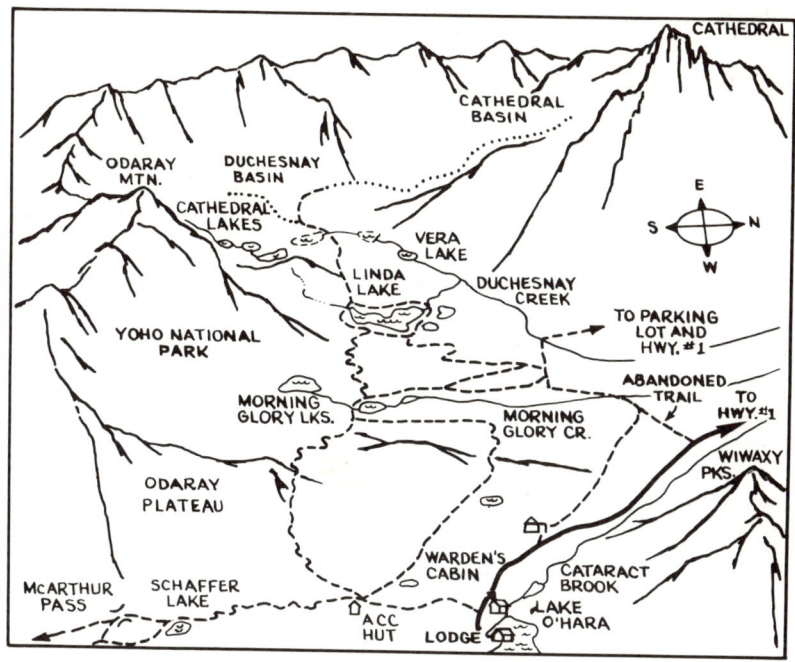

From Lake O'Hara (2034 m), follow the fire road 0.5 km downhill to the campground and find the unmarked trailhead near campsite 14. The trail descends gently for 1.5 km to pass an old horse trail on the right. Keep going straight and soon cross Morning Glory Creek (1981 m) and in about 50 m, reach a junction. The left fork goes to Morning Glory Lake; the right fork is the Cataract Brook Trail (Hike 19). Go straight ahead on the Cataract Brook Trail. In 100 m turn left on the Linda Lake Loop. The way steepens and reaches Linda Lake (2057 m) approximately 3 km from Lake O'Hara.

Follow the lakeshore trail around to the right, where a trail junction on the far shore marks an excellent side trip to Duchesnay and Cathedral basins. There, find more lakes, meadows and a climb to dramatic views.

The trail to the upper basins begins by climbing about 60 m in 1 km to reach Cathedral Lakes. Cross the outlet and look down to Vera Lake. Then follow the trail another 0.4 km to a junction: Duchesnay Basin to the left and Cathedral Basin to the right. The Cathedral Basin Trail deteriorates to a boot-beaten path marked by red and orange paint marks on rocks. It climbs very steeply, gaining over 200 m, then contours for 1.5 km to Cathedral Basin at 2316 m. Discover a tiny lake surrounded by pretty green meadows, with the bare rock buttress and spires of Cathedral Peak above.

Back at Linda Lake, continue around the shore, giving particular attention to crossing the boulder field. About three-quarters of the way around, find the Morning Glory Lake Trail. Follow this, climbing steeply about 4.5 km, then descend to middle Morning Glory Lake at 2012 m. Cross the inlet stream to another trail junction. The right-hand trail climbs very steeply over 304 m to Odaray Plateau (see Hike 23). Keep left following signs to Lake O'Hara, first climbing a bit and then descending back to the lakeshore.

YOHO

21 Lake McArthur Circuit

Distance: 8 km/5 mi loop
Hiking time: 4 hours
Elevation gain: 351 m/1150 ft
High point: 2408 m/7900 ft
Type: day hike
Best time: mid-July through mid-October
Map: Lake Louise 82 N/8 or Yoho
  Hiker's Map—Lake McArthur

Surrounded by cliffs and glacial ice, Lake McArthur is the largest and the most dramatic of the many lakes in the O'Hara Valley. Bounded on 2 sides by Mt. Schaffer and Park Mountain and blocked on a third by the Mt. Biddle Icefield, this rugged lake is a favored destination.

Using the interwoven trails of the O'Hara Valley, this circuit trip includes the best features of the area: meadows, larch forests, views and rocky, alpine slopes.

From the Lake O'Hara Campground (see Hike 19), follow the road up the valley for 1 km to the warden's cabin (2057 m). Strike out to the west, keeping right at the junction with the Big Larch Trail, which becomes the final leg of the return trip. Pass the ACC Hut on the left and a trail junction on the right at 1.2 km. Two trails head north from this junction, the Odaray/Grand View Prospect (Hike 23) and the Linda Lake Loop (Hike 20).

Continue straight across the meadow to begin the steep climb through trees. The Big Larch Trail meets the main route again, a kilometre beyond the hut. Continue past as the trail levels and bypass Schaffer Lake (2164 m). Stay on the main route, passing 2 more trails and crossing McArthur Meadows.

Approaching the McArthur Pass (2210 m) area, gain views of McArthur Creek (Hike 22) and down towards the Ottertail River. From the pass, head south on the lower trail, making the final ascent to the glacial cirque that holds the deep blue waters of Lake McArthur. It's easy to spend several hours here, enjoying the views and looking for goats on the rugged crags above.

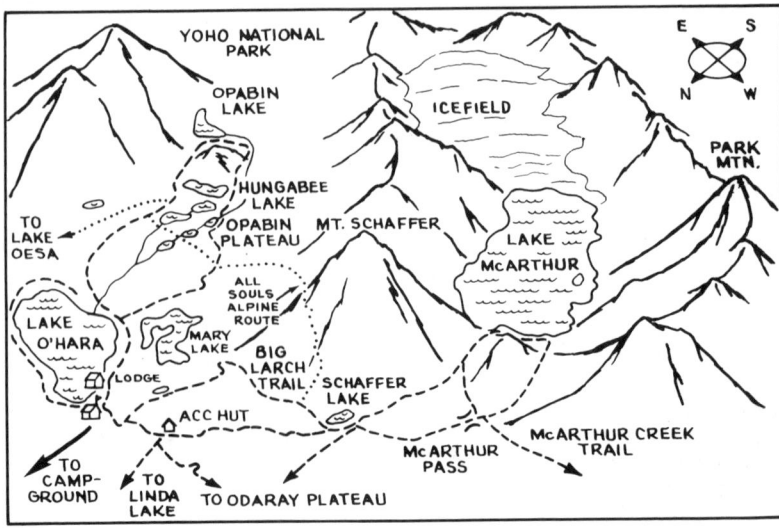

60

Lake McArthur and Mt. Biddle

To continue the high country survey and complete the Lake McArthur circuit, take the northernmost (right-hand) trail from the lake. Hiking around rocky barriers and skirting large rock walls, climb out of the lake basin to the trip's highest elevation point, 2407 m. Then descend stone steps along a ledge and wind across some boulder fields to a point above Schaffer Lake. Reaching Schaffer Lake, rejoin the main trail briefly, but bear right at the lake outflow to take the Big Larch Trail. Pass the All Soul's Alpine Route (see Hike 25) on the right and descend beside the Devil's Rockpile to a meadow below. Another meeting with the Lake McArthur Trail closes the circuit and a right turn returns you to the warden's cabin.

YOHO

22 McArthur Creek

Distance: 9 km/5.5 mi Ottertail River
 to McArthur Pass one way
Hiking time: 4 hours
Elevation gain: 835 m/2740 ft
High point: 2225 m/7300 ft
Type: day hike or backpack
Best time: mid-July through mid-October
Map: Lake Louise 82 N/8

Pass through a valley of forest and streams to an alpine world of craggy peaks, meadow-fringed lakes and a scattering of weathered trees. Here, some of the park's most well-known peaks stand out in barren splendor. Joined with the Ottertail River Trail (Hike 5), the McArthur Creek Trail provides an alternative access to Lake O'Hara. If an overnight fits into your plans, be sure to make advance reservations for a campsite in the O'Hara area.

Though the trail can be (and is) hiked in either direction, it will be described here from the forested Ottertail River Valley to the climactic views of McArthur Pass. The trail is reported to be a popular grizzly haunt; travel in a group and let the bears hear you coming!

See Hike 5 for driving directions and hike along the Ottertail River for 13 km to the trail junction at McArthur Creek. Climb in forest for 2 km around a long rib of Mt. Owen. The trail then levels and rambles in creekside greenery for several kilometres, passing marshes and crossing slide paths. At 7 km, the trail swings right, crossing McArthur Creek to climb towards the pass. Now the views finally begin. When the trail emerges between Odaray and Park mountains, pause for a breather and gaze south for a look at Mt. Goodsir, a well-placed focus for a rest stop.

Reach McArthur Pass (2210 m) at 9 km and find the toil is suddenly past. Lunch on scenic knolls or visit the lakes before continuing on. Overnighters, or those exiting via Cataract Brook, should proceed on the main trail, descending for 3 km through a maze of interconnected trails. The well-signed route passes Schaffer Lake and the ACC Hut to reach the warden's cabin. Turn left at the road to find the campground and hiking trail out to Highway 1. Turn right for the Lake O'Hara Lodge and bus service out of the valley.

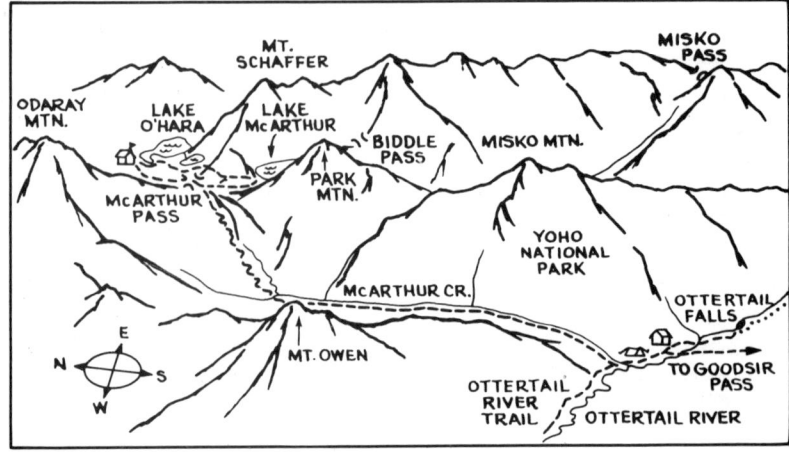

Mt. Goodsir

YOHO

23 Odaray/Grand View Prospect

Distance: 9.6 km/6 mi round trip to Grand View Prospect
Hiking time: 4 hours
Elevation gain: 472 m/1550 ft
High point: 2530 m/8300 ft
Type: day hike
Best time: mid-July through mid-October
Maps: Lake Louise 82 N/8, Yoho Hiker's Map—Linda Lake

Climb on hills, high above the O'Hara Basin, and wander out on broad plateaus to several outstanding overlooks. Then walk to a shoulder of Odaray Mountain, where the grand finale is the Grand View Prospect. Massive peaks of rock and ice stand deceptively close on steep-walled faces, while below the numerous lakes and ponds nestle into basins and protected valleys. In summer, myriad meadow flowers clothe the hills. Later the larches add splashes of gold.

Odaray Prospect

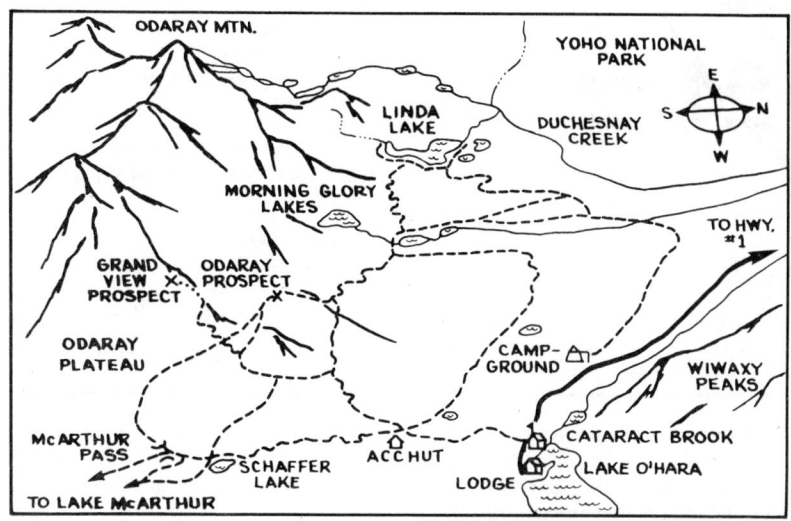

The Odaray/Grand View Prospect Trail is formed of several others, linked together to make a circuit. Though there are numerous intersections, the park has kept them well marked, so they should not be confusing.

Start in the Lake O'Hara Valley (see Hike 19), across the road from the warden's cabin. Follow the Lake McArthur Circuit (Hike 21) south for 1 km to the major 4-way intersection near the ACC Hut. The Lake McArthur Circuit Trail continues to the left. On the right, 2 trails depart from nearly the same spot. The lower trail goes to Linda Lake (see Hike 20). Take the upper trail.

Climb through mixed forest to a junction (signed) at 2.4 km, where the choice is whether to stay with the circuit route (left) or to add 1.5 km of distance and see some additional views by taking the right-hand trail (towards Morning Glory and Linda lakes).

If the right-hand trail is chosen, follow it towards Duchesnay Basin where it meets another trail. Then turn left to ascend to Odaray Plateau. The circuit route (left at first intersection after the hut) continues its climb. Pass a trail to Schaffer Lake on the left, and reach a spot where the trail forks, shortly thereafter. Stay right for the full circuit, climbing towards the plateau. Near the top, the Odaray Highline Trail merges on the left; continue straight ahead (north) to reach the Odaray Prospect (2286 m) and excellent views of the lakes below.

To continue the circuit, retrace steps to the Highline Trail, then keeping right, follow the higher plateau trail this time. Return to the Grand View Prospect Trail and go right for the last climb. Although it is an alpine route and is indeed steep, the trail is in good condition and is well-defined. It is highly recommended.

Marked by a large cairn and a superb panorama, Grand View Prospect is indeed rewarding. Alpinists may continue on a rough, cairn-marked route leading towards the summit of Odaray Mountain.

For the descent, return to the plateau trail and turn right towards McArthur Pass. Meet the Lake McArthur Trail (2210 m) and follow it to the left for a walk through bright meadows, past Schaffer Lake and back to the ACC Hut, completing the circuit. Bear right here to return to the warden's cabin.

YOHO

24 Lake Oesa

Primary Route
Distance: 6 km/3.8 mi round trip
Hiking time: 3 hours
Elevation gain: 253 m/831 ft
High point: 2288 m/7504 ft
Type: day hike
Best time: late June through September
Map: Lake Louise 82 N/8, Yoho Hiker's Map—Lake O'Hara

Wiwaxy Alpine Route
Distance: 8 km/5 mi round trip
Hiking time: 4.5 hours
Elevation gain: 496 m/1626 ft
High point: 2530 m/8300 ft
Best time: late July through September

A trail from the shores of Lake O'Hara climbing a series of cliffs past 3 small lakes and several waterfalls to a glacier-carved valley with a deep blue lake. The trail is as interesting as the views, with rock stairways and a path engineered across rock slides and boulder fields.

From Lake O'Hara take the lakeshore trail behind the warden's cabin, cross the outlet and follow the lakeshore. In 0.5 km, pass the Wiwaxy Alpine Route (more on this later) and about 1 km from the warden's cabin, reach a Y in the trail. Take the uphill trail, climbing steeply and gaining 150 m in 1 km. The way then moderates and crosses several boulder fields. The rocks that were moved to make this trail are impressive and one wonders how much some of the slabs must weigh and how many men it took to lift them.

After it crosses the boulder fields, the trail again climbs in earnest past 3 small

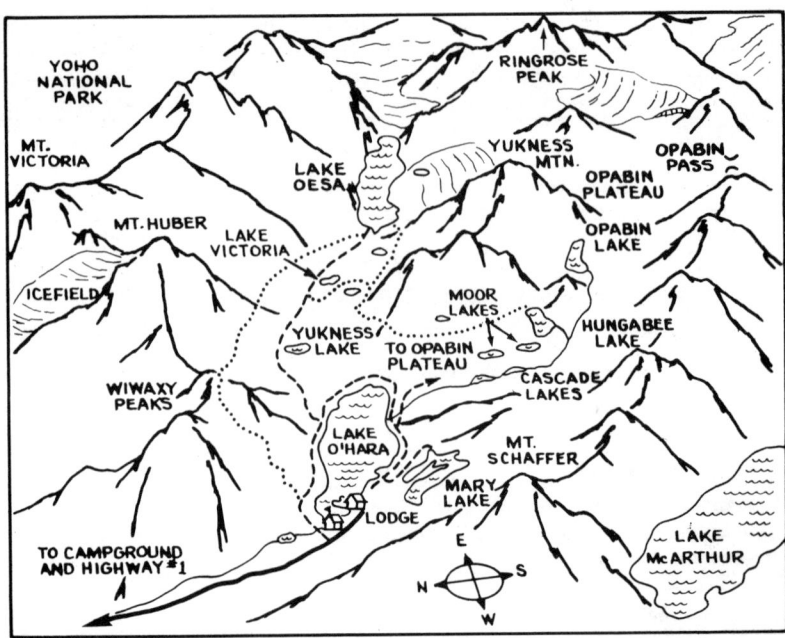

Mt. Biddle and Lake O'Hara from Lake Oesa Trail

lakes. Continue climbing over ledges on stone stairways to reach Lake Oesa (2287 m), about 3 km from the warden's cabin.

The lake can also be reached by the Wiwaxy Alpine Route, mentioned earlier. The views from this route are spectacular and the ledges traversed, airy. Though well-defined, the way is steep and difficult, adding an extra 244-m climb to the hike. The alpine route is no place for small children or the fainthearted and absolutely not for anyone when any part of the path is covered with snow. The route climbs a very steep 488 m to Wiwaxy Gap, then makes a gentle descent to Lake Oesa.

A second alpine route, encountered just west of Lake Victoria (the second of the 3 small lakes) provides an alternative return route from Lake Oesa to Lake O'Hara via the Opabin Plateau. Adding only 2-km distance over the standard return, the Yukness Ledge Route contours around the western side of Yukness Mountain to join the Opabin Lake Trail (Hike 25). This fine route has good views and high alpine flavor, without the strenuous climb involved on the Wiwaxy Route.

YOHO

25 Opabin Lake

Valley Route
Distance: 5.6 km/3.5 mi loop
Hiking time: 3 hours
Elevation gain: 252 m/826 ft
High point: 2286 m/7500 ft
Type: day hike
Best time: mid-July through October
Map: Lake Louise 82 N/8 (all trails not shown) or Yoho Hiker's Map—Lake McArthur

Alpine Route
Distance: 8 km/5 mi loop
Hiking time: 4 hours
Elevation gain: 435 m/1426 ft
High point: 2444 m/8100 ft
Best time: mid-July through September

Two hundred and forty metres above the Lake O'Hara Basin is a beautiful hanging valley, cradled between the steep walls of Mt. Hungabee and Yukness Mountain to the east and Mt. Schaffer to the southwest. Within lie 7 small alpine lakes, meadows, viewpoints and a glacier. Several scenic trails weave a circuit through the valley, connecting with other area trails and creating countless variations.

See Hike 19 for driving directions to the Cataract Brook parking area and hike or take the bus to Lake O'Hara. The Opabin trail branches from the southwest end of Lake O'Hara. A clockwise route around the lake will add a kilometre in total distance, but it offers a waterfall plus the option of side trips on the Wiwaxy Alpine Route and the Lake Oesa Trail (see Hike 24) before reaching the Opabin cutoff.

If the shorter direction is chosen, hike along the southwest shore of Lake O'Hara. At 0.5 km, pass a trail on the right. This will be the return leg of the loop

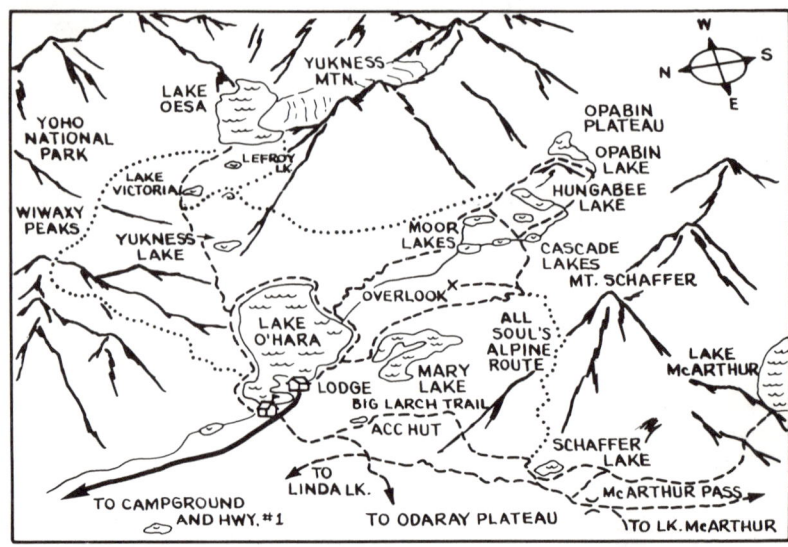

Hungabee and Moor lakes

(the West Opabin Trail). Continue along the shore for a total of 1.2 km to find the East Opabin Trail on the right.

Ascend on forested switchbacks for about 0.5 km and emerge into flower and rock gardens of the Opabin Plateau. The trail levels some as it penetrates the valley. At 2 km the Highline Scenic Route offers a diversion as it cuts right across the valley to the Cascade Lakes. Farther up the valley is Hungabee Lake (2255 m) and another trail. This one goes left to traverse Yukness Mountain to Lake Oesa (see Hike 24). Beyond Hungabee Lake the trail climbs around a small knoll, actually a terminal moraine, to arrive at the rock-and-ice-bound Opabin Lake.

Return by walking around the west side of the moraine-knoll and head towards Hungabee Lake. In a short 0.5 km from Opabin Lake find a viewpoint from which to observe the whole plateau, including the formerly hidden Moor Lakes. Cross the outflow of Hungabee Lake and continue along the east side of Opabin Creek. Where the trail crosses Opabin Creek, it intercepts 2 ill-defined paths. The one to the east of the creek leads to the Highline Trail and continues north to the East Opabin Trail. The one on the west of the creek, the Opabin Prospect Trail, leads to an overlook above Lake O'Hara and Mary Lake.

Just beyond is yet another trail, the All Soul's Alpine Route, which can be joined with the Opabin Lake Trail for a longer, more demanding hike. The name is something of a misnomer, as the path is rough, rocky, wet and poorly marked — certainly not for all. But those staunch souls who venture here will find a stiff climb to a breathtaking viewpoint on a shoulder of Mt. Schaffer. The descent route leads to the Big Larch Trail. Go left to Schaffer Lake, then right at the next trail to pass the ACC Hut and finish at the warden's cabin.

Descend the main trail from the junction with the Alpine Route by passing through a small cleft and onto a talus slope. Contour the west end of Mary Lake and return to Lake O'Hara, completing the loop.

YOHO

26 Ross Lake

Distance: 3 km/1.8 mi round trip
Hiking time: 1 hour
Elevation gain: 90 m/295 ft
High point: 1716 m/5628 ft
Type: short hike/nature walk
Best time: June through September
Map: Lake Louise 82 N/8

Though only 1.5 km from the nearest road, this lovely glacial tarn has remained remarkably unspoiled. Ross Lake's untrampled shores, turquoise waters and cool, lake-borne breezes are a delightful invitation to linger awhile and savor the scenery.

Drive 12.8 km east of Field along Highway 1 (Trans-Canada Highway) to the Highway 1A turnoff. Find the Ross Lake trailhead on Highway 1A, 1.9 km east of the Trans-Canada Highway. A small sign on the south side of the highway marks the trail's start. Park in a gravel pullout across the road from the trail.

For the first kilometre, the trail follows a corduroy road, parallelling the stream. It then bears right, onto a well-defined path that continues for most of the remaining distance. Just before reaching the lake, the trail merges with the fire road that runs from Lake O'Hara to Lake Louise. Together, the trail and the fire road skirt the open, north end of Ross Lake, crossing the outlet stream on an old, but sturdy log footbridge. For further exploration, follow the sketchy trail from the western end of the bridge along the western shoreline.

So close to the road, Ross Lake makes a perfect before-breakfast or after-dinner stroll to catch the first or last rays of the sun in the park.

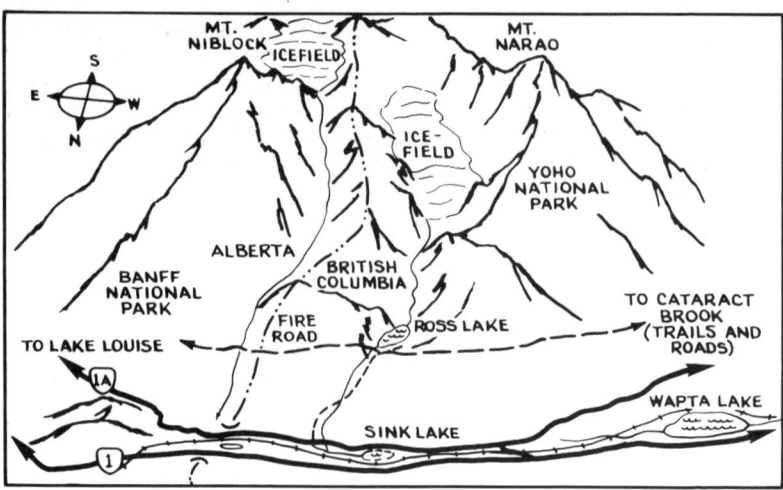

Ross Lake

Grouse

JASPER NATIONAL PARK

Of the 2 national parks described in this book, Jasper is the largest. In fact, its 10 878 square kilometres make it the largest of all Canada's Rocky Mountain parks. Its long backpacking trails, many of which interconnect, provide exceptional opportunities for extended tours, penetrating wild and remote corners of the mountainous backcountry. In addition, there are many short hikes and nature trails within easy access of Jasper townsite, the highways and the roadside campgrounds.

Jasper is the only park, of the 4 detailed here, in which extensive visitor services are available. In addition to the numerous campgrounds, hostels and picnic sites located throughout the park, grocery stores, service stations, hotels, restaurants and a post office are available at Jasper townsite. Park administration offices and a visitor information centre are also located in Jasper. Another visitor information source is the Icefields Centre, located near the Columbia Icefield at the southern end of the park. Visitors are encouraged to drop in for current trail conditions and suggestions on selecting a route. Park use permits (free), as well as maps and literature on natural and human history of the park, are available at either location.

Left: *Mt. Athabasca from Wilcox pass*
Above: *Hikers in Vine Creek Valley*

JASPER

27 Nigel Pass

Distance: 28.6 km/18 mi round trip to Four Point campsite
Hiking time: 2 days
Elevation gain: 298 m/977 ft
High point: 2208 m/7242 ft
Type: backpack
Best time: late June through September
Maps: Columbia Icefield 83 C/3, Sunwapta Peak 83 C/6

Climb a gentle slope through meadows and shrublands to a broad, rolling pass on the southern Jasper boundary. Sample superb high-country and unobstructed views of the massive glaciers flowing from the Columbia Icefield. Then make the steep descent to the Brazeau River while enjoying views of some of the most impressive and rugged peaks in the Front Ranges.

From the Jasper/Banff boundary at Sunwapta Pass, drive south on Highway 93. At 8 km turn left onto the gravel access road. Park along the road, but do not block the gateway. The trailhead is located about 90 m up this road on the right.

Making an almost immediate bridged crossing of Nigel Creek, the trail then swings northward to climb an easy grade. Walk through willowy shrubland and subalpine forest, ascending between Nigel Peak on the left and a large unnamed peak on the right. Still following Nigel Creek, at 5.6 km come to the first campsite—a small, sloping, less hospitable camp than those farther along the trail.

The last 2.5 km to Nigel Pass are gentle and open, crossing flowered meadows from which views of peaks and glaciers continue to grow with every step. Reach the pass at 8 km from the trailhead. Day trippers make this the turn-around spot, but those with time and energy to spare get to choose among several enticing options. Explore the spacious meadowland, or follow the Brazeau River upstream to a spot where its headwaters collect beneath huge, hanging glaciers. Or, climb to Cataract Pass for an afternoon of adventurous scrambling and more splendid vistas. Though a formal trail does not exist here, the route is easy to find.

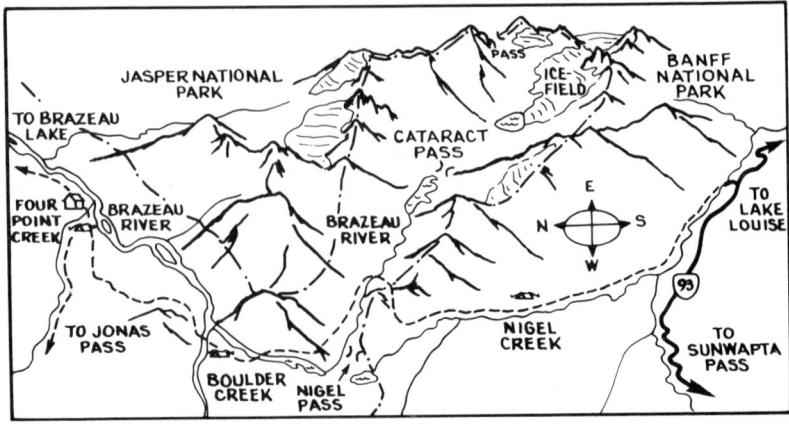

Nigel Pass

Backpackers follow the Brazeau River downstream, tracing its tumultuous descent to the open, green valley below. From the pass, descend the meadowed slopes to cross the river, then continue downstream, passing beneath a rock wall to the level valley bottom. Cross the river again at 10.3 km and come to the Boulder Creek campsite about 150 m beyond the crossing.

Boulder Creek is about 1.6 km beyond the camp area. Cross the creek on a small bridge, then climb a bit to a bench above the valley bottom. Continue along this terrace to the Four Point campsite and trail junction at 14.3 km.

Though the descent from the pass is much steeper than the approach, the route is not difficult, and all major river and creek crossings are bridged.

For a longer trip, proceed beyond Four Point along the Brazeau River, connecting with either the South Boundary Trail (Hike 63) or the Poboktan Pass Trail (Hike 31). Or, choose the Jonas Pass Trail (Hike 33), going west from the junction.

JASPER

28 Wilcox Pass

To Wilcox meadows
Distance: 12 km/7.5 mi round trip
Hiking time: 4 hours
Elevation gain: 318 m/1043 ft
High point: 2330 m/7642 ft
Type: half-day or day hike
Best time: late July through September
Maps: Sunwapta Peak 83 C/6, Columbia Icefield 83 C/3

To Tangle Creek
Distance: 9.6 km/6 mi one way
Hiking time: 2.5-3 hours
Elevation gain: 318 m/1043 ft,
loss 500 m/1640 ft

Scramble up a short, steep ridge to wide-open meadows. Then roam the trackless, rolling tundra between Mt. Wilcox and Nigel Peak. The Wilcox Pass area makes a superb vantage point for partial views of the Columbia Icefield and the many peaks and glaciers of the area. There are also excellent opportunities for spotting mountain goats, sheep, elk, eagles and ptarmigan.

The trailhead is located on the left side of the entrance road to the Wilcox Creek Campground, situated 2 km north of the Jasper/Banff boundary at Sunwapta Pass on Highway 93 (Icefields Parkway). Or, from the Icefields Centre, drive 2.5 km to the Wilcox Creek Campground. Roadside parking is available near the trailhead.

Climbing steeply at first, the trail passes through subalpine forest of spruce and fir. After about 1 km of walking, leave the trees for the meadows and views. The trail is well maintained and clearly marked through the lower meadows. Nearer the pass, the meadowland vegetation thins and the trail becomes fainter, but cairns mark the route through the summit area. Explore the rolling tundra and the small lakes and streams. Look for mountain goats on the ridges, or just relax on a grassy knoll to study the superb scenery.

The trail is actually a former route used by trappers and outfitters only 80 years ago when the Athabasca Glacier covered what is now the Icefields Parkway. It can still be followed in its entirety over the pass and down the Tangle Creek drainage where it joins again with the highway about 8 km northwest of the Wilcox trailhead.

To complete the route, bear to the right while descending from the pass area. The trail is not always obvious, but the general route becomes clear and is marked with

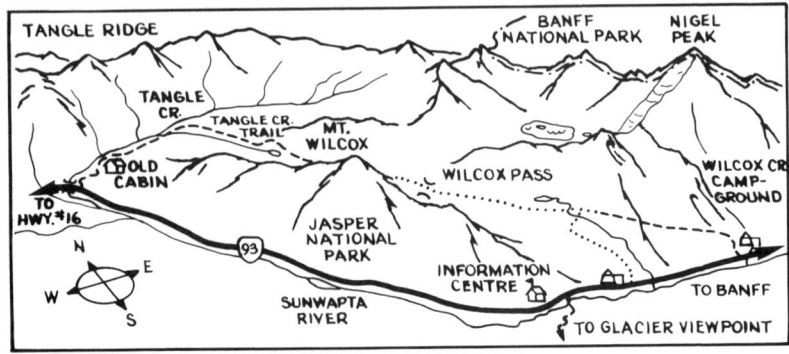

Athabasca Glacier

cairns at about 40-m intervals. The valley narrows near treeline, and the trail becomes well defined again. Follow it easily through the forest, crossing Tangle Creek about halfway, and passing the remains of an old cabin. Emerge near the old highway just above the present Icefields Parkway. Keep right and follow the old road to the Tangle Creek trailhead parking area, about 250 m from the point where it leaves the woods.

JASPER

29 Beauty Creek

Distance: 3.5 km/2 mi round trip to upper falls
Hiking time: 2 hours
Elevation gain: 40 m/131 ft
High point: 1660 m/5445 ft
Type: half-day or day hike
Best time: June through October
Map: Sunwapta Peak 83 C/6

Climb in forest beside spirited waters where 8 closely spaced falls tumble down this narrow gorge and race towards the Sunwapta River. Beauty Creek is indeed a beauty, and what's more, it is easily accessible from Highway 93 (Icefields Parkway). Parking, however, may be a tricky problem as there is no designated trailhead lot. The only convenient spot to leave a vehicle is a wide shoulder off the Icefields Parkway or along the nearby dike (not recommended for low-slung vehicles).

Beauty Creek Falls

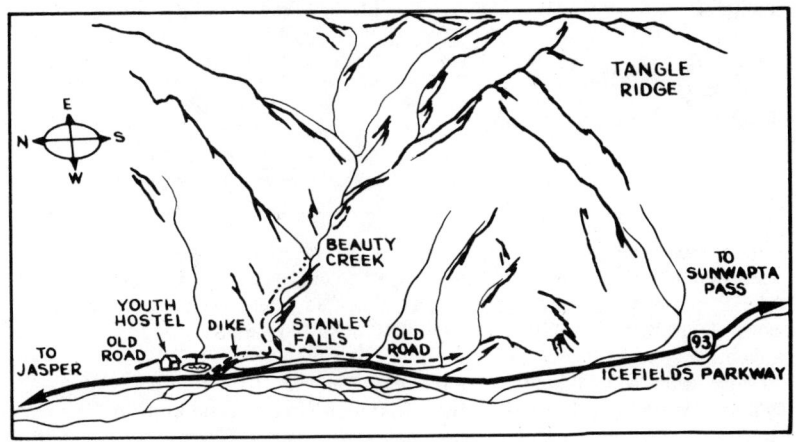

Drive north on the Icefields Parkway 15 km from the Icefields Centre, or 20 km from the Jasper/Banff boundary (Sunwapta Pass), to the Beauty Creek trailhead at a wide dike retaining a stream on the right. Going south on Highway 93, drive 88 km from Jasper to the Beauty Creek Youth Hostel and continue 2 km beyond, watching for the dike on the left. There are no trail signs, but the dike is fairly obvious.

Begin by walking along the dike about 500 m, watching closely for the unmarked trail that suddenly departs on the left. Follow it, passing through a narrow band of trees and emerging on the old Banff-Jasper Highway, now a dirt road. Turn right and walk about 250 m to the remains of an old bridge. Here the trail branches again to the left and climbs steeply for about 0.5 km, where it reaches the first falls. The sometimes steep incline continues past more falls, each more impressive than the previous. Meet the largest and final falls in this series at about 1.7 km. The trail has recently been brushed and upgraded, so it is in good condition; but due to irregular maintenance, be sure to check on current conditions at trail information centres. It is possible to walk a good deal farther upstream for more views and a delightfully secluded creek valley where one might plan to spend a peaceful day or so.

JASPER

30 Poboktan Creek Trail

Distance: 42.4 km/26 mi round trip
 Icefields Parkway to Jonas Pass cutoff
Hiking time: 3-4 days
Elevation gain: 559 m/1834 ft
High point: 2100 m/6888 ft
Type: backpack
Best time: July through October
Map: Sunwapta Peak 83 C/6

Long valley-vistas and cool, dark forests; waterfalls tumbling down rocky steps while lingering snow patches glisten on craggy peaks. A tantalizing show of sights and sounds await the explorer on this valley route. Spend a day, or several, investigating other trails and higher vantage points along the way. The views are superb.

Drive south from Jasper on the Icefields Parkway to the Sunwapta Warden's Station (70 km). Just beyond, on the left, find the trailhead parking lot. From the Jasper/Banff boundary at Sunwapta Pass, drive north for 35 km. Turn east off the highway to enter the parking lot just across the creek from the Sunwapta Warden's Station. Find the trailhead sign on the north side of the parking lot and descend the trail to the creek where it crosses on a sturdy suspension bridge. Then follow the trail along the creek, climbing and curving through thick forest, though occasional breaks in the canopy allow good views across the Sunwapta Valley and up into the Winston Churchill Range.

Heavily used by both hikers and horses, the trail shows the impact: It is often wide, wet and muddy. But most of the wetter areas and stream crossings have been improved with bridges and corduroy sections.

Crossing a small stream on the Poboktan Creek Trail

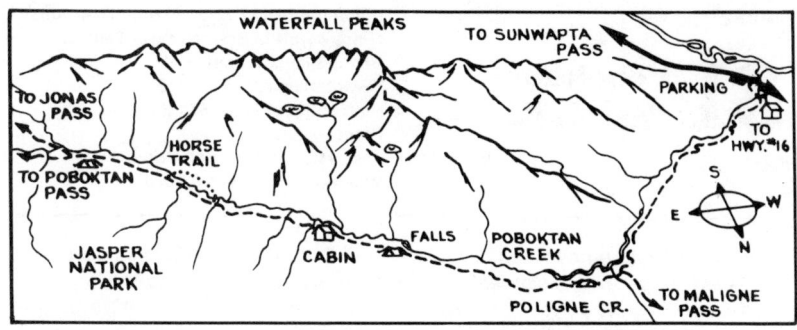

Gentle at first, the grade soon steepens and gains nearly half the total elevation of the trail in the first 6 km. At Poligne Creek (6 km), cross the bridge and bear right, passing the junction of the Maligne Pass Trail (Hike 34). In another kilometre reach the first campsite beside Poboktan Creek.

Beyond the campsite the trail continues its gentle-to-moderate grade, travelling above the creekbed, alternating between good and muddy stretches as it moves through forest and shrubland, an old burn and meadows. Then, it drops again towards the creek, passing through a drift fence and arriving at a beautifully terraced waterfall.

This spot makes a good turnaround for day trippers or a pleasant lunch site for those planning to do the entire trail in a day. The more leisurely hiker or the late-starter may decide to make camp at the small, forested campsite located just above the falls on the hillside.

The trail continues awhile at the forest's edge, passing behind the warden's cabin, then ascending again through trees to gain 120 m of elevation in less than 2 km. As the forest thins and open shrubland takes over, the trail becomes increasingly boggy. At one point the trail divides to separate horse and hiker traffic in an attempt to reduce muddiness. Little is gained by this, however, and from here on, the trail is relatively rough.

The last campsite is located at 20 km, on a small knoll in a clump of trees. The trail then descends to Poboktan Creek to join with the Poboktan Pass and Jonas Pass Trails.

JASPER

31 Poboktan Pass Trail

Distance: 34.4 km/21.4 mi round trip Jonas Pass cutoff to Brazeau River Trail
Hiking time: 2-4 days
Elevation gain: 524 m/1719 ft
High point: 2304 m/7560 ft
Type: backpack
Best time: July through October
Map: Sunwapta Peak 83 C/16

Walk this high route through spacious, rolling tundra to the 2304-m pass with its far-reaching views. Meander in gardens of flowers and grasses and lingering patches of snow. Then descend a scenic creek valley between 2 massive, brightly colored rock cliffs, to the chilly waters of Brazeau Lake.

The trail makes a link in the Poboktan Pass/Brazeau River/Jonas Pass Loop (Hikes 31, 32 and 33), or can be accessed via Nigel Pass (Hike 27) and the Brazeau River trails. It may also be hiked as an extension of the Poboktan Creek Trail, but because of snow, is not always accessible as early as the lower creek route. Hike this straightforward trail in either direction in 1 or 2 days, camping at either end or at the John-John Creek campsite about halfway. The hike is described here in a west-to-east direction but presents no major difficulty the opposite way. Even where the trail becomes indistinct in the sparse vegetation, the route is obvious.

Beginning at the Jonas cutoff (see Hike 30), follow the left fork along Poboktan Creek. Though horse traffic crosses and recrosses the creek, you can avoid fording by climbing the hillside above the creek and rejoining the trail upstream. After about 2 km, the trail moves away from the stream, traversing the soft, rolling tundra and moderate slope to reach the pass at about 3 km.

Trail conditions along this stretch vary from slightly damp to downright wet and muddy as the winter snows melt, the meadows flow and the streamlets run. Late August and September may be the prime time for this trip. In spite of the slog, the views are exceptional, so be forewarned and go prepared with well-sealed boots and extra dry socks.

Approaching the pass, watch for relics of the old telephone lines that used to run to the warden's cabin on John-John Creek. Then descend the steeper east slope. Views are of Le Grand Brazeau Mountains. About 3 km from the pass, the trail reaches treeline, marked by the appearance of scrub spruce that gradually blend into the thicker fir-and-lodgepole forests along the creek.

Traverse a small rock slide before passing the warden's cabin on the opposite side of the creek, and reach the John-John Creek campsite at 7.2 km. Located in a valley-bottom clearing between 2 steep and imposing rock faces, the small campsite offers a dry spot for tents and sleeping bags, but you'll have to climb the hillside

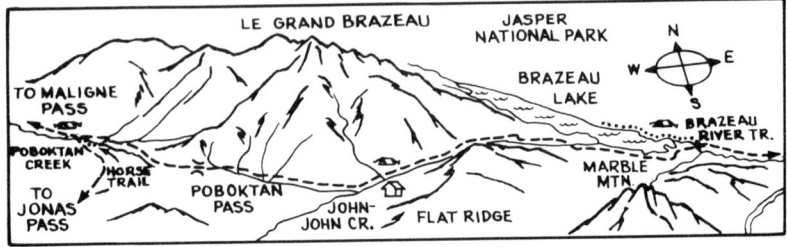

Brazeau Lake

across the trail to find trees for hanging food bags. At sunset, the jagged rock cliffs stage a grand show of color and light as they catch the alpenglow and toss it back to the darkening sky.

Beyond the campsite, the trail remains relatively well drained as it crosses several slide paths above the creek. Enter the forest again near the end of the valley, and continue a gradual descent to the bridge over John-John Creek, where a massive landslide has parted the forest, allowing captivating views of Brazeau Lake.

More views of the lake appear through the open forest as the trail skirts the southern shore, until it drops down to bridge the gushing, silty outflow waters. A comfortable campsite rests about 100 m upstream from the crossing, and trails wind along the northern lakeshore to views and secluded spots.

The main trail continues eastward for about 2 km, rolling gently through open spruce forest along the outlet stream. Reach the junction with the Brazeau River Trail at 17.2 km, where a left turn will join with the South Boundary Trail (Hike 63), while a right turn follows the Brazeau River, eventually meeting with the Nigel Pass Trail (Hike 27) to the Highway 93 (Icefields Parkway).

Brazeau River

JASPER

32 Brazeau River Trail

Distance: 31 km/19 mi round trip
Hiking time: 1-2 days
Elevation gain: 230 m/754 ft
High point: 1950 m/6396 ft
Type: long day hike or backpack
Best time: July through September
Map: Sunwapta Peak 83 C/6

Hard-to-beat views, gentle trail, and days of leisurely exploring are just a sampling of what one can expect to find here. Channeled by the rugged peaks of the Continental Ranges, the Brazeau River Valley has a lot to offer, in spite of its minimal elevation change.

Plan to camp at one of the comfortable sites along the river, or hold out for the Brazeau campsite at trail's end, which makes a superb base camp for roaming. Then take a short side trip to Brazeau Lake, or wander northward along the Brazeau River (South Boundary Trail, Hike 63) for peak-packed vistas.

The trail is easy to follow: no major problems and most river crossings are bridged. It is often hiked as a link in the Poboktan Pass/Brazeau River/Jonas Pass Loop, accessed via Poboktan Creek (Hikes 31, 32 and 33), or, more frequently, via the Nigel Pass Trail (Hike 27), as described here.

See Hike 27 for driving directions and follow the trail 14.3 km to the Four Point campsite and trail junction. Heading northeast from the junction, the trail is a rambling delight of terraced meadows and sparse, open forests. The way is flat and moves easily along, crossing 2 bridged streams and making the first crossing of Brazeau River at 4.7 km. Views of nearby peaks persist, providing bait to continue.

Reach an inviting campsite, nestled in a small grove of trees, at 6.9 km. Beyond, more delightful meadows stretch on beside the Brazeau as it scores the base of Marble Mountain. Occasionally passing through patches of pine and spruce, the trail finally recrosses the river at 12.4 km and remains in forest for the duration of the trip. In the last 3 km, the trail descends about 100 m through a rocky forest to reach the Brazeau campsite between Brazeau River and the Brazeau Lake outflow. If high waters and heavy rainfall have left the campsite a bit soggy, continue on to the Brazeau Lake campsite, just 2 km down the Poboktan Pass Trail.

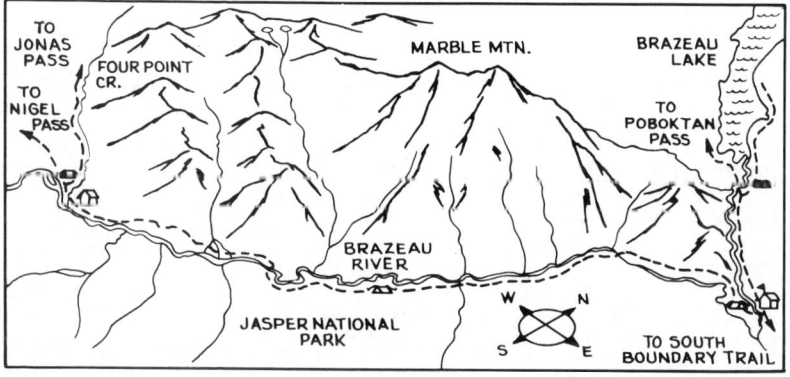

JASPER

33 Jonas Pass Trail

Distance: 19.3 km/12 mi one way
Hiking time: 8 hrs
Elevation gain: 550 m/1804 ft
High point: 2460 m/8069 ft
Type: backpack
Best time: August through mid-October
Map: Sunwapta Peak 83 C/6

Vast alpine meadows laced with streams and strewn with wildflowers. Icy waterfalls tumbling from remnant glaciers and lingering snowfields. Cirques, valleys, tarns and ridges fill the horizons on this stretch of Jasper highlands.

The delicate nature of the fragile alpine environment has made it necessary for the park to establish quotas for the trail, restrict camping to areas located at either end of the 19-km stretch and ask visitors to move through the area in a day. Originally cut by horses' hooves, the trail is now primarily a hikers' trail, the indirect result, no doubt, of the restrictions placed on grazing animals in the pass area.

A particularly scenic link in the Poboktan Pass/Brazeau River/Jonas Pass Loop (Hikes 31, 32 and 33), the trail may be approached from either the Four Point Creek drainage and Nigel Pass or from the Poboktan Creek drainage (see Hikes 27 and 30 for driving directions).

From the Four Point Campground, follow the trail westward over marshy valley flats into dry lodgepole forest and up a moderately steep grade. The rest of the trail represents some of the driest of Jasper's alpine routes. Climb steadily through forest for about 1 km, then level out as the forest changes to subalpine fir and spruce, finally thinning to scattered clumps. The thick ground cover near treeline is a luxuriant bed of grasses, heather and moss that continues for some distance into the valley but gradually becomes more scarce and fragile as the trail gains elevation.

Scenery is constantly unfolding as the slow grade climbs through the wide, glacier-carved valley towards the pass area. At the pass are small tarns, knolls strewn with wildflowers and new views down the Jonas Creek Valley. Descend westward along Jonas Creek for about 2 km before angling right to begin the ascent towards the long ridge known as Jonas Shoulder, which separates the Poboktan and Jonas Creek valleys. Steep, but relatively short, the climb to the ridge crest traverses sections of scree and snow, making it more difficult to follow, though it is marked with rock cairns. Work towards the narrow notch through which the trail must pass. Take a few moments at the ridge crest to enjoy the views down both the Jonas and Poboktan creek valleys.

Pass through the notch and descend the steep switchback over loose talus and scree, then continue into wet alpine vegetation on the long slopes. Though the trail tends to fade in spots, follow the general course of runoff streams, crossing them

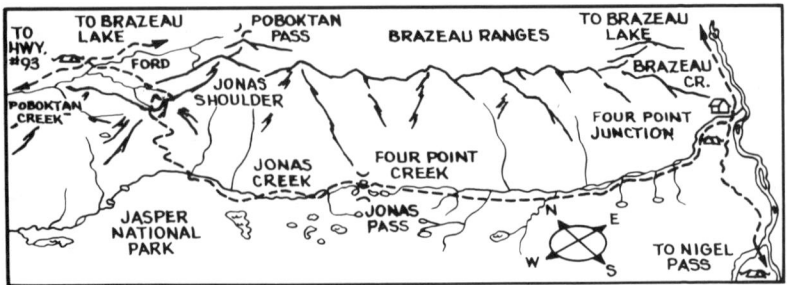

when necessary to stay on the east side. Near treeline, the trail again becomes visible and descends quickly to cross Poboktan Creek and join the Poboktan Creek and Poboktan Pass trails. A second campsite is located just 1 km downstream from this junction.

Approaching from the Poboktan Creek drainage, watch for the old Jonas Pass Trail sign atop a knoll across Poboktan Creek from the junction of Poboktan Creek and Poboktan Pass trails. The Jonas Pass Trail ascends to the right of the knoll following the watercourse to treeline and on towards Jonas Shoulder. Where the trail begins to fade in the spongy tundra, a map and compass may be helpful in locating the notch above the steep talus slope.

Jonas Creek Valley and a shoulder of Sunwapta Peak

JASPER

34. Maligne Pass Trail

Distance: 41 km/25.4 mi one way
Hiking time: 2-3 days
Elevation gain: 759 m/2490 ft
High point: 2300 m/7544 ft
Type: backpack
Best time: August through mid-October
Maps: Athabasca Falls 83 C/12, Southesk 83 C/11, Sunwapta Peak 83 C/6

Expansive views of nearby mountain ranges unfold as the trail wanders through flowers, mosses and lichens. Follow the Maligne River almost to its headwaters at Maligne Pass, beneath the craggy shapes of the Endless Chain Ridge. These excellent grazing lands are popular foraging sites for local herds of elk, moose, caribou and mountain goat. The Maligne Pass Trail is a fine trip in itself, but many hikers choose to combine it with the somewhat more spectacular Skyline, Poboktan Pass or Jonas Pass trails. The wet, boggy trail is best travelled in late season when runoff waters are at a minimum. Even then, be prepared for numerous stream crossings and infinitely soggy stretches, though most major stream crossings are bridged.

Beginning at Maligne Lake (see Hike 67 for driving directions), walk the Bald Hills Fire Road for 250 m to the trailhead on the left. Follow the trail through pleasant forests of spruce and pine for about 5 km. The grade here is gentle and the forest floor dry (enjoy it while you can). As the trail gains elevation, the forest thins, finally changing to large open meadows and willowy shrubland interspersed with pine and spruce forests.

Cross Trapper Creek (bridged) at 5.7 km and reach the first campsite just beyond. Then continue through level-to-rolling meadowlands with patches of pine and

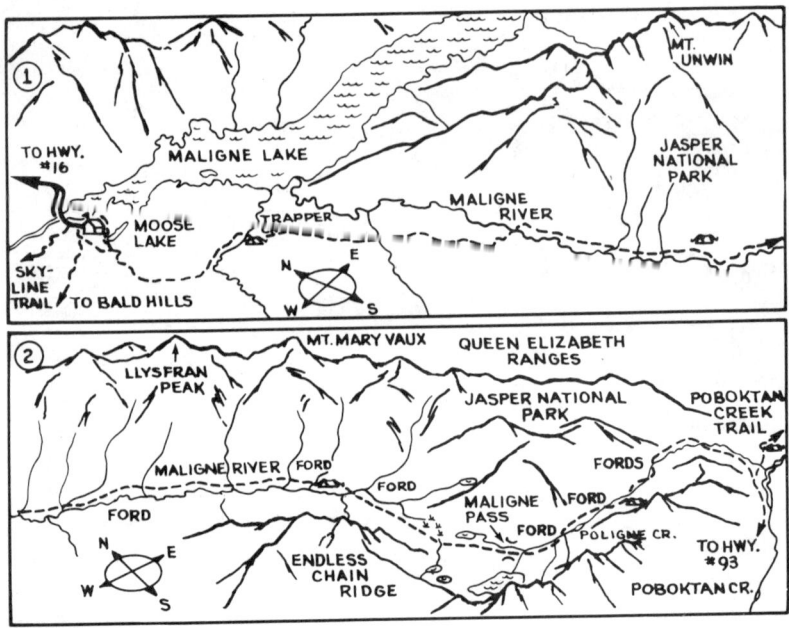

A chilly crossing

spruce, and cross a large bridged stream at 9 km. At 13 km cross the Maligne River. Fortunately this once-difficult task has been lessened with the aid of a sturdy suspension bridge located just downstream from the horse crossing.

A cool spruce forest provides a pleasant change as the trail snakes along at the foot of Mt. Unwin, parting briefly here and there to reveal the mountains above. Reach a second campsite at 17.1 km, then follow the Maligne River along the valley floor, passing through the edges of forest and willow flats and rising gradually to the subalpine regions. Cross several avalanche areas on the flanks of Mt. Mary Vaux as the trail continues to climb gently.

Now the increased moisture in the area may become a bit troublesome, as numerous stream crossings are necessary. A third campsite is located just beyond a ford of a rather large stream, and 1 more kilometre will present another crossing of the Maligne River, this time without the aid of a bridge. Sometimes difficult, this ford is most safely made during late season and dry weather when large boulders in the streambed are sufficiently exposed to provide good stepping stones.

Continue through trees below Replica Peak, then out again into flowery gardens that roll along beneath views of surrounding peaks and passes. To the east appear the snowy tops of Mts. Brazeau and Warren, and southward the towering Endless Chain Ridge presents an imposing backdrop to the Maligne Pass area. Open, alpine

Poligne Creek

Bull moose

and invariably boggy, the meadows roll on towards the wide pass where a small lake graces the summit. Reaching the pass at 31.7 km, the trail traverses above the northeast side of the lake.

Descend over scree and sparse vegetation to follow Poligne Creek, continuing into spruce forest. A stretch of solid footing here is a welcome change, though the inevitable wet conditions return as the trail continues along the stream. The trail crosses Poligne Creek without the aid of a bridge, shortly before reaching another campsite at 36 km—a pleasant spot on the edge of a meadow. Ford the creek again, then follow a ridgeline above the creek for a short distance before descending to make several more stream crossings which are increasingly difficult. The last 3 crossings of Poligne Creek are bridged, the final one being at the junction of the Maligne Pass and Poboktan Creek trails at 41 km.

A moderate-to-gentle grade down the Poboktan Creek Trail leads to the Sunwapta Warden's Station and Highway 93 (Icefields Parkway) in 6 km. Or, choose to continue southwest along the Poboktan Creek Trail (Hike 30) and on to the junction with the Poboktan Pass (Hike 31) and Jonas Pass (Hike 33) trails.

Sunwapta Falls

JASPER

35 Lower Sunwapta Falls

Distance: 4 km/2.5 mi round trip
Hiking time: 1 hour
Elevation gain: 80 m/262 ft
High point: 1400 m/4592 ft
Type: nature hike
Best time: May through November
Map: Athabasca Falls 83 C/12

Here's an exciting little leg-stretcher along the thunderous Sunwapta River. Saunter along beside the flood of silty, jade waters as they batter away at potholes and caves en route to join forces with the Athabasca some 2.5 km downstream.

The Sunwapta Falls turnoff is located 22.8 km southeast of the intersection of Highways 16 and 93. Turn off 93 and drive 0.6 km to the Sunwapta Falls parking area. The trail begins at the south end of the parking lot.

The moderately downsloping trail follows the north side of the tumultuous stream, passing a series of falls and rapids. Though unpaved, the trail is easy walking and features several scenic overlooks on the way to the most impressive Lower Sunwapta Falls. Though the trail officially ends here, it is possible to explore farther along the riverbank.

Picnic spots and interpretive signs near the parking area provide a comfortable setting for an afternoon of leisurely activities for the whole family.

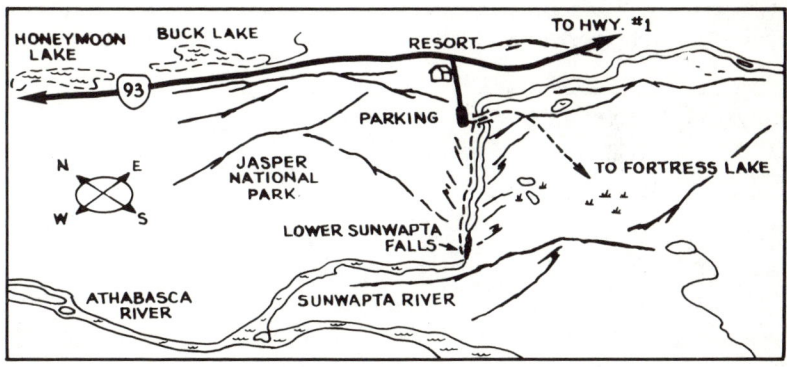

JASPER

36 Fortress Lake Trail

To Fortress Lake
Distance: 45 km/28 mi round trip
Hiking time: 2-3 days
Elevation gain: 960 m/3150 ft
High point: 1386 m/4550 ft
Type: backpack
Best time: late August through mid-October
Maps: Athabasca Falls 83 C/12, Fortress Lake 83 C/5

To Athabasca River crossing
Distance: 28 km/17 mi round trip
Hiking time: 2 days
Type: backpack
Best time: July through October

Steep cliffs and icy peaks surround the 11-km-long Fortress Lake, which guards the only trail into this vicinity. This pocket of pristine beauty, indeed a hikers' paradise, unfortunately is inaccessible to most foot travellers during the major part of the hiking season. Without bridges to aid the otherwise formidable crossings of the Athabasca and Chaba rivers, the unspoiled backcountry receives few visitors. Horse packers sometimes swim their horses across, but the only foot access to the area must be left to those with mountaineering skills, who can cross over from the upper Fryatt Valley (see Hike 40) or Geraldine Lakes (Hike 41).

Park officials feel that this should remain an area for the hardy, and they do not presently plan to construct any bridges here. Those strong and experienced hikers

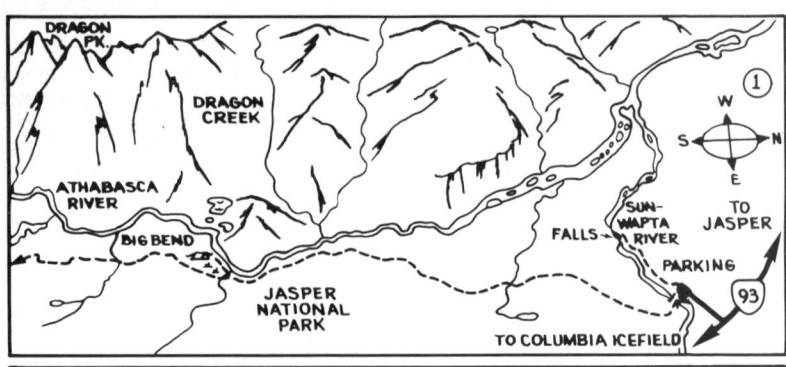

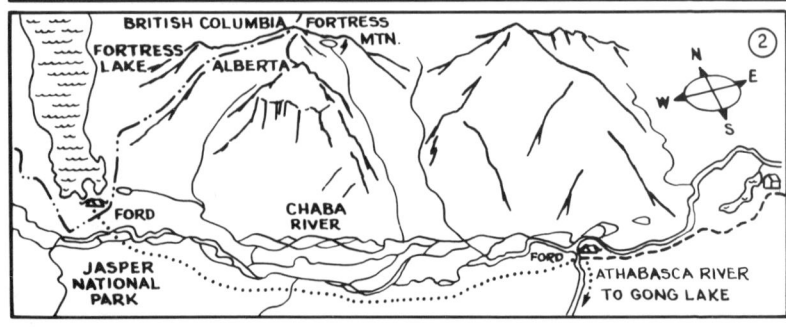

Athabasca River at Big Bend

who wish to make this trip are advised to wait until late season after a particularly dry stretch, when waters are lowest.

Unless a more reasonable hikers' route into Hamber Provincial Park becomes available, most foot travellers must be content to turn around at the crossing. The near-level walk along the Athabasca River is a beautiful trip itself, with tantalizing views up the Chaba River and into the upper Athabasca River Valley.

The trail begins at the Lower Sunwapta Falls parking area (Hike 35). Cross the bridge over the upper falls and continue along the old road on the other side. Pass through dense lodgepole forest on old river terraces, and descend gradually for about 6.5 km, finally reaching the Athabasca River at Big Bend. A scenic campsite lies on a small point 0.3 km off the main trail: a good destination for day hikers.

The next 5.5 km are mostly forested as the trail stays away from the often marshy river's edge. Then, it closely parallels the river for the final 2 km to the crossing. Though this is the natural turnaround for most hikers, the more adventurous may want to explore farther up the Athabasca, perhaps searching out Gong Lake. Keep in mind that this is map-and-compass country as there is no maintained trail.

JASPER

37 Wabasso Lake

Distance: 5.7 km/3.5 mi round trip
Hiking time: 1.5 hours
Elevation gain: 40 m/131 ft
High point: 1260 m/4133 ft
Type: Picnic or short hike
Best time: May through October
Map: Medicine Lake 83 C/13

A quick-and-easy trip through pine forest, grassy meadows, and patches of wildflowers to a delightful lake on the Prairie de la Vache. With little change in elevation, this pleasant route travels along flower-lined streams, allowing glimpses of snow-topped peaks before reaching the teal blue waters of Wabasso Lake. Although overnight camping is not permitted, the peaceful lake and grassy shorelines, scattered with wild rose and Indian paintbrush, make a perfect setting to while away a lazy afternoon.

Drive south on Highway 93 (Icefields Parkway) from the intersection of Highways 16 and 93. At 14 km, turn left off the highway into a small parking lot. The trailhead is located at the south end of the parking lot.

The trail parallels the highway for a brief distance before swinging east to crest a small rise. Delightful pine and aspen forest gives way to open meadowlands as the trail enters the Prairie de la Vache, a level stretch of land also known as Buffalo Prairie. Cross a small stream on a log bridge at the far side of the meadow, then continue upstream for a short distance and recross to climb beside the cascading water. One more crossing and the trail levels, approaching lush, grassy marshes at the head of Wabasso Lake.

Reach the first picnic spot just beyond the marshes, near the shore. Here the trail meets the Wabasso Lake to Big Shovel Pass Trail (Hike 39), which connects the Valley of the Five Lakes area to the Skyline Trail (Hike 66). Sometimes merging, sometimes parallelling, the 2 trails wind around the shoreline to the north and east shores for better views and more picnic sites.

Wabasso Lake

Mule deer in velvet

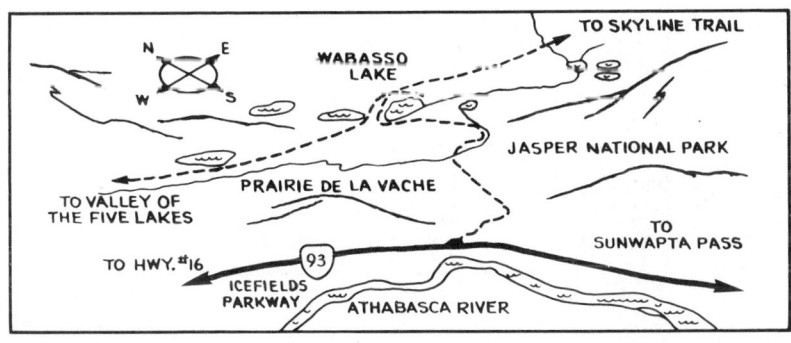

Prairie de la Vache

JASPER

38 Valley of The Five Lakes

Long Loop
Distance: 18.5 km/11.5 mi round trip
Hiking time: 6 hours
Elevation gain: 130 m/426 ft
High point: 1160 m/3806 ft
Type: day hike
Best time: late June through October
Map: Jasper 83 D/16 (trail not shown)

Short Loop
Distance: 5.5 km/3.5 mi round trip
Hiking time: 2 hours
Elevation gain: 60 m/197 ft
High point: 1130 m/3707 ft

A lovely lowland valley, embracing 5 small, closely set lakes, is the destination here. Labled Wabasso Lakes on the topographic map, this aquatic little troupe is a lake-lover's dream and a perfect destination for a family excursion. Lots of room to picnic and explore, fish for trout, or just relax and drink in the beautiful reflections of the Jasper Rockies, visible in all directions.

Two separate loops access the area; and while both offer the diversity of views, aspen groves, pine forests, marshlands and beaver ponds, the longer is recommended for a greater sampling of the area's charms. Both trails are fairly gentle with some moderately steep sections.

Begin the longer loop at the Old Fort Point trailhead and parking area (Hike 75). From the intersection of Highways 93 and 16, drive south on 93 for 2 km and turn left on the Highway 93A cutoff. Proceed for 1.6 km, then turn right onto Beauvert Lake Road. Go another 0.8 km to cross the Athabasca River, then enter the first parking area on the right, situated below Old Fort Point.

Begin the hike at the rear of the parking lot at the trail marked 1A, keeping left at the junction. Following the Old Fort Point Trail for the first 1.5 km, climb through aspen and willow along a gentle draw to a rocky cliffband and narrow pass where the Valley of the Five Lakes Trail continues straight while the Old Fort Point Trail branches right. Go straight, heading south over rolling hills, through more aspen groves, and cross Tekarra Creek at 4 km. Shortly after crossing the creek, pass near a large marsh and begin a steep but short climb.

Reach another intersection at 5.5 km and keep left for another kilometre to reach the first and largest of the 5 lakes. Encircled by forest, this makes a pleasant picnic or fishing spot. Just beyond the lake, the trail encounters the shorter loop trail, which merges to circle the rest of the lakes. Continue on to find the small, rockbound second lake—hardly more than a puddle by late summer. This one, along with the third and fourth lakes (separated only by a thin strip of land), has an open feeling with few trees. The fifth lake is once again in the forest and large enough (like the first) to permit several boats, which hikers can arrange to rent in advance at sporting goods stores in Jasper.

Choose to follow a rough trail around the fifth lake, or turn right at the northern tip of the lake to reach the picnic area and start the return loop.

Follow the trail along the lakes to another intersection with the short loop trail and turn left to descend a gentle slope into grassland. In a short distance, encounter the Wabasso Lake to Big Shovel Pass Trail (Hike 39), and turn right for a meadowy stroll of about 3 km to rejoin the lakes trail.

If time is limited, try the shorter loop, beginning on Highway 93 at 8.7 km south of the intersection of Highways 93 and 16. From the signed trailhead on the east side of the highway, start the walk in a band of pine forest, which soon thins to grassland. At about 1 km, the trail must negotiate an ever-expanding, beaver-engineered impoundment (expect wet feet here). Arriving shortly at the intersection with the Wabasso Lake to Big Shovel Pass Trail, cross the trail and climb a minor ridge with excellent views, to reach the loop trail.

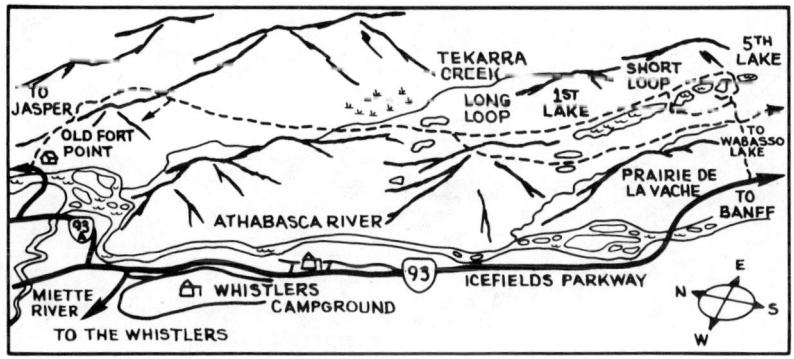

JASPER

39 Wabasso Lake to Big Shovel Pass

Distance: 28.6 km/17.8 mi round trip from Wabasso Lake trailhead
Hiking time: 2 days
Elevation gain: 1120 m/3674 ft
High point: 2200 m/7216 ft
Type: backpack
Best time: June through October
Maps: Jasper 83 D/16,
  Medicine Lake 83 C/13

Serene, lowland, open forest wandering past numerous lakes, streams and meadows, a steep and rocky climb, a subalpine valley parkland and finally the splendid heights of the Maligne Range. In spite of some stretches of poor trail, this is an interesting and scenic alternative to the ever-popular and ever-crowded Skyline Trail (Hike 66). Though most of the trail is in relatively good shape, it is used frequently by horse packers and has some boot-grabbing

Unnamed stream below Curator Lake

mucky stretches until late season. And the mosquitos and biting flies can be enough to try any hiker's patience.

The trail can be accessed from any of 3 different starting points, each significantly altering the total distance to be hiked. The shortest and most frequently used access is the Wabasso Lake Trail (Hike 37), which proceeds from the northeast side of the lake towards the Maligne Range. The second access point is the same as that for the Valley of the Five Lakes. See Hike 38 (short loop) for driving directions, then follow the trail to its intersection with the access link to the Wabasso Lake to Big Shovel Pass Trail. This trail rambles through forest and meadows of the Prairie de la Vache for about 7 km to reach Wabasso Lake.

The third and longest access route begins at the Old Fort Point parking area and the Valley of the Five Lakes trailhead (Hike 38, long loop). The trail traces the Valley of the Five Lakes Trail for 5.5 km, where it divides to form the lake loop. Bear right on the trail leading through the Prairie de la Vache and continue for 13 km to Wabasso Lake.

Leaving the lake, the trail begins to climb the 1000+ m to the skyline, slowly at first, then steepening to climb nearly 900 toilsome metres in 8 km of switchbacks. Be sure to carry enough water on this dry, rocky stretch, as there is no dependable source, and available supplies may be contaminated by horses.

As the trail breaks out of the forest zone, the terrain soon levels and enters a lovely alpine valley complete with sparkling stream, patches of wildflowers and superb views. Unfortunately, here is the worst of the horse-churned trail. Keep left of the stream, amid the sparse trees for the last 2 km. Follow the trail past the horse corral to another steep but short climb. This one leads out of the valley and the mud, to Curator campsite, beside a peaceful pond fed by cascading waters from Curator Lake.

From the campsite, hike to the Big Shovel Pass area (2286 m) or visit The Notch (2530 m) above Curator Lake for breathtaking views. If transportation can be arranged, consider a cross-range trip that descends to the north through the Watchtower Basin (Hike 61) for long rambles through more alpine meadows. This route can be accessed from the Skyline Trail (Hike 66) near Big Shovel Pass.

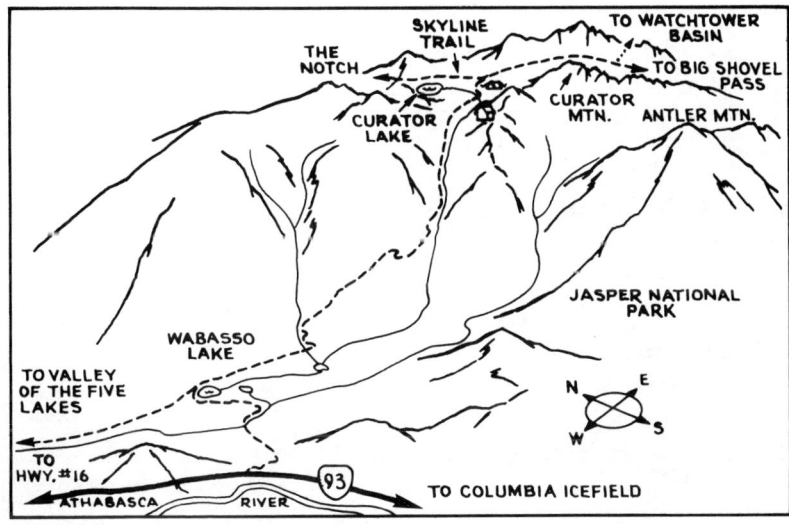

JASPER

40 Fryatt Creek

Distance: 43 km/26.7 mi round trip
Hiking time: 2-3 days
Elevation gain: 820 m/2690 ft
High point: 2000 m/6560 ft
Type: backpack
Best time: June through October
Map: Athabasca Falls 83 C/12

Hard won, but worth every gruelling step, the upper Fryatt Valley is one of the most beautiful alpine valleys in the Jasper Park area. Discover a glacier-fed jewel of a lake, trimmed by alpine buttercups, mountain avens and heather, and closely guarded by a court of craggy peaks. The upper valley is a splendid focal point from which days of high-country rambling and exploring are possible. The beauty, serenity and charm of this basin should be savored, so plan to spend more than a day here. The trip itself is quite long, and the full impact of what this unique place has to offer would be difficult to absorb in a day.

Drive south on Highway 93 (Icefields Parkway) from the junction with Highway 16. At about 6.4 km turn right onto route 93A and continue 17 km to the intersection with the Geraldine Fire Lookout Road (Geraldine Lakes Road). Make another right, then follow the gravel road 2 km to the trailhead on the left.

Begin the walk along an old dirt road which persists for 2 to 3 km before dwindling to a single track, and continue on flat terrain through almost invariable lodgepole pine forest. Not an exciting start, and not made any more tolerable by the fact that nearly 9 km of the trail lies directly across the river from the Icefields Parkway, both visible and audible from the trail.

Pass a small marshy meadow area 0.5 km from the trailhead. In another 1.5 km make the first stream crossing and another in 0.5 km. Split-log bridges aid in the crossing of most streams along the trail. More stream crossings are necessary at 5.5 and 6 km. At 8.5 km the trail makes a sharp right turn and ascends a small plateau area, making a long switchback before levelling off. Upon reaching the buttes (9 km), where the combined waters of Fryatt and Lick creeks join the Athabasca River, the trail turns southwest and proceeds towards the Fryatt Valley.

At 11 km, reach Lower Fryatt campsite near Fryatt Creek, the first designated

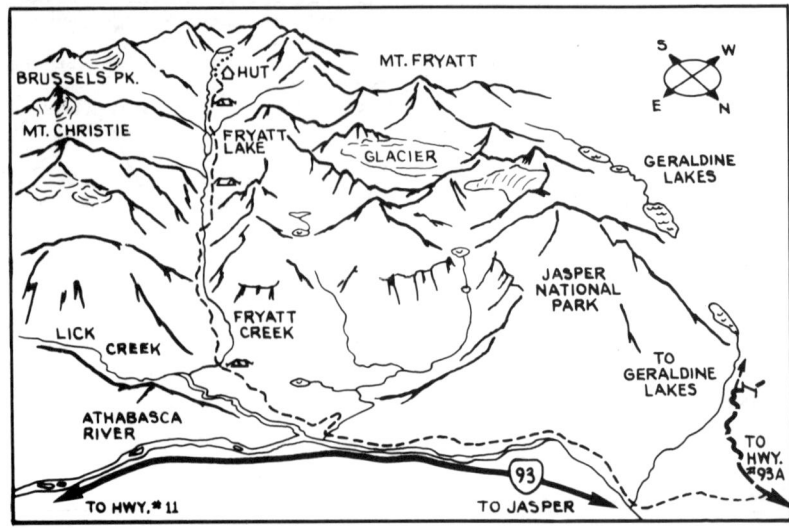

Fryatt Lake

backcountry campsite. Cross the creek on a wooden bridge and follow the trail into the Fryatt Creek drainage. Notice the distinct change in vegetation as the trail gains elevation.

Ascend steadily now through spruce and fir along the base of Mt. Christie, catching glimpses of the creek. Cross Fryatt Creek again at 14.5 km, this time on a split-log bridge, and continue along the creek. This is a tiresome, ankle-wrenching walk on rounded river rocks, but the magnificent headwall waterworks, now visible from the creekbed, offer a pleasant distraction. Reach the Brussels campsite at 17 km, then cross a large fan of scree and talus. Cairns may be difficult to follow, but as you crest the rock pile, Fryatt Lake becomes visible and the trail soon emerges to follow the right shoreline. The last 3 km to the headwall travel beyond the lake through lovely meadows, past the last designated (and most popular) campsites and into the scrub forest at the head of the valley.

An ascent of the headwall requires sturdy legs and perseverance. The trail is good and presents no major difficulties other than being steep, but views are exceptional and worth every step. Many hikers prefer to camp below and make the climb without a heavy pack. An alternative is to stay in the Parks Canada Hut at the top of the headwall. Reservations are required, however, and this popular spot fills up fast during peak season. Many climbers frequent the area, using the hut as a base of operations from which days of climbing in rugged country can be planned. Cross-country skiing is also becoming a popular activity both in the lower valley and in the alpine terrain; however, this location is recommended only for experienced winter travellers due to avalanche hazards.

JASPER

41 Geraldine Lakes

Distance: 12 km/7 mi to Second Geraldine Lake
Hiking time: 4 hours
Elevation gain: 400 m/1312 ft
High point: 1900 m/6232 ft
Type: day hike or backpack
Best time: June through mid-October
Map: Athabasca Falls 83 C/12

Forest and flowers, then views all around of a glacially terraced valley. Meltwaters cascade down Mt. Fryatt and surrounding ridges to feed the chain of stepped lakes and waterfalls. A full spectrum of sights and challenges awaits, packed tightly into a few square kilometres and set snugly between 2 prominent mountain ridges. Possibilities range from a few hours of easy rambling to several days of rugged scrambling and cross-country exploring.

Drive south on Highway 93 (Icefields Parkway) from the junction with

Waterfall below second Geraldine Lake

Highway 16. At 6 km turn right onto route 93A and continue 17 km to the junction with the Geraldine Fire Lookout Road (Geraldine Lakes Road), and make another right. Follow the gravel road for 5.3 km to the parking area next to the trailhead. From the Jasper/Banff border (Sunwapta Pass), drive north on Highway 93 to the southern junction of 93 and 93A. Turn left and drive 1 km to the Geraldine Fire Lookout Road.

Begin on a good trail that winds and climbs through thick pine and spruce forest. It's a pleasant walk of only 2 km to the first Geraldine Lake, but be forewarned: Mosquitoes can be ferocious along this stretch. Find excellent spots along the shady shoreline for lunch or fishing (in season).

Overnighters must carry on a bit farther to find campsites located near the second and third Geraldine Lakes. Follow the trail along the western shoreline of the first lake for about 0.8 km. Though still obvious, the trail begins to lose some of its well-travelled quality. Roots and stumps in the path make walking tricky, especially in damp weather. Beyond the lake, climb through trees and rocks to a large boulder field. Travelling slows as unstable boulders must be negotiated; sturdy boots are strongly recommended. Follow cairns and watch carefully for the trail to cross the stream below the tarn, then continue on the opposite side.

Don't be confused by the trail that follows along the right of the stream. Although this will lead to the lake, the way is poorly marked, merges with game trails or completely fades in places, resulting in considerable boulder-hopping and bushwhacking before reaching the second Geraldine Lake. The trail on the left side of the stream follows a steep but well-defined route to the top of the waterfall and on to the lake. Campsites are located at the far end of the lake.

A sharp contrast to the forest-enclosed lake below, these rocky shores are nearly barren of vegetation. With the exception of a few hardy tufts of heather and alpine flowers, a starkness prevails and yet views continue to expand and intrigue the adventurous hiker. The way to the third Geraldine Lake and beyond is little more than a rough cross-country route requiring considerable scrambling on steep and rocky terrain. But the experienced backcountry traveller, proficient with map and compass, will find it an exhilarating challenge with remote alpine scenery as a reward.

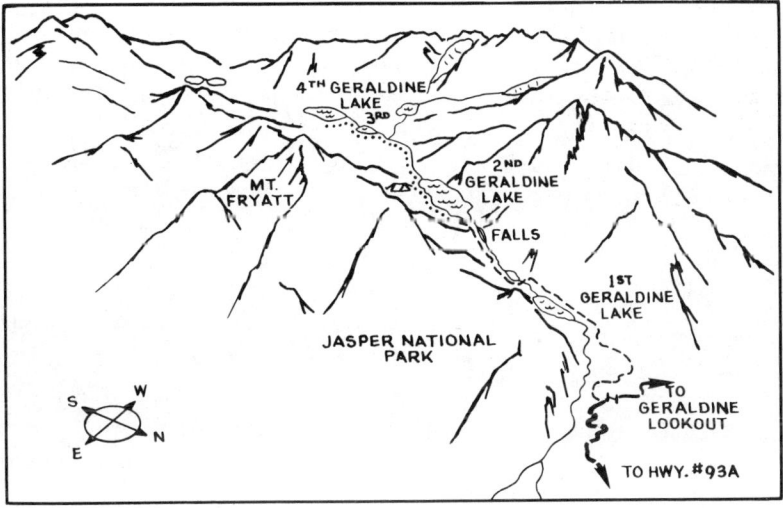

Geraldine Lookout

JASPER

42 Geraldine Lookout

Distance: 4.8 km/3 mi round trip
Hiking time: 2 hours
Elevation gain: 200 m/656 ft
High point: 1700 m/5576 ft
Type: half-day hike
Best time: June through October
Map: Athabasca Falls 83 C/12

At 1700 m, the Geraldine Lookout stands vigilant upon the shoulder of a rugged, unnamed peak, guardian over rivers and lakes, forests and flatlands. Below, the Whirlpool and Athabasca rivers deeply score the countryside in serpentine style. Views from these pleasant hillsides are a welcome surprise after a relatively unscenic road walk.

Follow the driving directions for the Geraldine Lakes Trail (Hike 41) and park in the same parking area. Walk around the gate and continue walking along the road. Heading in a general westerly direction, the way switchbacks and climbs, steeply at times, for 2 km to the forested high point of the trip. It then takes a short dip as the forest opens out to a small alp, holding lookout buildings and a tall, spindly fire tower.

The "front yard" of the lookout has been arranged for picnickers and includes a small fire box for cooking. Visitors should bring water. Several chairs are set on the eastern side of the promontory, for viewing the Athabasca River and Maligne Range. To the south, the aptly named Endless Chain Ridge marks the confluence of the Athabasca and Sunwapta rivers. The greatest treat, however, is discovered by roaming over to the north side of the alp to view Mt. Edith Cavell.

There's plenty of inspiration here to plan a wilderness adventure. While scanning the countryside from this lofty overlook, design a trip to ramble on distant ridges or explore the river valleys below.

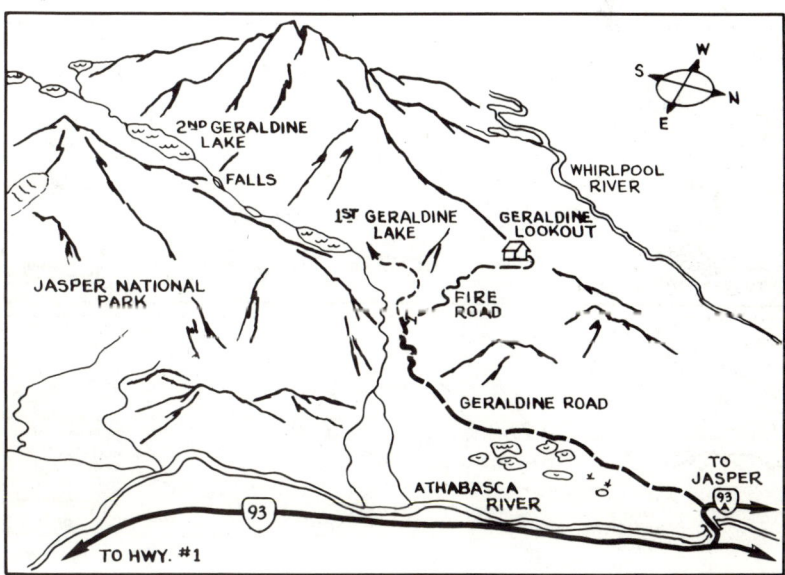

JASPER

43 Athabasca Pass

Distance: 102 km/62 mi round trip
Hiking time: 5-7 days
Elevation gain: 528 m/1732 ft
High point: 1768 m/5800 ft
Type: backpack
Best time: late June through October
Maps: Athabasca Falls 83 C/12, Amethyst Lakes 83 D/9 (trail not shown), Athabasca Pass 83 D/8 (trail not shown)

Situated at the headwaters of the Whirlpool River on the Continental Divide, Athabasca Pass separates the massive Kane Glacier to the northeast from the Mt. Brown Glacier to the south. Unfortunately these awesome masses of ice are visible only in spots from the forested river trail. But the popularity of the route rests in the historical significance of this former fur-traders' route, pioneered by David Thompson in 1810-1811.

Hikers to Athabasca Pass should be well equipped and physically prepared for this arduous trip. Plan to be self-sufficient and out of touch with all but your own party for the duration of the hike. Campsites are numerous and spaced at easy intervals. Water supply is abundant throughout the trip.

Leave Highway 93 at Athabasca Falls and drive 93A north for 8.6 km. Turn left onto the Moab Lake Fire Road and follow it 6.7 km to the parking lot and gate. Walk around the gate and continue along the dirt road, meandering through the long, low valley and crossing occasional streams. Although much of the pioneer spirit has been lost to the long stretch of fire road that serves as the trail for the first 16 km, the remaining distance rambles along on a moderately rough horse trail. It crosses large gravel flats and marshes and provides numerous occasions to recall the essence of those early treks to the pass.

At 24 km, 3 km beyond the crossing of the Middle Whirlpool River, the broad channel narrows and the scenery gets better. The trail, now a hoof-beaten track, fades and reappears as it crosses numerous gravel bars, but the objective remains clear.

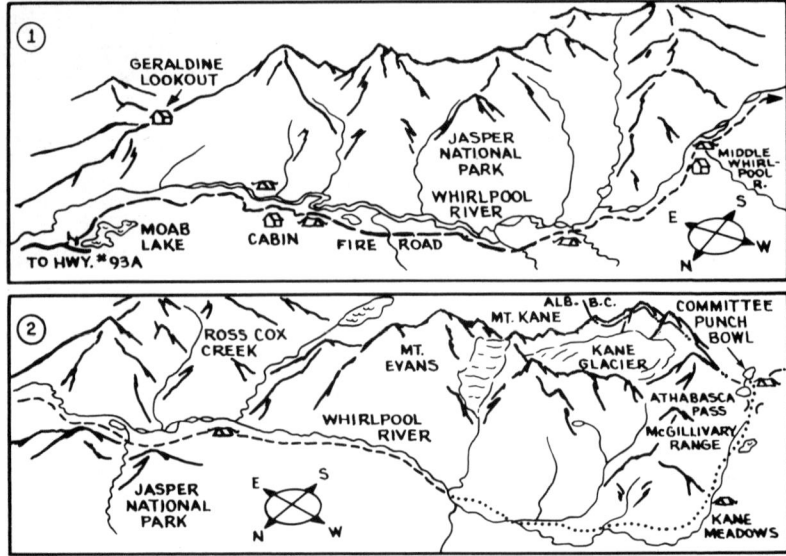

Fire road serves as the trail for the first 16 km up the Whirlpool River

Stay on the north side of the river until 40 km, below Mt. Kane, where the trail crosses to the left side of the valley and remains there for the rest of the trip.

Near the Alberta/British Columbia boundary, the trail fades, delivering its travellers near the famous gathering place, the Committee Punch Bowl. Beginning in 1826, furs were brought here from as far away as Fort Astoria at the Pacific end of the Columbia River, to be passed on by emissaries of the Hudson's Bay Company for transport to the east.

JASPER

44 Angel Glacier

Distance: 9 km/5.6 mi round trip
 to upper meadows
Hiking time: 3 hours
Elevation gain: 400 m/1312 ft
High point: 2073 m/6800 ft
Type: day hike
Best time: mid-July through October
Map: Amethyst Lakes 83 D/9
 (trail not shown)

Mt. Edith Cavell would be worth a visit, even without the famous Angel Glacier, but this dynamic interplay of blue ice, snow and rock should not be missed. Tourists have long since discovered it, though, and come in droves to view the splendor, so don't expect a lonely refuge.

It is possible to drive within a few metres of where the glacier lay only decades ago, and good views are possible from the viewpoint just south of the parking area. The most spectacular sights, however, are the rewards of those who hike the trails to the basin and upper meadows where the soaring "angel" and surrounding landscape can be viewed from new and intriguing viewpoints.

Drive Highway 93 for 7 km south of Jasper townsite, and turn right at Highway 93A. Follow it for 5 km to Edith Cavell Road. Continue on this winding mountain highway (no trailers allowed) for 13.8 km to its end at the Angel Glacier Viewpoint parking lot.

Begin the hike with a visit to the monument honoring Edith Cavell, World War I heroine, then turn left and follow the paved nature trail along the moraine for 0.6 km. At the sign and trail intersection, take the unpaved trail heading uphill. Climb over the morainal rubble, working past auto-sized boulders, then pass through a band of subalpine forest before emerging at the base of Cavell Meadows (2.5 km). The trail continues to make a wide loop through these colorful fields, providing splendid viewpoints from which to watch the rumbling avalanches and icefalls across the valley.

Snow often lingers here in the meadows until late July, frequently covering the trail and causing generally wet, muddy conditions as wandering feet seek drier ground or lose the trail. This further complicates the job of preserving and restoring

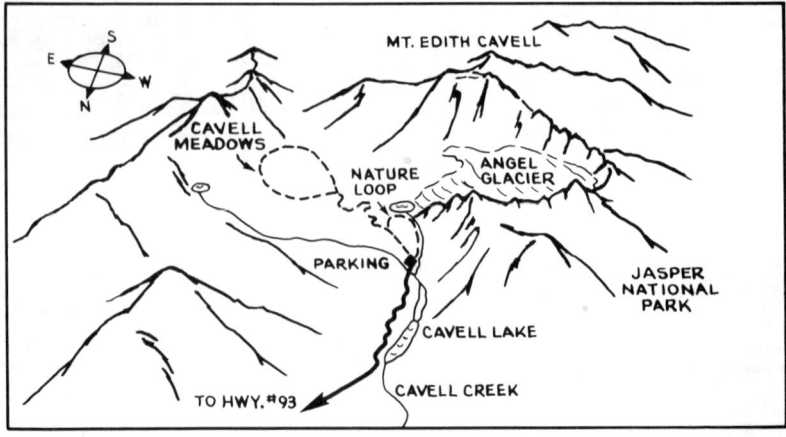

fragile alpine environments. Therefore, this portion of the hike is not recommended until snow has left the trail, especially since excellent viewpoints are available prior to reaching the meadow area.

Save time to complete the nature trail to the small terminal lake at the toe of the glacier and on through the rest of the basin. This additional kilometre of trail features interpretive signs describing the recent glacial history and the rebirth of vegetation to this nearly sterile valley. Do not venture across the small stream, however, because of the danger of intercepting falling rocks and ice, constantly being dislodged from above.

Angel Glacier

JASPER

45 Tonquin Valley via Astoria River

Distance: 36 km/22.5 miles round trip to Amethyst Lakes campsite
Hiking time: 2-3 days
Elevation gain: 427 m/1400 ft
High point: 2118 m/6950 ft
Type: backpack
Best time: July through October
Map: Amethyst Lakes 83 D/9

The Tonquin Valley evokes visions of medieval castles and citadels of stone. Images of spires and minarets slither across the waters of Amethyst and Moat lakes, while glaciers and icefields shift and groan, sending powerful loads of snow and ice crashing to the foot of the ramparts.

Both new and seasoned visitors to the Tonquin Valley continue to be amazed by the scenery, so plan to spend enough time here to ramble the side trails and visit the out-of-the-way lakes and viewpoints during your stay.

The Tonquin Valley is accessible by 2 popular routes from within Jasper National Park: the Astoria River Trail, described here, and the Maccarib Pass Trail (Hike 46).

The Astoria River Trail travels a richly forested river valley, providing only limited views of the mountainous terrain for much of the way. But the trail itself is pleasant with smaller-scale variety all along. Of the 2 trails into the Tonquin Valley, this one has the advantages of being drier, shorter by 4 km (one way) and lower in elevation (allowing earlier access).

The trail begins near Cavell Lake on Edith Cavell Road. Drive south on Highway 93 for 7 km to the 93A turnoff on the right. Follow 93A to Edith Cavell Road (5.2 km), then take this winding mountain highway 12 km to the trailhead located on the right, just past the youth hostel.

Leaving the parking area, the trail drops immediately to Cavell Lake and crosses Cavell Creek on a wooden bridge just below the lake. Turn right before reaching the horse corral and begin the 4-km contour along the northwest slope of Mt. Edith Cavell. At about 5 km the trail makes 2 crossings, first over Verdant Creek and then over the Astoria River, both bridged.

At 7.2 km, reach the first campsite. Just beyond is the rustic Old Horn Warden's Cabin and an intersection in the trail. The left branch recrosses the Astoria River on a log bridge, then follows the river valley to Chrome Lake and Eremite Valley from which optional routes into the Tonquin Valley and to Out-

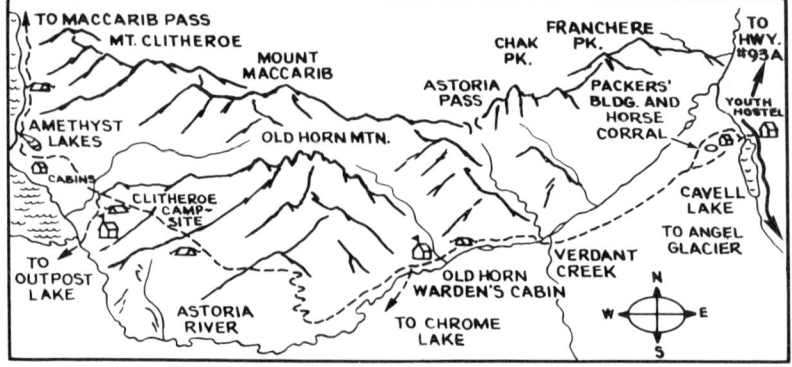

Amethyst Lake and the Ramparts

post Lake are possible. The route is approximately 6 km to Chrome Lake and another 6 km to the Amethyst Lakes campsite, much of which is wet, soggy travelling.

Passing Old Horn Warden's Cabin, the Astoria River Trail begins to climb away from the river, gently at first, then switchbacking steeply up the southern side of Old Horn Mountain to treeline and alpine meadows. Here, the real views begin and the rest of the way is pure joy. The Switchback campsite, located at 13.5 km provides a welcome stop with exciting views of mountains and glaciers. Continuing on, the walk through the meadows is level to gently downsloping with views unfolding grandly as the trail contours around the base of Mt. Maccarib. Pass the junction leading to Clitheroe campsite and Outpost Lake at 15.4 km, continuing on another 2.6 km for lakeview camping at the Amethyst Lakes campsite.

The need to curb impact in these alpine areas has made it necessary for the park to establish quotas (60 people per night), which fill rapidly in peak season. Also, available fuel is quickly used up, so plan to use a stove.

The Ramparts

JASPER

46 Tonquin Valley via Maccarib Pass

Distance: 44 km/27 mi round trip to Amethyst Lakes campsite
Hiking time: 2-3 days
Elevation gain: 740 m/2427 ft
High point: 2210 m/7250 ft
Type: backpack
Best time: August through mid-October
Maps: Jasper 83 D/16, Amethyst Lakes 83 D/9

Though slightly longer than the Astoria River Trail (see Hike 45), the Maccarib Pass Trail offers superb alpine scenery, being above timberline or within a high alpine valley most of the way. In addition, the long, gentle grade presents an attractive alternative to the laborious switchbacks on the Astoria River Trail. Those hikers who can arrange transportation can enter the area via one trail and exit on the other. The pass area, however, often harbors considerable amounts of snow well into midsummer, making travel difficult and very wet.

Though it is possible to get to the Tonquin Valley as early as June or July, consider making this trip a late-season venture. Long recognized for its scenic splendor, the Tonquin draws hundreds of visitors each year, both on foot and on horseback, and by midseason, when rains, hikers and horses are most abundant, the trail becomes a wide, ankle-deep, mud highway through the meadows—a miserable foot-slog for hikers. Presently, efforts are under way to remedy this situation, but it might be wise to check progress before planning an early season trip.

Drive south from the intersection of Highways 16 and 93 near Jasper, to the junction with 93A at 6.4 km. Turning right onto 93A, drive 2.4 km to the Marmot Basin Ski Area Road and make another right. At 5.8 km up this road, reach Portal Creek and a parking area on the left near the horse corral.

Begin the trail at the far end of the parking area. Cross the creek on a wooden bridge about 0.5 km up the trail and continue on the north side of Portal Creek. Elevation gain is constant, though not too steep. Travelling through open forest just above the creekbed, this trail passes through a narrow canyon for 4 km and then crosses Circus Creek.

Follow the left side of Circus Creek for 0.5 km, then swing left and climb towards the talus slope on the lower flanks of Peveril Peak. Here the forest thins and the peaks surrounding the Portal Creek/Maccarib Pass area display their jagged profiles and spill coffee-colored fans of scree to the valley floor. Crossing the talus slope below Peveril Peak, descend again to the creek and reach the Portal campsite area at 7.6 km. Beyond this point the trail begins to show the impact of thousands of horseshoes and lug soles as it meanders through the soft, wet meadowland. Though snow may linger on this eastern slope of the pass, the open alpine tundra allows good visibility, and route finding is not a problem.

Climb now towards the rugged Old Horn Mountain (2987 m) for about 3.5 km before veering west again for the last kilometre to Maccarib Pass (2210 m). Though far from ordinary to this point, the views now acquire an extraordinary aspect as the first peaks of the Ramparts and Tonquin Pass come into view on the western horizon and the Tonquin Valley further unfolds with each kilometre.

Continuing along the Maccarib Creek drainage, hikers may find it quite boggy, especially in early season. The trail may also seem confusing as horses and hikers initiate numerous trails in their search for drier, firmer terrain. Try to keep to the northern (right) slope, where a relatively dry route has been established, until trail improvements, presently under way over this section, have corrected the problem.

Follow the general course of Maccarib Creek for about 7 km where the trail crosses the footbridge and turns left towards Amethyst Lakes. This is the site of the cutoff to the old Meadow Creek Trail, which still exists on some maps. Although the route is shorter by about 10 km than the Maccarib Route, it is no longer maintained or recommended by the park as an acceptable hikers' trail, and is reported to be inhabited by a large grizzly population.

In 1 km reach the northern end of Amethyst Lakes where the trail branches—the right fork going on to Moat Lake, the left to skirt the eastern shore of Amethyst Lakes and the Amethyst Lakes campsite.

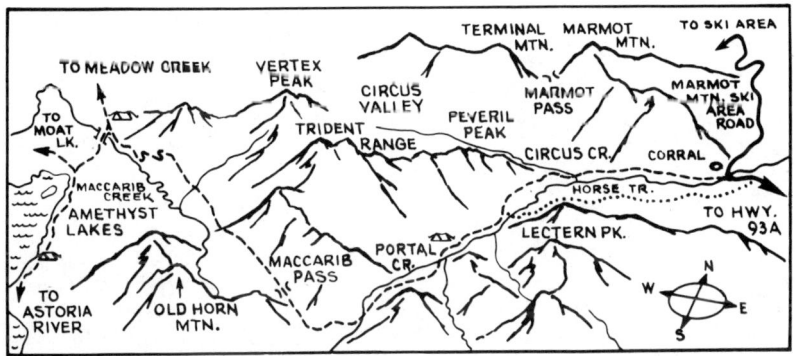

JASPER

47 Outpost Lake

Distance: 13 km/8 mi round trip from Clitheroe campsite
Hiking time: 5 hours
Elevation gain: 91 m/300 ft in, 488 m/1600 ft out
High point: 1981 m/6500 ft
Type: day hike or backpack
Best time: July through mid-October
Map: Amethyst Lakes 83 D/9

A small gem of a lake, caught in a rugged, rockbound basin and hidden by a fringe of subalpine forest. All around are knolls to climb for seldom-seen views of summits and glaciers. A popular day hike from the Tonquin Valley, but the way is not easy. The trail is often wet and boggy, generally rough and sometimes steep. A worthwhile objective, however, is not without struggle, so don't get discouraged.

At the southern end of Amethyst Lakes, leave the Astoria River Trail (Hike 45) for the well-defined trail to Clitheroe campsite. Pass through the camp area and follow the trail towards the warden's cabin. Turn right at the corral and descend

Outpost Lake from a shoulder of Outpost Peak

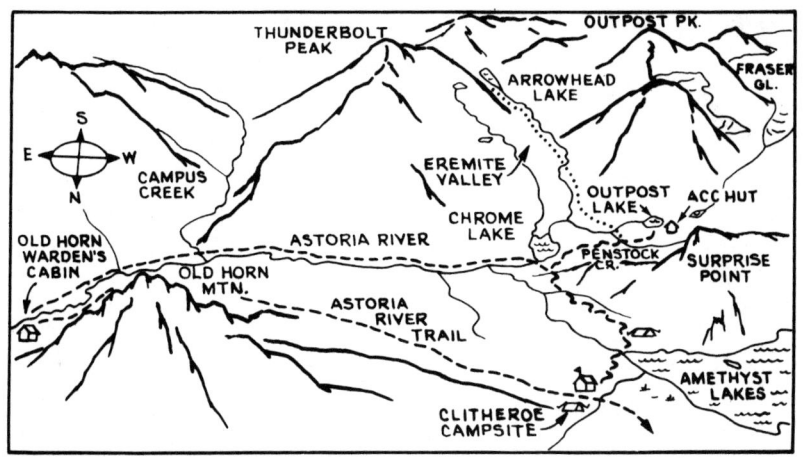

to the marsh flats. As indicated by a small sign, there really is a bridge crossing the major outlet stream near the southeastern tip of Amethyst Lakes, but getting to it with dry feet is tricky. You may wish to walk down the marsh (to the left) until the small meandering stream becomes narrow enough to jump. Then walk back up to the bridge.

Beyond the bridge, things remain drier for awhile as the trail climbs gently past the Surprise Point campsite and enters the forest for a 1.5-km descent to the valley floor. At 4.5 km the trail is joined by the valley route from the Old Horn Warden's Cabin (see Hike 45). Here, the bright turquoise waters of Chrome Lake gleam through the trees, but the trail will not touch its shores. Instead, it turns right to skirt a marsh and cross Penstock Creek.

Keep right at the next intersection for the final 1-km climb through forest to Outpost Lake. An ACC cabin stands above the northern shore. (Those interested in staying at the cabin must make prior arrangements with the ACC.) Walk to the left around the lake, crossing the outlet stream which, suddenly unrestrained, leaps down a rocky precipice. Then, wander up the small knoll behind for a view of the whole area.

Other options include an exploration of the Penstock Creek valley, which leads to 2 small tarns below massive glaciers. Or, try an ambitious journey up the Eremite Valley. A good trail leads the way but gives out after some distance into the valley; carry a map for further travel. This hike leads to rugged high-country and Arrowhead Lake resting below massive, glacier-draped peaks.

Open meadows near Moat Lake

JASPER

48 Moat Lake

Distance: 6 km/3.7 mi round trip
from Maccarib Pass Trail
Hiking time: 2 hours
Elevation loss: 46 m/150 ft
High point: 1981 m/6500 ft
Type: day hike from Tonquin Valley
Best time: July through October
Map: Amethyst Lakes 83 D/9

Easily accessible from the north end of Amethyst Lakes, the trail to Moat Lake is a pleasant walk through sparse trees, meadow and tundra, offering exceptional views and new perspectives on the magnificent Ramparts.

Find the trail to Moat Lake at 2 km to the north of the Amethyst Lakes campsite, or 1 km south of the Maccarib Creek bridge. The boggy area at the north end of Amethyst Lakes may make it difficult to follow the trail during extremely wet periods. But the trail soon becomes well defined as it reaches firmer ground among the lodgepoles. Near the far western end of the lake, a short spur trail will lead past the horse corral and outfitters' cabins to a small promontory on the lake. From this spot, excellent views into both ends of the great curving Tonquin Valley are possible.

Back onto the main trail, begin the gradual descent to Moat Lake, which is now only 1.2 km away and quite visible. It stretches westward beneath the near vertical walls of Bastion and Drawbridge peaks. Beyond the lake, on either side are the 2 passes, Moat and Tonquin, which point the way to a backcountry route into Mt. Robson Park along Tonquin Creek and the Fraser River. These are not regularly maintained routes, however, and should be left to the experienced cross-country traveller.

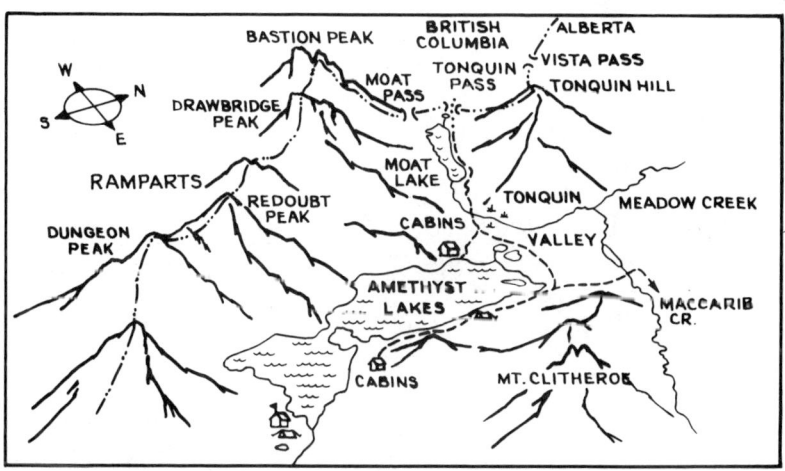

JASPER

49 The Whistlers

Distance: 4.5 km/2.8 mi one way
Hiking time: 3 hours
Elevation gain: 1244 m/4083 ft
High point: 2464 m/8085 ft
Type: half-day hike
Best time: June through mid-October
Map: Jasper 83 D/16

Endless diversity on this steep but rewarding climb to the summit of The Whistlers. At the top, a 360-degree panorama. Views of the Athabasca and Miette River valleys expand to encompass distant mountain ranges, while rugged, icy peaks demand close-up inspection. From the lush vegetation of valley forests to the starkness of the alpine tundra, this trail has it all.

While a counterbalance cable tramway carries visitors to the 2500-m level, leaving only a short hike to the summit, most hikers prefer to walk at least 1 way on the trail, leaving the tram for those with less time, ambition or fortitude. A small investment, however, will secure a spot on the tramcar for either a 1-way or round-trip ride. For those ardent hikers, we recommend a walk up and then perhaps a ride down in order to experience fully the subtleties of the changing life-zones and ecosystems with the change in elevation.

Drive south on Highway 93 from Jasper. From the intersection of Highways 93 and 16, continue south for 1.7 km to The Whistlers Road on the right. Follow The Whistlers Road 2.8 km to the gravel road on the left leading to the parking lot, just before the hostel. The trailhead is located at the far end of the parking lot about 10 m to the left of the service road.

The walk begins in a woodland of aspen and lodgepole, featuring a lush undergrowth of wildflowers, grasses and shrubs. After several switchbacks, the trail levels some before turning west to cross beneath the tramway. Ascending

View east over the Athabasca River Valley from The Whistlers

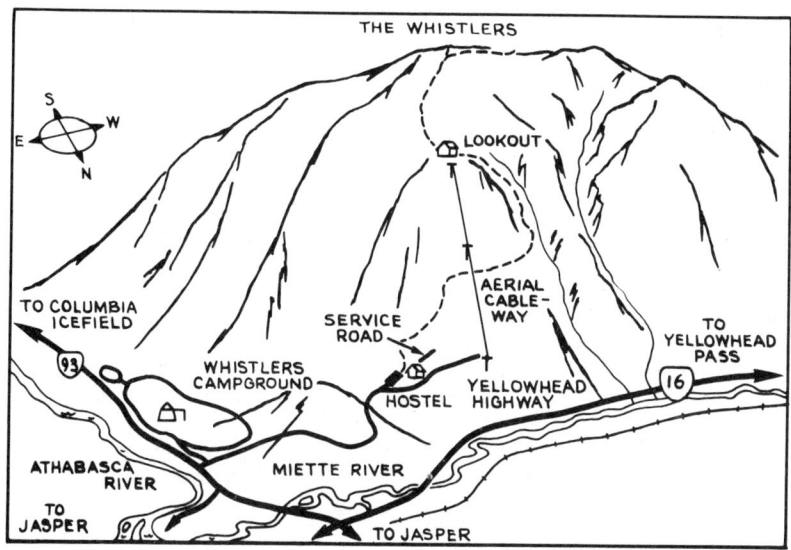

again on the other side, enter subalpine forest and enjoy brief views as the forest thins. Passing into the alpine environment of the summit region, watch for pikas and hoary marmots that live among the rocky debris, and listen for their piercing whistles that echo frequently across the slopes. Arrival at the summit meadows will likely be heralded by multitudes of ground squirrels "tamed" by the thousands of visitors who feel compelled to feed them, even though it is unlawful to do so.

To the right of the upper tram terminal, the trail merges with the main summit trail. A leisurely 30 minutes allows plenty of time for photographs and rest stops along the sometimes-steep trail to the summit. The broad summit meadows invite easy wandering on kilometres of scenic trails. Bear in mind, though, that this fragile ecosystem is very susceptible to damage by trampling. Some delicate plants here take 25 years or longer to bloom. The park, therefore, requests your help in maintaining the area by staying on the established trails.

Descend either by retracing steps along the trail, or by riding the tram back to the lower terminal, then walking the short distance along the road to the trailhead parking lot.

JASPER

50 Sulphur Skyline Trail

Distance: 9.6 km/6 mi round trip
Hiking time: 3-4 hours
Elevation gain: 625 m/2050 ft
High point: 2062 m/6763 ft
Type: half-day hike
Best time: May through mid-October
Maps: Miette 83 F/4 W, Miette 83 F/4 E

Close-up views of multihued mountains towering above green wilderness valleys are the prime features to enjoy along this trail. Good views are possible at several spots along the way, though the ultimate panoramas are the reward of those who make the steep, dry climb to the summit where peaks of the Miette Range seem to crowd around, displaying bands of color and texture. Below are numerous deep valleys where the Fiddle River, Sulphur Creek and many other streams and waterworks have cut and ruffled the forested flanks of the mountains.

To get to the Miette Hot Springs complex, drive 6.7 km on Highway 16 (Yellowhead Highway) from the Jasper Park northeast boundary to Pocahontas

Fiddle River from the Sulphur Skyline Trail

Bighorn sheep

and the Miette Hot Springs Road. Drive 16 km along the Miette Hot Springs Road to the parking area at the end of the road. Approached from the southwest, the Miette Hot Springs Road is 43.9 km from the junction of Highways 16 and 93 near Jasper.

The trail begins as a dirt road leading eastward from the rear of the former campground (now officially closed). Bypassing any smaller trails that join or crisscross, continue on the most obvious path, which climbs and switchbacks for about 2.5 km to a junction and narrow pass. The left fork continues on to Mystery Lake; the right swings south and steepens as it ascends the rocky hillside towards Sulphur Ridge. Be sure to carry water, for although the trail is short and offers ample, scenic rest spots, the climb is laborious and dry. Near the summit, only the hardiest of alpine flowers, mosses and lichens persist on the rocky landscape, providing sustenance for mountain goats, bighorn sheep and numerous small mammals that live among the boulders.

Hikers can descend by retracing the main trail, or the more adventurous can follow the ridgeline to the west towards the hot springs area. A little bushwhacking may be necessary near the base of the ridge to follow the sketchy route, which ultimately intersects the Fiddle River Trail (Hike 52) leading from the complex area above the swimming pool.

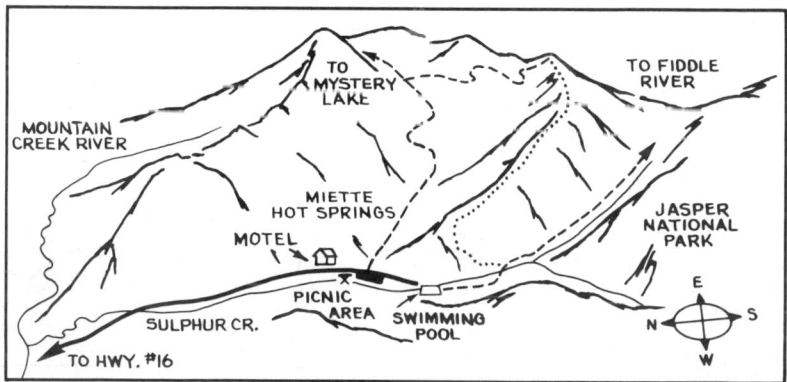

51 Mystery Lake

Distance: 21 km/12 mi round trip
Hiking time: 8-9 hours
Elevation gain: 473 m/1550 ft in;
  350 m/1150 ft out
High point: 1661 m/5450 ft
Type: long day hike or backpack
Best time: late July to mid-October
Maps: Miette 83 F/4E, Miette 83 F/4W

As diverse as it is challenging, the Mystery Lake Trail holds a plethora of hiker delights: forest and flowers, a pass and a view, a river with a challenge and a quiet mountain lake. Those who have timed it right to make the ford of the Fiddle River (sometimes unmanageable on foot until August or later) will find their prize: a secluded lake, a peaceful backcountry campsite and a fine chance for some uncrowded trout fishing.

For those who choose not to try the ford, the lake will remain a mystery. Nevertheless, the 4.5 km to the river make an enjoyable and scenic day hike with time to spare for a leisurely lunch or some riverside prowling before making the steep climb back to the pass.

Follow directions for the Sulphur Skyline Trail (Hike 50) to the junction at the pass (1661 m) for 2.5 km. Here, the Skyline Trail branches right. Continue straight, descending through forest gently at first and then more steeply for the last 0.5 km to reach the river at 4.5 km (1311 m).

To ford the river, walk downstream 0.5 km or so. But make sure to cross before the steep walls of the gorge converge, confining the waters in a deep, swift torrent.

The trail is essentially a horse trail from this point on, paying little heed to the foot traveller's preference for dry feet. Remain on the east bank whenever the trail switches sides. The minor bushwhacking involved is usually preferable to several risky fords.

After about 1.5 km of riverside tramping, follow the trail away from the water and begin the climb to the lake (1494 m), reaching it at 10.5 km.

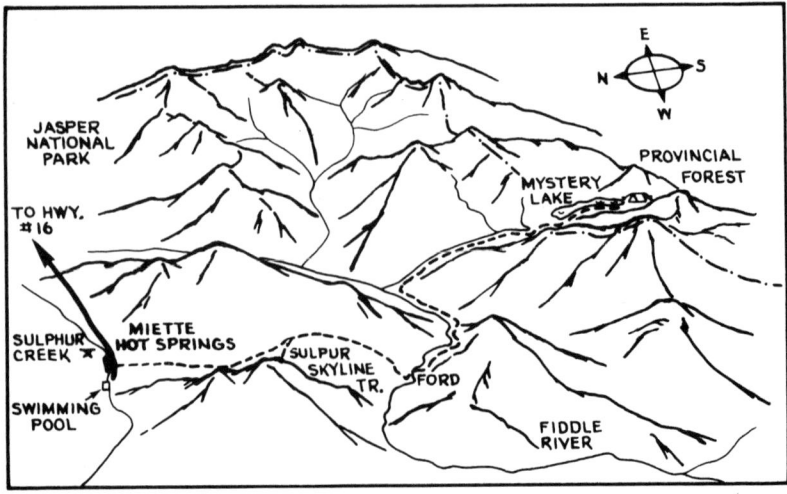

Small valley descending to Fiddle River

JASPER

52 Fiddle River

Distance: 45 km/28 mi one way from Miette Hot Springs to Whitehorse Pass
Hiking time: 2 days
Elevation gain: 747 m/2450 ft
High point: 2118 m/6950 ft
Type: backpack
Best time: August to mid-October
Maps: Miette 83 F/4 E, Miette 83 F/4 W

A fine wilderness trip through rugged backcountry with challenge for the experienced traveller and a chance to test route-finding skills. This colorful river gorge makes for exciting scenery, though fords are often difficult and dangerous due to high waters before midsummer. Consequently, this trip is not recommended before that time.

Beginning as a horse trail, the original route swings back and forth across the boisterous waters, often losing definition in the process and making foot travel difficult. The recent influx of backpackers, however, has begun to redesign the trail in favor of the foot traveller and may soon result in a well-defined trail that makes the entire trip without the treacherous ford of the Fiddle River. At present this route requires considerable bushwhacking in order to avoid the river fords.

From the Miette Hot Springs pool area (see Hike 50, Sulphur Skyline, for driving directions), walk the trail leading east. Follow the boardwalk to its end and continue on a good dirt path, crossing a small stream and Sulphur Creek before heading up the draw beneath the northern slopes of Utopia Mountain. The forest here is dense and mossy, lichen hangs from tree limbs and the thick undergrowth crowds the trail with bluebells and bunchberry. In spite of the dampness, a freshness prevails. Nevertheless, regular horse traffic has created a wide muddy track, which remains quite wet most of the season. Consequently alternative footpaths have developed in places to skirt the deep trenches and washboard-like surfaces where foot logs or bridges have not been added.

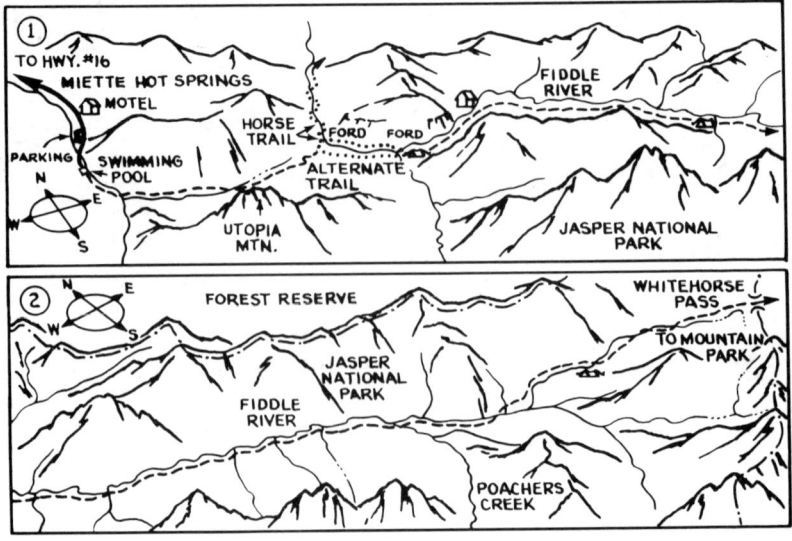

At 3 km, the trail levels to cross the small pass and traverse beneath a large rockslide on the left. It then begins a rapid descent to the river, the last 0.5 km being exceptionally steep. Those not wishing to make the river fords or the toilsome climb back to the top of the canyon can stop at the edge for views of the river gorge. These first 5 km from the Hot Springs to the Fiddle River make a good half-day trip and, though wet in places, this portion of the trail can be done much earlier in the season.

Upon reaching the canyon floor, the trail crosses the river and continues upstream, coming to the Utopia campsite at 7 km (2 km from the crossing.) From here numerous crossings present moderate-to-serious difficulties in keeping on trail. These fords can be avoided by following a faint boot path that branches right just before the final steep descent to the river. Expect to do some bushwhacking.

The route should be obvious to experienced wilderness travellers, although a map and compass may be helpful. At approximately 18 km, the trail veers to the left to follow the northern tributary stream eastward to Whitehorse Pass. From the pass, hikers may follow an alternative route to Mountain Park, using old forest roads.

Fiddle River Valley

JASPER

53 Merlin Creek

Distance: 69 km/43 mi round trip to Jacques Lake
Hiking time: 2-3 days
Elevation gain: 871 m/2856 ft
High point: 1930 m/6330 ft
Type: backpack
Best time: June through October
Maps: Snaring 83 E/1, Miette 83 F/4 W, Medicine Lake 83 C/13

A cool, forested creek valley peppered with patches of meadow and flowers. Catch glimpses north and south to the Jacques and Colin ranges and climb to 2 high passes before reaching the junction with the Jacques Lake Trail (Hike 62). To hard-core hikers, the Merlin Creek Trail is the true beginning of the South Boundary Trail. Most, however, prefer to use the shorter Jacques Lake Trail, beginning on the Maligne Lake Road, to get to the South Boundary Trail. Con-

Jacques Creek drainage

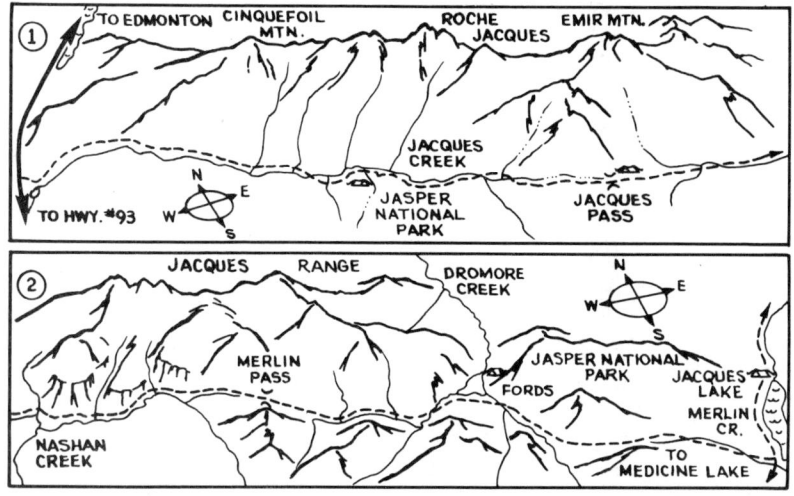

sequently, the Merlin Trail receives only moderate use from end-to-end, making it an excellent getaway with lots of easy rambling and exploring from campsites along the way.

Drive northeast on Highway 16 for 26 km from the intersection of Highways 16 and 93. The trailhead is located on the right side of the road, about 3 km northeast of the Athabasca River crossing and 2.7 km northeast of Cold Sulphur Springs.

From the parking area the trail slips quickly through a band of lodgepole and aspen and passes a small lake as it leaves the woods to ramble through fragrant meadowlands. Pass bright green stands of aspen and willow, then work up the Jacques Creek valley, moving in and out of the forest and skirting a deep chasm cut in the rock by creek waters.

Continue through deeper forest on a gentle but continuous grade, occasionally leaving the canopy to cross the stream or ramble along the bank. Creek fords are not difficult and trail markers help you pick up the trail easily at crossings.

At 6 km, come to the Cinquefoil campsite on the right bank near the point where an unnamed side creek merges with Jacques Creek. This isolated spot makes an ideal getaway with possibilities for exploring up side creeks to peaks in the Colin and Jacques ranges. Or, continue along the Merlin Trail an additional 3.8 km to Jacques Pass (1783 m) where views begin to open up. At 18.2 km Merlin Pass offers an even higher vantage point along an otherwise deeply wooded valley trail. Beyond the passes, the trail becomes less distinct though not difficult to follow. Still traveling through dense forest, pass the Dromore campsite (26 km) and intersect the Jacques Lake Trail at 32 km, near the south end of Jacques Lake. The Jacques Lake campsite is located near the north end of the lake.

From Jacques Lake, return either via the same route or continue southward an additional 12 km along the Jacques Lake Trail to the Maligne Road, though this requires prior arrangements for vehicle shuttles or other transportation. The quota on this trail is 20 people per night.

Overlander Trail

JASPER

54 Overlander Trail

Distance: 6.4 km/4 mi round tr
  to Morro Creek
Hiking time: 2 hours
Elevation gain: 92 m/300 ft
High point: 1067 m/3500 ft
Type: short hike
Best time: June through October
Map: Snaring 83 E/1 (trail not shown)

Trace a small section of the route pioneered in 1862 by 250 gold seekers, en route from eastern Canada to British Columbia. Today only a small, but particularly scenic, section of this historic route through the park is maintained for hiking. The majority of users seem to be rock climbers heading for the near vertical slabs of dolomite that typify the Colin Range, but the casual hiker will no doubt enjoy the quickly accessible views of the wildly contorted Athabasca River and the splendid summits of the main ranges of the Canadian Rockies.

Follow Highway 16 east for 22 km from the intersection of 16 and 93 near Jasper. The broad, gravel turnout on the south side of the road at Cold Sulphur Springs just after crossing the Athabasca River is the parking area. The trailhead is at the west end of the lot.

Gaining nearly all of its elevation in the first 0.5 km, the trail requires faith and determination. But the grind is soon over and the slope levels as a broad, grassy terrace is reached. The toil is forgotten as grand views spread across the river valley to Esplanade Mountain (2286 m) and Chetamon Mountain (2591 m). Below, the widely braided Athabasca River seems to have tangled itself into an impossible string of knots as it wraps itself around numerous islands.

Possible picnic spots are plentiful along the open, grassy hillsides here below the Colin Range. Just beyond the 1-km point, another trail intersects the main route and leads to a memorial plaque about 50 m off the trail to the left.

Between 2.5 and 3 km, several faint trails branch left towards the scenic Morro Creek Canyon between Morro Peak and Hawk Mountain. The only water along the route, Morro Creek is reached at 3.2 km and represents the usual turnaround point. The trail continues faintly for an indefinite distance beyond the creek but does not receive regular use or maintenance.

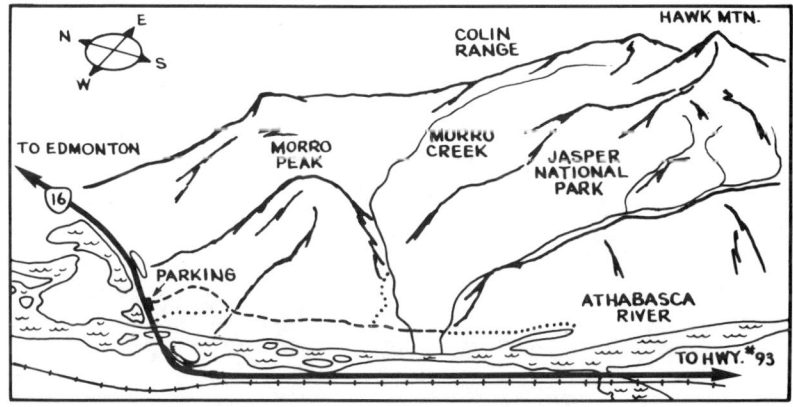

55 Devona Lookout

Distance: 8.4 km/5.2 mi round trip from Celestine Lake parking lot
Hiking time: 3 hours
Elevation gain: 154 m/505 ft
High point: 1404 m/4605 ft
Type: short or half-day hike
Best time: June through October
Map: Snaring 83 E/1

A breezy overlook in the heart of the Front Ranges above the confluence of the Snake Indian and Athabasca rivers. Views stretch across the valley to the Fiddle, Miette and Jacques ranges where thrust-faulted bands of limestone, dolomite and sandstone stand in frieze-like relief. This grassy ridge, peppered with wildflowers through midsummer, provides excellent opportunities for a peaceful afternoon of photography, nature study or easy rambling along the hillsides. Examine the fossil shale that laces the ridge rock or just enjoy the excellent views from the bench beyond the lookout station. The watch has gone the way of the roving fire patrolman and the lookout is no longer manned on a regular basis. But, the quaint buildings are well maintained for use during high fire-danger periods. The access road also is in good condition, making the walk an easy journey along a gentle grade.

Though the hike is relatively short and undemanding, the drive to the parking area is quite another matter. Nearly 27 km of narrow dirt track, rough and often exposed, require strict adherance to the 1-way travel schedules, which should be checked in advance. Extremely low-slung vehicles may experience difficulties at unbridged creek crossings and at particularly rough spots in the road. Nevertheless, the drive is somewhat scenic and provides access to a number of other trailheads along the way before terminating at the Celestine Lake parking lot.

Beginning at the intersection of Highways 16 and 93, drive east from Jasper for 13 km to the Celestine Lake Road. Turn left and proceed 5 km to the Snaring Campground registration booth. If you have not done so already, check here for current road conditions before continuing. Drive 1.3 km to the end of the pavement and the

Jasper Lake and Jacques Range

Band of fossils in rocky outcrop near lookout

beginning of the 1-way road. Make note of travel times (also available at park information centres) as these are strictly enforced. Then, observing the regulations, proceed for 26.6 km along the narrow track to the Celestine Lake parking lot.

The fire lookout access road, which is closed to vehicles, is the trail—a wide, flat track that makes for easy walking. Passing 2 scenic lakes, reach the Celestine Lake Campground at 1.6 km. About 2 km beyond Celestine Lake, the forest thins, permitting views of softly rounded peaks in the De Smet Range to the southwest. A bit farther, the snowy summit of Edith Cavell is visible to the south.

If time permits, camp at the well-equipped Celestine Lake Campground. Wildlife seems to abound in the area, from the abundant fish in Celestine Lake, to the sound of bugling elk in the forest. Early evening and morning hours come alive with small marshland animals, while the ever-present camp-robbing nutcrackers and squirrels noisily test the unwary camper. These lakes also are breeding grounds for the common loon, often heard piercing the still night air with their eerie tremolos.

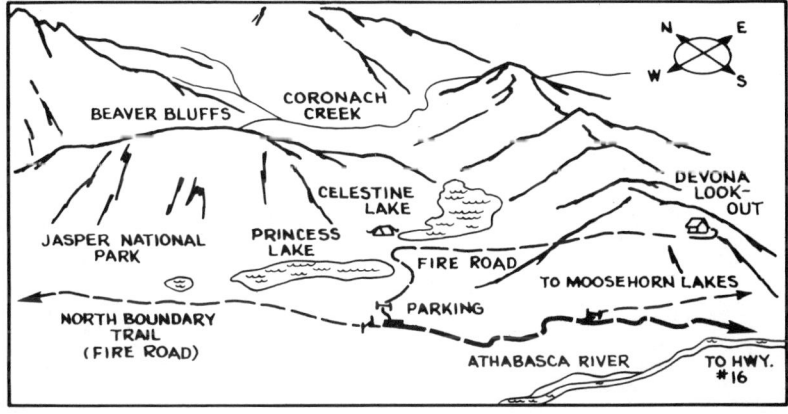

56 North Boundary Trail

Distance: 185 km/114.7 mi one way
Hiking time: 10 days to 2 weeks
Elevation gain: 1006 m/3300 ft,
 loss 1372 m/4500 ft
High point: 2019 m/6625 ft
Type: extended backpack
Best time: mid-July through mid-October
Maps: Snaring 83 E/1, Rock Lake 83 E/8,
 Blue Creek 83 E/7 E, Blue Creek 83 E/7 W,
 Twintree Lake 83 E/6 E, Twintree Lake 83
 E/6 W, Mount Robson 83 E/3

This is a trail for a special kind of backcountry lover. Certainly not those with only a short time to spend in the park, who must dash from highlight to highlight. The character of the North Boundary Trail is more subtle, gradually revealing its wilderness secrets to the patient, steady traveller who will take the time to walk it end-to-end. A trek of impressive duration through long, forested valleys and high alpine passes, it will surprise and delight you with a tremendous waterfall, glittering lakes, rugged mountains of ice and rock and a variety of life zones and ecosystems. The wildlife enthusiast or photographer will delight in knowing the area is inhabited by deer, moose, caribou, bear and wolves as well as many smaller species. And, there are unlimited opportunities for seeking out little-travelled side trails and hard-to-find hideaways for days of peaceful solitude.

Campsites are located at regular intervals, no more than 14 km apart. Hikers are required to stay at these sites, which fortunately are well located near water and generally quite comfortable.

Spectacular alpine scenery is lacking for much of the way and the hiker should be prepared for several long days of river-valley trudging. Though sometimes tedious and sometimes rough and treacherous, the trail's biggest challenge is the distance—and the preparations required to make such a trip. Food, extra food for emergencies, warm clothing, protection from all kinds of weather conditions, map and compass for anyone planning to leave the main

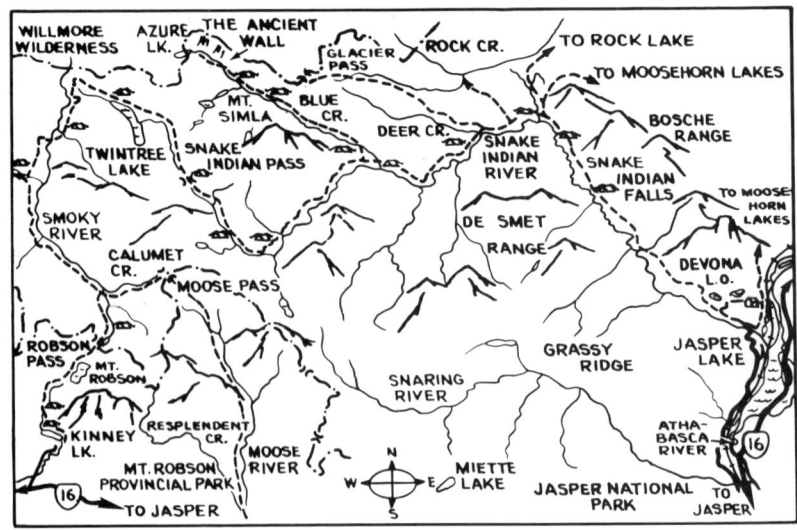

Eastern end of the North Boundary Trail

route and first aid equipment for treating everything from blisters to major injuries should all be included in a reasonable-sized pack. There is also the probability of wildlife encounters and finally, not a minor consideration, is the vehicle shuttle or transportation at trail's end. Obviously, this is not a trip for first-time backpackers or others who are unsure of their wilderness expertise.

Hiking the trail from east to west seems to be the preferred direction, primarily because it presents a gradual approach to the elevation gain, as well as saving the scenic climax for the end.

See Hike 55, Devona Lookout, for driving directions to the trailhead, located at the Celestine Lake parking lot. Then begin by following the fire road on its seemingly endless journey into the forest. Scenic interest is marginal at best until the thunder-

Porcupine looking for tender bark to eat

ing Snake Indian Falls are reached at about 21 km. Shortly thereafter, the way leaves the road and finally the forest to ramble into spacious meadows.

At about 32 km, the river makes a wide turn to head west, while the Willow Creek Trail (Hike 86) enters from the north via Rock Lake and Willmore Wilderness Park. Here is the first exit from the trail, or more probably, an alternative beginning, which, although it misses the falls, also avoids that tedious stretch of road walking. Transportation or vehicle shuttles may be more difficult to arrange, however, from this more remote trailhead.

Following the river west now, find a second trail, branching north at 34 km and leading up to Rock Creek and over Eagles Nest Pass (Hike 89). At 41 km reach the junction with the Deer Creek Trail to Glacier Pass (2286 m), a 26-km trip.

Views improve as meadow and shrubland persist, adding interest with patches of pine, aspen and willow. These continue while the trail moves west up the river valley to slip between the 2 steep faces of Mts. Kelsey (2482 m) and Simla (2785 m), where it meets the Blue Creek junction. If time is not crucial, a worthwhile side trip follows the Blue Creek Trail below the Ancient Wall to Azure Lake. The trip is a 32-km walk along mostly good and well-used trail. It offers superb scenery, as well as 3 trailside camps and numerous lakes to fish or explore.

Crossing Blue Creek, the main route swings south, around the base of Mt. Simla, still gaining almost no elevation. At about 79 km, the trail bends west again. Pass the campground and begin the slow, steady climb to Snake Indian Pass (2019 m). As elevation increases, the forest thins and the rolling, alpine objective is visible beneath rugged limestone peaks. Reach the pass at 91 km.

Descend the opposite slope beside Twintree Creek to Twintree Lake. Back in forest now, the trail gets rougher as it crosses a ridge and descends to the Smoky River. A horse trail continues downriver but is not recommended for hikers.

Crossing the river, the trail soon meets with another trail to Bess Pass, a rough but scenic diversion. But scenery is better all around, here beneath the rugged peaks and glaciers of the Jasper/Robson boundary region. At the confluence of Calumet Creek and the Smoky River is the final option for altering route exit. The trail leads to Moose Pass and down the Moose River (Hike 80) to Highway 16. The trail is rough, though, not maintained and may require some bushwhacking to avoid dangerous fords.

The wilderness section of the trip comes to an abrupt end when the trail reaches the park boundary area, but hikers may still choose to stay several days in the Mt. Robson/Berg Lake area, taking in the views and side trails. The final stretch is a wide, well-used and meticulously maintained trail (Hike 82) to the Berg Lake Trail parking lot, approximately 2 km from Highway 16 (Yellowhead Highway) and about 85 km west of Jasper townsite. Bus service is available to Jasper townsite, but the return to the Celestine Lake parking area (if necessary) must be left to ingenuity. There are campsites along the road, but the road walk is rather tedious.

Mule deer

JASPER

57 Moosehorn Creek Trail

Distance: 64 km/40 mi round trip to Moosehorn Lakes
Hiking time: 4 days
Elevation gain: 610 m/2000 ft
High point: 1616 m/5300 ft
Type: backpack
Best time: June through October
Maps: Snaring 83 E/1, Miette 83 F/4W, Entrance 83 F/5, Rock Lake 83 E/8

A superb trail for a day of solitary rambling or an extended trip to a remote, seldom-visited lake. Saunter along sloughs and waterways of the Snake Indian and Athabasca rivers to photograph the lush marshes and flowers of the flats. Enjoy grassy hillside meadows overlooking the wide Athabasca River Valley before journeying on to the remote Moosehorn Creek and Moosehorn Lake.

From Jasper, drive Highway 16 (Yellowhead Highway) east from its intersection with Highway 93 (Icefields Parkway). At 13 km, turn left onto the Celestine Lake Road and proceed 6 km through the Snaring Campground and on to the beginning of the

Coronach Creek bridge below Roche Ronde

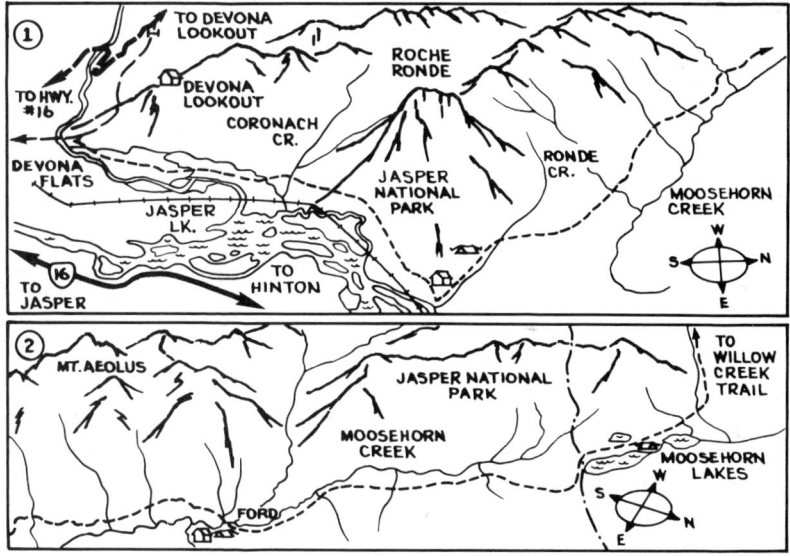

1-way section. See Hike 55, Devona Lookout, for travel restrictions beyond this point. Observing the limited-access regulations, proceed on gravel road. At 17.5 km, pass the gated Devona Flats Road on the right and continue, crossing the Snake Indian River and reaching the trailhead (marked by another dirt road merging on the right) at 23 km from the beginning of the limited-access road.

Leave cars here and walk along the old road for 3.8 km, descending to a point across the Snake Indian River from Devona Flats. The trail fades a bit as it meanders through the flats along the river valley but becomes more distinct as it enters valley-edge vegetation. Following the river downstream, the trail snakes through patches of aspen, willows and grasslands, skirting pools and crossing tributary streams. Canoeists sometimes make their way up these waterways from the Athabasca, slipping quietly through the peaceful waters to fish or picnic along shady river-banks.

At about 8 km, the trail crosses a medium-sized creek on a bridge and begins to climb north out of the lowlands towards the base of Roche Ronde in the Bosche Range. Traversing grassy hillsides, follow the trail to a point where it branches off to the left and follows the creek up the valley. Just beyond is the Miette Warden's Cabin. Here, and at other critical spots, watch for the yellow trail markers to help keep you on route. Find a campsite near Ronde Creek at 13 km. Ford Moosehorn Creek at about 24 km, and find a second campsite and a warden's cabin on the other side. Reach Moosehorn Lakes, just beyond the park boundary in another 8 km. There are more campsites here.

From Moosehorn Lakes, it is possible to follow a route westward, through the north end of the Bosche Range. The route joins the Willow Creek portion of the North Boundary Trail (Hike 56), which continues along the Snake Indian River and back to the Celestine Lake Road, making a large loop of 104 km. Allow about 6 days to complete the entire loop.

Experienced backpackers will find this seldom-travelled route through the creek valley a challenge in route finding and patience, as the trail crosses creeks and park boundaries. Though most critical fords are marked, it would be wise to check with park officials on current trail conditions before embarking on this hike, since the trail is not regularly maintained.

JASPER

58 Vine Creek

Distance: 19 km/12 mi round trip
  to Vine Creek campsite
Hiking time: 7 hours
Elevation gain: 625 m/2050 ft
High point: 1692 m/5550 ft
Type: day hike or backpack
Best time: July through mid-October
Map: Snaring 83 E/1

A cool, forested valley trail, refreshing and secluded, where visible human impact takes a back seat to nature. Situated beneath several 3000-m peaks of the De Smet Range, the woodsy valley ends in a small subalpine meadow with 1 small backcountry campsite. Here is a great place to look for animal tracks, as bear, wolves and elk are the trail's most frequent travellers.

From the intersection of Highways 16 and 93, drive east on 16 for 13 km to the Celestine Lake Road. Follow this road for 6 km east, past the Snaring Campground registration booth, to the end of the pavement. The road narrows to a 1-way dirt road on which access is strictly regulated and enforced. The travel times should be checked in advance and retained for the return trip. The regulations are available at the Jasper Information Centre, and they are posted at the beginning of the road. The trailhead is located 7.7 km up this dirt road, and parking is available off the road just beyond the Vine Creek bridge.

Begin the hike on the old road to the right of the creek. When the road terminates in a loop, look to the right for a cairn marking the trail. Although the trail receives infrequent use, it is not difficult to follow, as it rambles along beside the creek for most of the distance.

The way actually makes only 2 crossings of the creek, although numerous

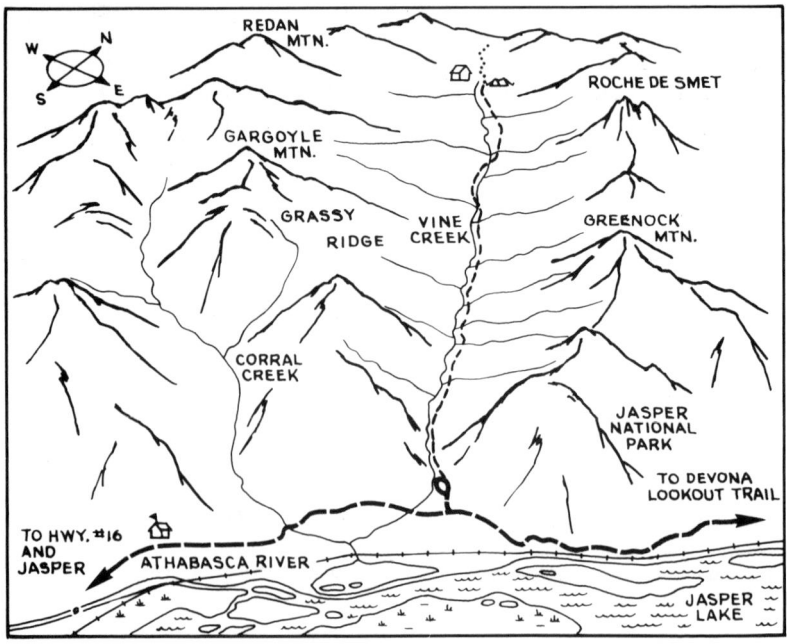

intersecting game trails may lead one to believe it makes several more. The first ford occurs after passing beneath Gargoyle Mountain at 7.2 km, and the trail remains on the left bank for about 0.5 km before crossing back. The crossings are not bridged.

As the trail proceeds upstream, it is sometimes obscured by merging side streams. These areas are usually marked by blazes or cairns and do not present a problem in crossing them.

Views of Redan Mountain and Roche De Smet and a long shoulder of Mt. Thornton become visible from the upper valley. The official trail ends at the Vine Creek campsite at 9.7 km. An obvious path continues, however, to pass the Vine Creek Warden's Cabin and wander towards the end of the valley and more difficult terrain beyond.

Upper Vine Creek Valley

JASPER

59 Signal Mountain Lookout

Distance: 17 km/10.5 mi round trip
Hiking time: 1-2 days
Elevation gain: 980 m/3215 ft
High point: 2120 m/6955 ft
Type: long day hike or backpack
Best time: mid-June through mid-October
Maps: Jasper 83 D/16,
   Medicine Lake 83 C/13

Lookout sites, by their function, are located in areas that command expansive views of the surrounding countryside. Signal Mountain Lookout is certainly no exception, as it rests a lofty 1100 m above the broad Athabasca River Valley.

An impressive bit of scenery, but the hiker can gain it only by walking a long, steep fire road or by following an even steeper, unsigned trail. The road is mercilessly hot and dry, so remember to fill canteens before setting out. There is some relief under the trees along the trail, but water is unreliable throughout the season.

Follow Highway 16 east for 6 km from the intersection of Highways 16 and 93. Turn right at the Maligne Lake Road sign, crossing the river and bearing left just after the bridge. Continue for 5 km to a gated, dirt road on the right, which leads

Colin Range from Signal Mountain Lookout

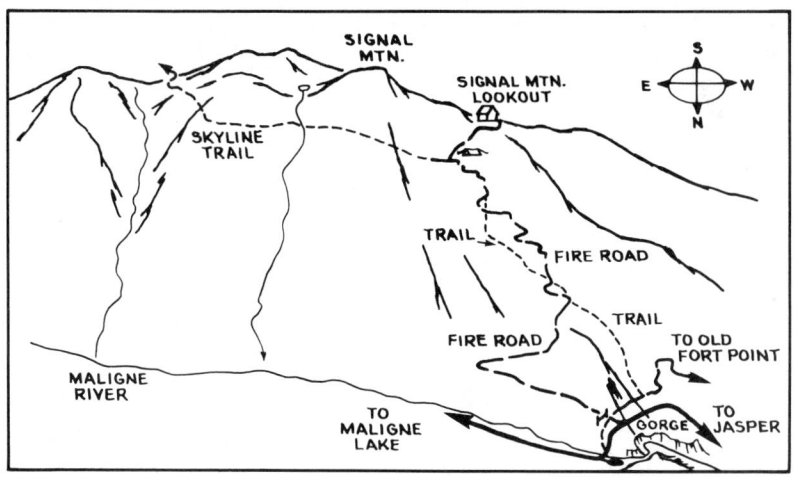

to a parking area beneath the trees. Trail signs indicate this is also part of the Skyline Trail (Hike 66).

To begin at the parking lot, find the trail marked #7 just before the gate on the right and follow it downhill for about 0.5 km. In a small hollow, find an unmarked trail that heads abruptly uphill, sometimes switchbacking, sometimes short-cutting, always up. Some may find it easier to use the gentler road for hiking up, saving the trail for the descent.

The fire road is straightforward and easy to follow. It climbs steadily and relentlessly to the top, with limited views and little variety. At 0.5 km below the lookout, find a much-appreciated campsite on the edge of the open meadows, near a small stream. Just beyond, on the left, the Skyline Trail branches off towards Mt. Tekarra.

Hikers wishing to forsake the hard, hot, road walk for the steep, but wooded trail, may do so at the trailhead, or pick up the trail at any of the points where it intersects the road. It is well defined throughout, blazed, shorter by a couple of kilometres and well used. It is not, however, maintained at present, so be prepared to step over some downed trees.

The lookout is worth as much time as one can spare. Look south to the Winston Churchill Range stretching northward from the Columbia Icefield, separating the Athabasca and Sunwapta rivers until they merge at the northern tip of the range. Scan southwest across the Rockies' main ranges, picking out the snowy crowns of Mts. Christie and Edith Cavell. A little closer are Marmot Mountain and The Whistlers. From the west, the Miette River rushes down from the Continental Divide to join with the Athabasca. Jasper sprawls below as the panorama swings north, then northeast with still more peaks and valleys rolling off towards Alberta's boreal forest. Open hillsides surrounding the site are excellent for picnics, siestas and exploratory rambles. A short walk out the Skyline Trail further expands possibilities for discovery.

The condition of the present routes to the scenic vista have discouraged more than a few hikers. So, those wishing for a more scenic and enjoyable access will join in encouraging the park to complete the planned trail from Old Fort Point to the lookout.

Maligne Canyon

JASPER

60 Maligne Canyon

Distance: 8.2 km/5 mi round trip, sixth bridge to Maligne parking lot
Hiking time: 2.5 hours
Elevation gain: 210 m/689 ft
High point: 1240 m/4067 ft
Type: nature walk/short hike
Best time: May through November
Maps: Jasper 83 D/16,
  Medicine Lake 83 C/13

A dramatic gorge, with walls of multicolored dolomite and limestone that fall steeply to the boiling waters of the Maligne River some 15 m below the canyon rim. An awesome testimonial to its name, the silty excavator continues to carve its geologic signature below hanging gardens and rainbow falls.

Even a short stay in Jasper should not fail to include a walk along the Maligne Canyon, as the best part of this impressive trail is easily accessible and can be hiked in a short time. Walk this popular, well-maintained, self-guided tour in its entirety from the sixth bridge to the Maligne Canyon parking lot. Or, shorten it somewhat by beginning the walk at the fifth bridge parking lot.

The trail may be shortened even further and still contain the most spectacular part of the canyon. Drive to the Maligne Canyon parking lot and then walk as far as time permits down the trail. It is recommended, though, that one travel at least as far as the emergence of the underground stream beyond the fourth bridge to witness the most impressive hydrologic forces at work here.

To begin at the sixth bridge, drive northeast on Highway 16 from the intersection of 16 and 93 near Jasper. At 4.7 km turn right at the sign for Maligne Lake Road and Lodge Road. Cross the bridge and bear left at the Y to follow the Maligne Lake Road. Proceed 1.7 km to a road on the left leading to the Sixth Bridge Warden's Station. At 1 km down this road another left turn leads to the parking lot.

Though the recommended walk begins here, it is also possible to continue along the Maligne Lake Road an additional 1 km to the fifth bridge road. The parking lot and trail are 1 km down this road. To begin at the head of the Maligne Canyon near the first bridge, drive 3 km beyond the fifth bridge road to the turn-off on the left and the parking area just beyond the intersection.

An interpretive exhibit near the parking lot and self-guided trail signs along the way detail the interaction of nature's artists and point out exceptional features. Bridges cross and recross the chasm, providing excellent viewpoints from which to examine or photograph the many caves, potholes and sculptures. Below the fourth bridge several underground streams gush from the canyon walls with waters from as far away as Medicine Lake, and greatly increase the volume of water in the river as it travels the last few kilometres to the Athabasca River.

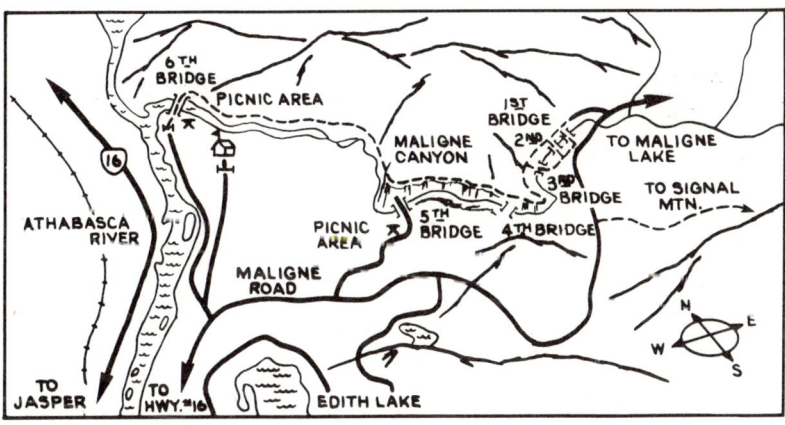

JASPER

61 Watchtower Basin

Distance: 20 km/12.4 mi round trip to Watchtower campsite
Hiking time: 7 hours
Elevation gain: 670 m/2198 ft
High point: 2075 m/6806 ft
Type: day hike or backpack
Best time: June through October
Map: Medicine Lake 83 C/13

A moderately strenuous trip through a pleasant mix of lowland meadows, sparkling streams, dense forest and alpine tundra. Good for a weekender or just a day of scenic wandering. The trail terminates in a scenic basin below the massive monolith of The Watchtower. Standing vigilant over the valley at 2791 m, the rocky structure invites exploration. Or, roam the high meadows and climb to the Skyline Trail near Big Shovel Pass for excellent views.

Drive 6 km on Highway 16, northeast from the intersection of 16 and 93. At the sign to Maligne Lake Road, turn right, cross the bridge, then bear left at the Y to follow Maligne Lake Road. At 17.5 km make a right turn on a short spur road leading to the Watchtower trailhead and parking area.

The trail begins near the back of the parking lot and joins another trail almost immediately. Keep right past the junction and descend the bank to cross the Maligne River on a sturdy log footbridge. Then follow the trail downstream a short distance (0.2 km) to another junction and turn left, heading south now, into dense pine and fir forest.

The trail climbs along a moderately steep grade for about 0.5 km, then levels somewhat as it enters an open, marshy stretch. Most of this wet area is bridged with split logs or corduroy walkways. Entering the forest again, begin the steady ascent to the lower Watchtower Basin. At about 6 km the trail emerges from the forest and approaches the creek, turning south to follow the right bank. Winding through scrub trees and low streamside vegetation, continue up the creek for about 2 km where the trail crosses an old rockslide area. Then, proceed for about

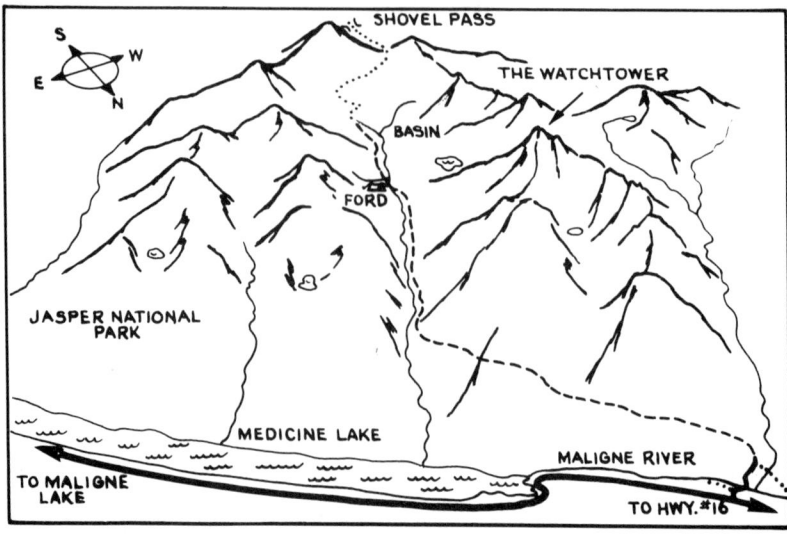

Entrance to Watchtower Basin

2 more kilometres, until streamside vegetation on the right is noticeably diminished and the stream widens considerably. At this point, water is usually shallow enough to cross without topping boots. Scan the left bank here for the yellow sign that marks the trail and the Watchtower campsite, where the quota is 10 people per night.

JASPER

62 Jacques Lake

Distance: 26 km/16 mi round trip
Hiking time: 2 days
Elevation gain: 60 m/197 ft
High point: 1560 m/5117 ft
Type: backpack
Best time: July through November
Map: Medicine Lake 83 C/13

Diversions unlimited on this favorite Jasper backpack. The popularity of the Jacques Lake trip stems from the several trailside points of interest and the relatively minor elevation gain required to reach the lovely, forested lakeshore.

At the junction of Highways 16 and 93, drive east on 16 for 6 km. Turn right to follow the Maligne Lake Road another 26.5 km to the trailhead parking area just across Beaver Creek at the south end of Medicine Lake. From the parking lot, recross the creek, walk through the small picnic area and then up the gated road. The road passes several small cabins and a corral before turning north and leaving civilization behind.

One and one-half kilometres of walking bring the hiker to the forested shores of Beaver Lake. A picnic shelter 0.5 km beyond is the first of several possible lunch or rest spots. Heading northwest now, the trail travels up the steep-walled

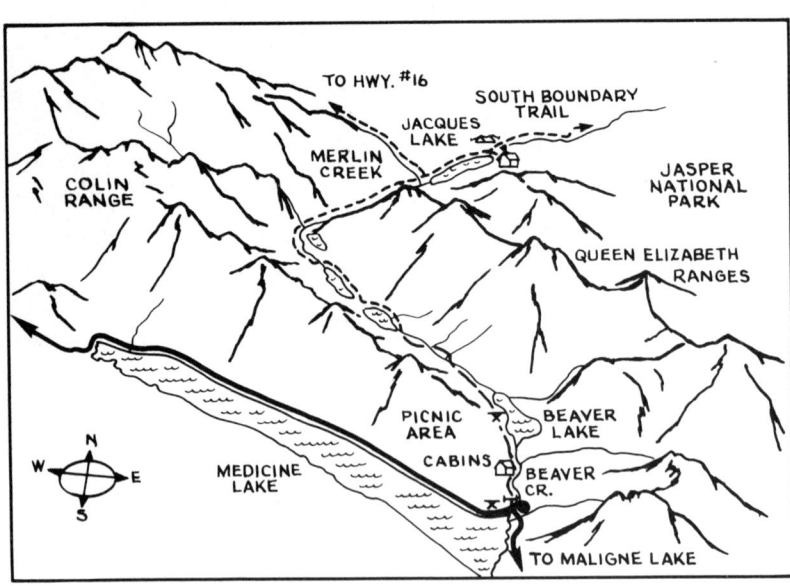

Jacques Lake

valley between Oolin and Queen Elizabeth ranges. The road ends at the first of the 3 Summit Lakes, none of which have a visible outlet. A boot-beaten path skirts the shoreline on the right, although the main trail travels through the grove of cottonwoods fringing the lake.

Beyond the 3 lakes, the valley turns to the northeast and crosses a low divide. Then the old trail branches to the right, the newer one continuing left to avoid several fords. The Merlin Creek Trail (Hike 53) merges at 12 km, and the lake is visible shortly thereafter. In 1 more kilometre, find the well-groomed campsite, situated at the far end of the lake, where views of surrounding peaks and landscape are best.

The Jacques Lake Trail is often hiked as the first leg in the 176-km South Boundary Trail (Hike 63).

JASPER

63 South Boundary Trail

Distance: 176 km/110 mi one way
Hiking time: 10 days to 2 weeks
Elevation gain: 1219 m/4000 ft
High point: 2255 m/7400 ft
Type: extended backpack
Best time: mid-July through mid-October
Maps: Medicine Lake 83 C/13, Mountain Park 83 C/14, Southesk 83 C/11, George Creek 83 C/11, Job Creek 83 C/7, Sunwapta Peak 83 C/6, Columbia Icefield 83 C/3

Providing a unique and challenging opportunity for a major wilderness hike, the South Boundary Trail travels through regions of near-pristine quality. It is considerably less travelled than its counterpart, the North Boundary Trail (Hike 56), and hikers here are frequently on their own to roam the wilds of southern Jasper. While there is no grand finale of beautiful alpine scenery, such as on the North Boundary Trail, there are many kilometres of uncrowded open country, fine views, and abundant evidence of the large wildlife population— appropriate rewards for the venturesome explorer who is not deterred by solitude and the lack of an easy trail.

This trip requires a major commitment in preparations (both physical and psychological), as well as in time allowed. There is only 1 reasonable escape route if conditions turn bad.

The trip is probably most often hiked from Camp Parker and Nigel Pass, north to Medicine Lake. However, as scenery improves to the south, we suggest starting at Medicine Lake in spite of the extra 300-m climb.

Beginning in the north end, the journey starts at the Jacques Lake trailhead (Hike 62) and follows this trail 13 km to Jacques Lake. An alternative start is the Merlin Creek Trail (Hike 53), a predominantly forested 34.5-km walk that connects at Jacques Lake.

Jacques Lake marks the entrance to the true wilderness. From here the trail

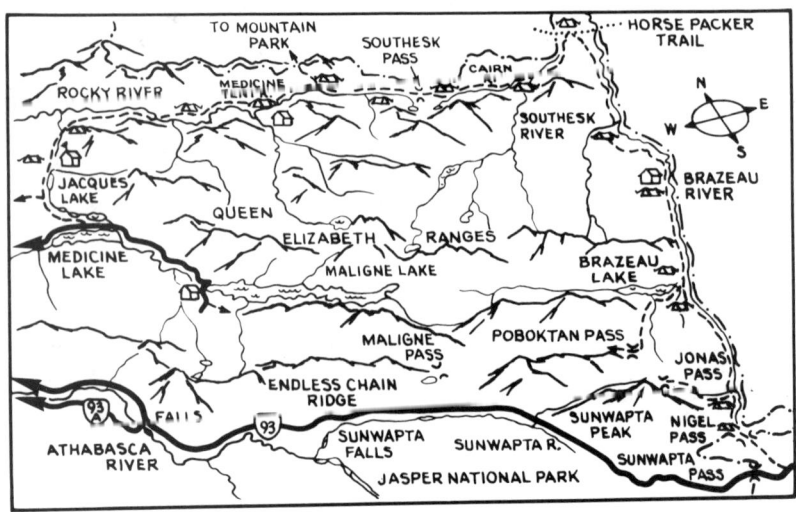

South Boundary Trail in the Brazeau River Valley

Jacques Lake near the northern end of the South Boundary Trail

heads northeast, running through the forested creek valley, to meet the Rocky River and Grizzly Camp at 24 km.

The way proceeds beside the Rocky River, making a long, gentle ascent out of dense forest to the subalpine zone. Cross a bridge at about 34 km and continue on the east side of the river. Passing a campsite at Climax Creek, continue about 10 more kilometres to reach the confluence of the Rocky and Medicine Tent rivers. Here, the trail swings east to follow the Medicine Tent River. Be careful to stay on the hiker paths (follow blazes) to avoid the fords that horse trails often encounter.

This valley is narrower and the climb becomes more pronounced. At about 60 km, just before the Medicine Tent campsite, a trail cuts off through the Miette Range and meets a forest road south of Mountain Park. It is the only escape route off the South Boundary.

Continuing south, pass the La Grace campsite and complete the ascent to the apex of the trip. At 77 km, Southesk Pass (or Cairn Pass—2255 m) is surrounded by meadows and fine alpine scenery.

Beyond the pass, follow the gentle descent of the Cairn River, passing another campsite and making 2 fords before reaching the Southesk River at 97 km. As the trail approaches the second ford, pass a campsite and meet a junction. Walk east here, making the ford and continuing along the north bank of the Southesk River.

At about 103 km, a bridged crossing takes hikers to the south bank, where the trail makes a wide bend around the base of Mt. Dalhousie. It passes a campsite and warden's cabin and meets the Brazeau River.

The route stays close to the Brazeau River for most of the remaining distance. Passing through forest and intermittent meadows, the trail reaches 119 km, marked by the Isaac Creek Warden's Cabin and campsite. It rolls along in similar terrain, but with mountainous views continually improving, and then passes another campsite about 15 km beyond.

Km 146 marks the end of the wilderness and the hiker's reentrance into the world of numerous hikers. Reaching the outflow stream from Brazeau Lake, the trail meets with the Poboktan Pass Trail (Hike 31) to the right and the Brazeau River Trail (Hike 32) to the left. The right-hand route leads 2.5 km to the Brazeau Lake campsite near the shore of Brazeau Lake. The left-hand route continues up the Brazeau River, to the Four Point campsite. Here is the junction with the Nigel Pass Trail (Hike 27), the last leg of the South Boundary trip. Hike over scenic Nigel Pass to reach the exit on the Icefields Parkway just inside Banff National Park.

Bear track

JASPER

64 Maligne Lake Shoreline Trail

Distance: 3.2 km/2 mi loop
Hiking time: 1 hour
Elevation gain: 30 m/98 ft
High point: 1710 m/5609 ft
Type: nature walk
Best time: May through October
Map: Athabasca Falls 83 C/12

Mecca for photographers and seekers of beauty, this blue green, inland fiord hugs the flanks of the Queen Elizabeth Ranges and reaches deep into the heart of the mountains. It is unfortunate that hikers must be content with a few short kilometres of trail on which to enjoy the lake's beauty. Those wishing to see more must rent a canoe or take the tour boat. But here is a short and easy loop trail that captures an intriguing bit of the views.

Drive east on Highway 16 from the intersection with Highway 93. At 5.9 km, turn right to follow the Maligne Lake Road and drive 42 km to the tour boat parking area.

Easy to reach from the lower parking lot, the paved trail parallels the shoreline, heading south. For the first 0.5 km, watch the trail, not the view! Hundreds of ground squirrels have made the area their home and consider the trail to be their private sunbathing spot.

Views get better as the trail approaches the end of the loop. A small lagoon marks the end of the lakeside portion of the trip, and a practical park staff has provided benches here to give view-gazers a place to sit off the trail. This spot is known as Mary Schaffer Viewpoint and interpretive signs tell about early travellers in the area. Views are across the lake to the Maligne Range, to the twin summits of Mts. Unwin and Charlton and to the softly rounded Bald Hills.

An old pony trail may be followed along the forested lakeshore for another 1.5 km, but the main trail turns away from the lake here, making a mild climb into forest. As it swings around to complete the loop, the trail passes from forest into a flowered meadow and then joins the Opal Hills Loop (Hike 65) briefly before returning to the lakeshore and parking area. Follow the trail around the tip of the lake for about 2 km for more lakeside walking.

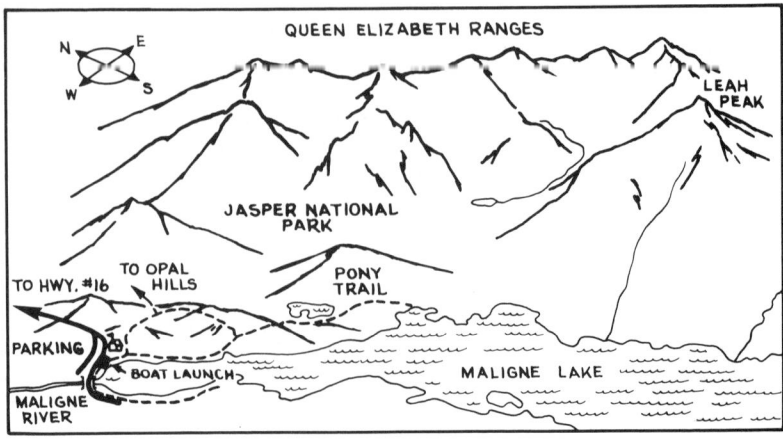

Right: *Maligne Lake*

Maligne Lake from Opal Hills

JASPER

65 Opal Hills Loop

Distance: 8.2 km/5 mi round trip
Hiking time: 4 hours
Elevation gain: 470 m/1541 ft
High point: 2140 m/7019 ft
Best time: July through mid-October
Type: day hike
Maps: Athabasca Falls 83 C/12
(trail not shown), Medicine Lake 83C/13
(trail not shown)

Overlooking the largest glacier-fed lake in the Canadian Rockies, these alpine meadows are a wide rambling parkland of blossoms and greenery. Climb knolls to relax on broad hillsides among myriad wildflowers. The dramatic views will impress even the most seasoned adventurer, so don't be discouraged when the trail seems to ignore the laws of gravity to travel nearly straight up.

From the junction of Highways 16 and 93, drive east on 16 for 5.9 km. Turn right to follow the Maligne Lake Road for 42 km to the tour boat parking area. Keep left and go up the hill to the third and last parking lot.

The trail starts from the southeast end of the parking lot and descends a short distance to meet the Maligne Lake Shoreline Trail (Hike 64). The 2 trails join for about 100 m before the Opal Hills Loop splits off, heading across the meadow. Upon reaching the trees, the trail begins the real climb and even the shade of dense lodgepole forest offers little relief from the arduous escalade.

Just when you feel tempted to abandon efforts on a thus-far unscenic and toilsome trail, things begin to happen. At about 3 km the trail levels and enters a small meadow where it divides to form the loop through the upper meadows. The right branch makes a steeper but quicker ascent to treeline and the lovely meadows. The left branch rambles more gently, taking longer and climbing less directly through forest and hillside meadows to the splendid scenery above.

The meadows stretch out along a large bench and the trail encircles 2 distinct hills perched near the southern end of this bench. Spend a little more effort and climb 1 of these hills for the best views of the lake and the valley, to the Bald Hills and beyond to the Maligne Range. Continue through the meadows, then descend through forest to close the loop. The final descent is steep and quick, returning to the parking lot to complete the tour. Wildflowers are best from mid-July to August.

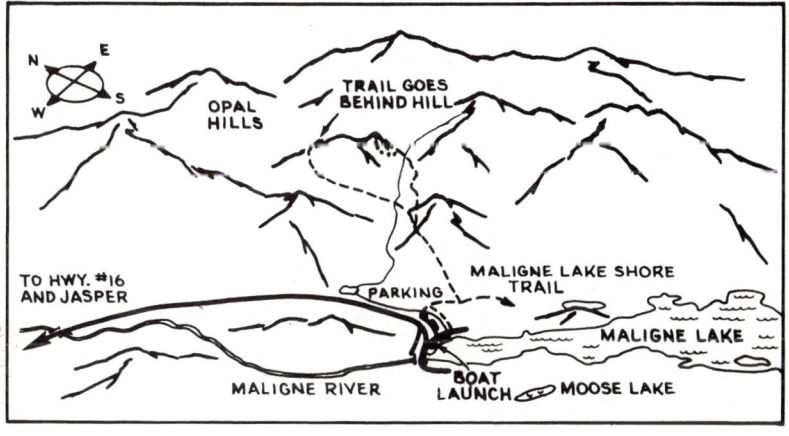

Mt. Edith Cavell

JASPER

66 Skyline Trail

Distance: 53 km/33 mi one way from
 Maligne Lake to Maligne Lake Road
Hiking time: 2-3 days
Elevation gain: 850 m/2788 ft
High point: 2530 m/8298 ft
Type: backpack
Best time: August through mid-October
Maps: Athabasca Falls 83 C/12,
 Medicine Lake 83 C/13

Winding along ridge tops high above the valleys of the Maligne and Athabasca rivers, this trail penetrates the heart of the Maligne Range. Enjoy vantage points from which to view mountain peaks and valleys, tarns, heather meadows and stark, rocky slopes. Though it has its share of wet, muddy trail, creek fords, steep slopes and other challenges, this trail is exceptional in its scenic variety and splendor all along the way.

From the junction of Highways 93 and 16, take 16 east for 5.9 km, then turn south to cross the bridge and meet the Maligne Lake Road. Follow it for 42.5 km to Maligne Lake and the parking area at the road's end (1650 m).

From the trailhead just above the parking lot, begin a gentle walk through an old burn area, now succeeded by lodgepole forest. Slowly gaining elevation, the trail passes several small lakes, ponds and meadows, including 2 popular fishing lakes—Lorraine and Mona. But you will want to move quickly through here during mosquito season since the dampness brings them out in force. Fortunately the trail follows a gentle grade and within 4.4 km, reaches Evelyn Creek, a good spot to fill canteens and take a quick breather.

Cross the creek on a bridge, pass a campsite on the right, then begin a series of switchbacks leading up the next 4.8 km. Reach another campsite at 8.4 km, and soon the forest opens and views to the southwest begin to unfold. Look out to the brown and rounded Bald Hills, down to deep blue Maligne Lake and

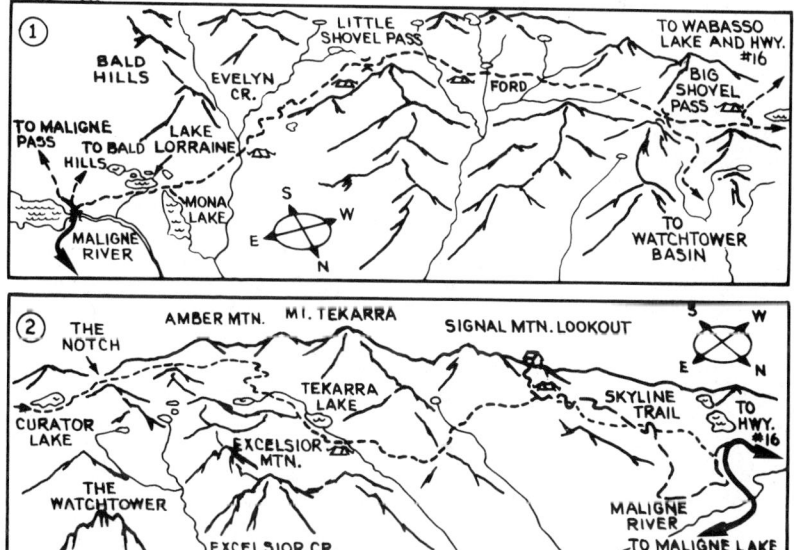

Bighorn sheep below Amber Mountain

across to jagged, glaciated peaks in the Queen Elizabeth Ranges. Leaving the forest at about 9.5 km, exchange trees for heather gardens. In full bloom in mid-July, the soft heather dominates the hillsides with a carpet of color near Little Shovel Pass (2225 m). Descend into the gigantic Snowbowl, where the subalpine meadows attract large numbers of elk, deer, mountain goat and the occasional grizzly.

Travelling across these high meadowlands is usually wet business due to abundant fresh streamflow from surrounding peaks and snowfields. The trip is recommended for August or later, though the soft, spongy earth remains sodden most of the season and the large numbers of hikers and horses on this route have been instrumental in reducing the trail to a deep, muddy trench in places. Park plans to upgrade the trail appear to be slow in coming and present management must rely on quotas (60 people per night) to monitor visitation to the area. Open campfires are prohibited due to the fragile nature of the alpine environment and the scarcity of fuel at this elevation. Stove use is mandatory for the length of the Skyline Trail.

Hikers may have to ford at least 1 stream on the walk through the meadows; explore to find a convenient spot. Then continue on through rolling terrain, ascending slightly to Big Shovel Pass (2286 m), where the vegetation has all but disappeared. From the pass, which lies sheltered beneath Curator Mountain (2623 m), one might choose to descend into Watchtower Basin (see Hike 61) and out to the Maligne Lake Road, or continue on towards Curator Lake and The Notch. At 19.5 km the trail forks, the left fork descending a steep switchback trail to the Curator campsite and then on down into the Athabasca Valley (see Hike 39).

The right fork ascends a steep, rocky slope to Curator Lake. The trail passes to the right of the milky waters, climbing steeply towards The Notch (2530 m), which often retains snow well into late summer. Breathtaking views appear near the crest, though the inevitable exclamation you make may actually be in relief at having completed the gruelling climb. Traverse sterile hillsides on sharply fragmented rock, passing just below the summit of Amber Mountain, then switchback down towards Centre Lakes. Following the valley bottom, pass Tekarra Lake and Tekarra campsite, located between Mt. Tekarra and Excelsior Mountain, which dominate either side of the valley. Cross the stream below the lake and gradually ascend again to skirt the northern flanks of Mt. Tekarra and exit on the Signal Mountain Fire Road. From here an 8.5-km walk on the fire road will bring you to the gate and parking lot near Maligne Lake Road.

A trail exists, which more or less cuts switchbacks on the fire road, thus shortening the less than desirable road walk. The trail descends steeply to a hollow about 0.5 km southwest of the trailhead, then parallels the highway back to the parking area. Park plans to construct an alternative route from the Signal Mountain Lookout area to Old Fort Point near Jasper are presently being developed. Such a trail would not only provide a more pleasing finish to the trip, but could simplify the problems of transportation and vehicle shuttles.

The skyline near Snowbowl

Maligne Range from the Bald Hills

Arnica

JASPER

67 Bald Hills Lookout

Distance: 10 km/6 mi round trip
Hiking time: 3 hours
Elevation gain: 520 m/1706 ft
High point: 2170 m/7118 ft
Type: day hike
Best time: July through September
Map: Athabasca Falls 83 C/12

In an area so rich with scenic trails, Bald Hills Lookout ranks near the top. A park-like atmosphere prevails around the old lookout site, with its trim spruce trees and alpine meadows.

From the junction of Highways 93 and 16, take 16 east for 5.9 km, then turn south to cross the bridge and meet the Maligne Lake Road. Follow it for 42.5 km to a large parking area at the road's end (1650 m).

The Bald Hills Lookout Trail starts directly opposite the parking lot entrance on a gated fire road. During the first 0.5 km, pass the Maligne Pass (Hike 34) and Moose Lake (Hike 68) trail sign on the left, and a packers' cabin on the right.

The road climbs gently throughout the first 1.5 km and steeply for the next kilometre. At 2.5 km the road levels and takes a sharp turn to the northwest. At this point, hikers may choose to stay on the road or follow an unsigned but well-defined trail up the hillside. The road is well-graded, easy walking—the trail, much steeper, but shorter and more scenic. Watch closely on the left side of the road for a pile of rocks and sticks that mark the otherwise inconspicuous trail.

Be prepared to spend some time at the top. The mountain-filled panorama and lovely meadows make for excellent picnicking and unrestrained alpine wandering.

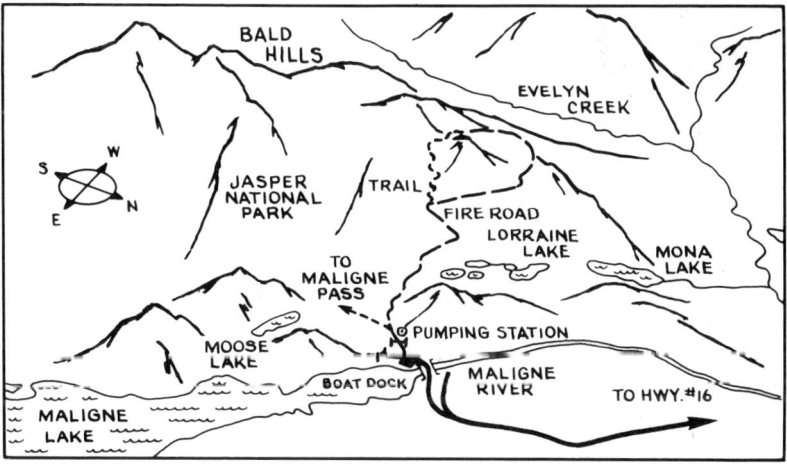

JASPER

68 Moose Lake

Distance: 2.6 km/1.6 mi loop
Hiking time: I hour
Elevation gain: 62 m/203 ft
High point: 1742 m/5714 ft
Type: short hike or nature walk
Best time: June through October
Map: Athabasca Falls 83 C/12

Walk a quiet, easy path to a peaceful little lakelet in a pocket of forested hills. Reflecting the snowy tops of Samson and Leah peaks, the still, green waters of Moose Lake are a favorite feeding area for local moose. The cautious and quiet hiker might catch a look at these magnificent creatures browsing the aquatic meadows. Choose the quiet hours of dawn or dusk, or perhaps a grey, drizzly day, for best wildlife viewing. Be sure to come armed with camera and insect repellent, for the ubiquitous mosquitoes and biting flies have also discovered the plentiful foraging here.

See Hike 67 for driving directions. From the parking area, cross the road and follow the gated Bald Hills Fire Road for 250 m to the Maligne Pass Trail junction on the left. Walk this trail for 0.8 km to the intersection (signed) where the Moose Lake Trail branches to the left. Views are scarce as the way travels through dense lodgepole forest, gaining little elevation or hiker interest. The final 0.4 km to the lake descends a gentle slope, then tops a small ridge crest to make a sudden appearance at the lake.

Have lunch, or explore the grassy shoreline on the numerous game trails and footpaths winding through the trees. Then return to the parking lot by retracing your steps, or make the loop trip, following the well-defined main trail as it continues its gentle downslope through forest to Maligne Lake and back to the parking area.

Moose feeding on lake bottom grass

Moose Lake

S
E
W
N
BALD HILLS
JASPER NATIONAL PARK
TRAPPER CREEK
TO MALIGNE PASS
TO BALD HILLS
LAKE LORRAINE
MOOSE LAKE
SKYLINE TRAIL
MONA LAKE
MALIGNE LAKE
TO HWY. #16

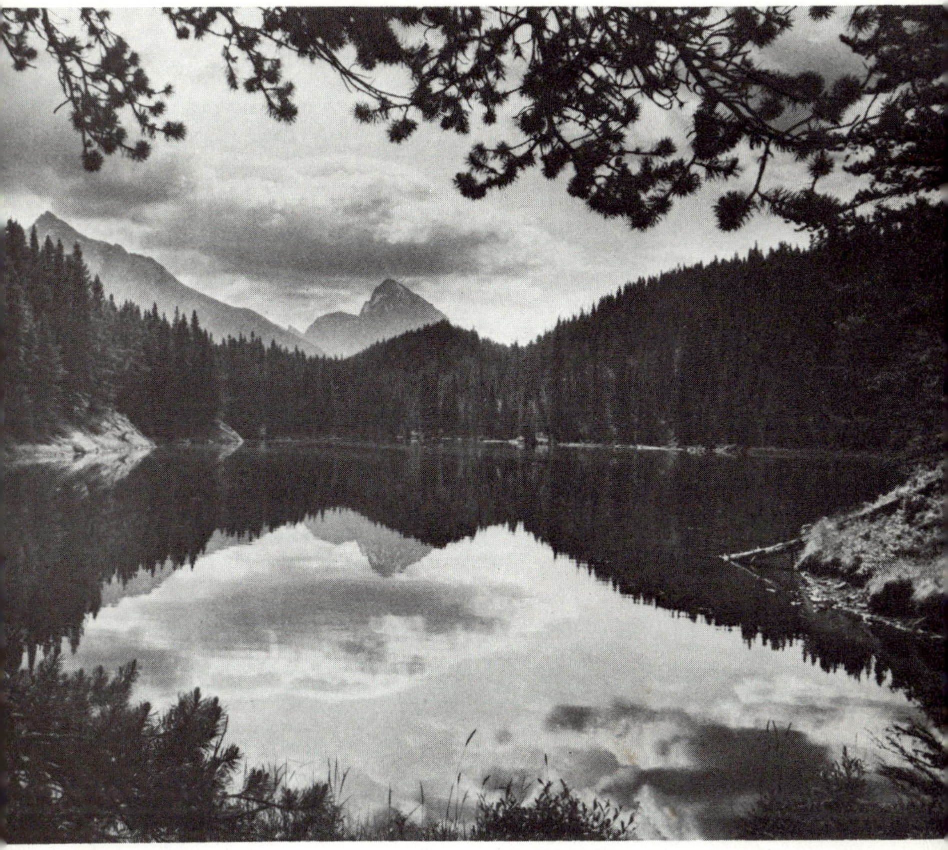

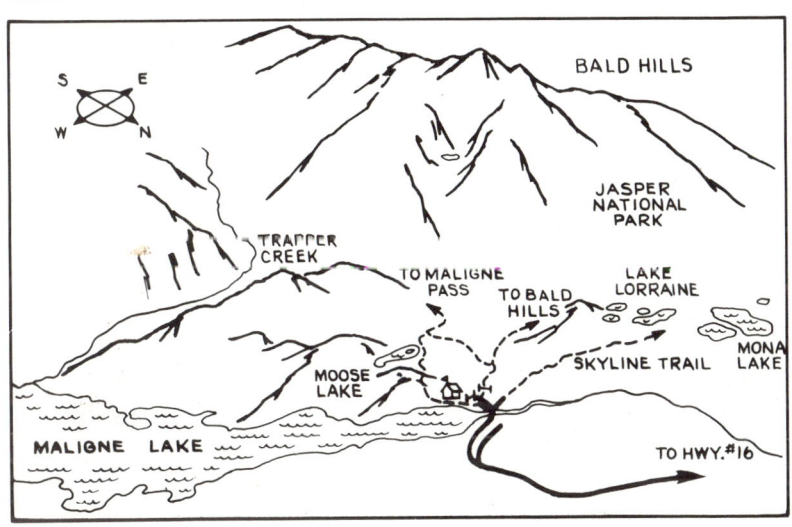

JASPER

69 Marjorie and Caledonia Lakes

Distance: 10 km/6.2 mi round trip
Hiking time: 2.5 hours
Elevation gain: 100 m/328 ft
High point: 1180 m/3870 ft
Type: half-day hike or nature walk
Best time: May through October
Map: Jasper 83 D/16

Easy access, gentle terrain and good picnic and fishing sites make this area ideal for the whole family. The modest incline rambles past small patches of meadow and marshland, into a delightfully cool forest of lodgepole pine and brightly contrasting aspen poplar. Lush wildflowers persist well into midsummer and lots of small wildlife as well as deer, elk and moose inhabit the area.

Starting low and gaining little elevation, this trail becomes accessible very early in the season, offering excellent opportunities for picnics and day hikes, photography and nature study when time or weather hinder travel to more remote areas. During fishing season, Caledonia Lake is a popular destination for those in search of that prized trout. Small rental boats are available at both lakes through local sporting goods stores in Jasper. Picnickers will find a pleasant selection of spots at either Marjorie or Caledonia Lake, though Marjorie's popularity has left the lakeshores a bit shy of ground cover vegetation.

Drive north towards Jasper townsite from the intersection of Highways 93 and 16. At 0.8 km, turn left on Pine Avenue and continue 0.4 km to Cabin Creek Road. Another left turn and 0.6 km will bring you to the parking lot beside the mobile-home subdivision at the far west end of town. Leave vehicles here and walk west a short distance up a dirt road leading from the parking area to the trailhead (marked Saturday Night Lake Loop) on the left side of the road.

The walk begins on an easy trail following a subtle incline past marsh and meadowlands for approximately 1 km. Then, ascending more rapidly, it climbs the next 1.5 km to Marjorie Lake. Near the far west end of Marjorie Lake, a short spur trail (0.5 km) leads to another small lake, Hibernia Lake.

From this junction, continue another 2 km of nearly flat trail to Caledonia Lake, passing an intersecting trail on the left at about 1 km past Marjorie Lake. There are good picnic spots here and lots of shoreline to explore, but keep in mind that these marshy shores are home to a large number of small wildland creatures—walk softly! Overnight camping is not permitted at either Marjorie or Caledonia Lake.

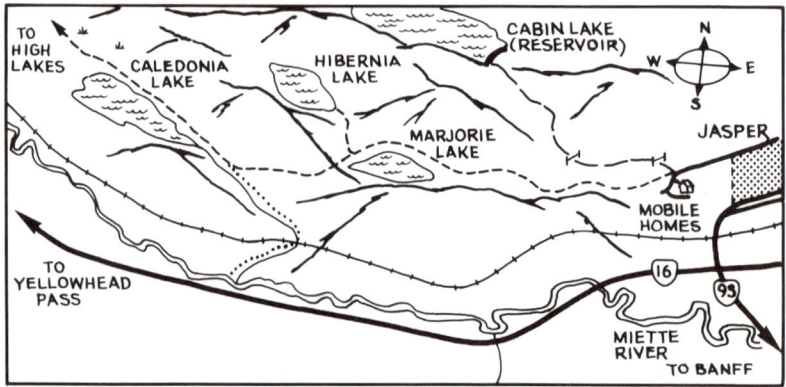

Park Ranges

JASPER

70 Saturday Night Lake Loop

Distance: 27 km/16.7 mi loop
Hiking time: 1-2 days
Elevation gain: 580 m/1902 ft
High point: 1640 m/5379 ft
Type: long day hike or backpack
Best time: June through October
Map: Jasper 83 D/16

A pleasant trail through gently rolling forest provides the ambitious hiker with a long but not-too-strenuous day trip that rambles past lakes, waterfalls, marshes and meadows and offers fleeting views of nearby peaks. But countless possibilities for exploration may convince you to linger awhile, camp at 1 of several primitive campsites along the way and invest some time discovering the area.

See Hike 69, Marjorie and Caledonia Lakes, for driving directions and location of the trailhead, then follow the trail to Caledonia Lake. Continue along the trail, ascending slightly as the forest thickens and becomes predominantly lodgepole pine. Pass 2 marshy areas with small lakes (in early season) and reach the junction of the Minnow Lake Trail at about 9.5 km, 4.5 km beyond Caledonia Lake. The 1-km side trail to Minnow Lake offers popular camping and excellent trout fishing (in season).

Saturday Night Lake

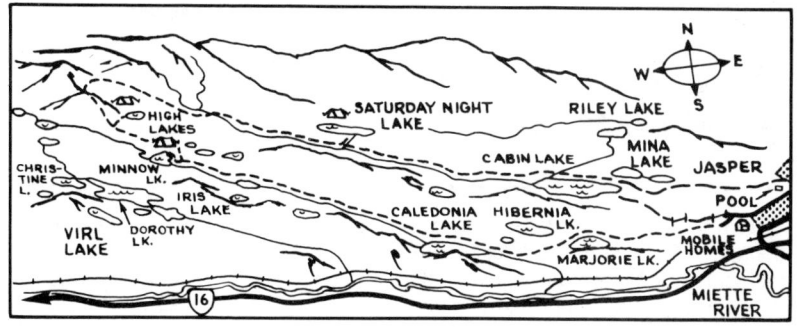

Turning right from the junction, climb a bit and reach the High Lakes junction in approximately 3 km. A 0.2-km spur from the main trail emerges in meadows and marshes, encircling 1 of the small, sparkling High Lakes. Open shorelines here allow the best views yet along this trail. Rocky mountain ridges and snowy peaks reflect across the waters as local and migrant waterfowl feed near the grassy shore. A pleasant campsite is located near the spur trail.

On level terrain now, make the short walk to the stream and waterfall at the far end of the loop and find a pleasant spot for lunch, beside ferns and cascading waters. Then begin the gradual descent along the stream, skirting marshes and passing through stands of spruce and lodgepole. About 5 km will bring you to the junction with the Saturday Night Lake Loop, which ascends steeply to the left for 0.5 km to reach the lake. A pleasant contrast to the lower, forest-enclosed lakes, the open shoreline here permits views to snowy peaks beyond.

The main trail continues a gradual descent about 6 km to the ridge above picturesque Cabin Lake. No point in descending the hillside to the shoreline, however, as this lake is a reservoir for Jasper's water supply and is closed to recreational activity. Besides, views are from the trail, which eventually does pass near the lower end of the lake on returning to the trailhead.

An alternative trailhead exists at the parking lot opposite the town pool (see Hike 71, Mina and Riley Lakes Loop). The quota for this trail is 24 people per night.

JASPER

71 Mina and Riley Lakes Loop

Distance: 9 km/5.6 mi round trip
Hiking time: 3 hours
Elevation gain: 180 m/590 ft
High point: 1240 m/4067 ft
Type: nature hike
Best time: May through October
Map: Jasper 83 D/16 (trail not shown)

Surrounded by dense forest and set upon a broad plateau above Jasper townsite, Mina and Riley lakes offer popular year-round destinations for residents and visitors alike. The trail is wide and pleasant underfoot, winding through varied woodlands to good picnic spots on the lakes. This peaceful area offers good opportunities for wildlife viewing to the quiet and lucky hiker.

From the intersection of Highways 16 and 93, drive 0.8 km towards Jasper townsite and turn left on Pine Avenue (at police station directional sign). Drive 0.5 km on Pine, turning right when it ends at Pyramid Lake Avenue. Continue for 0.6 km to the activity centre parking lot on the left, and park here (1060 m).

The trailhead, located at the rear of the parking lot, is at an intersection where the Saturday Night Lake Loop and the Mina and Riley Lakes Loop trails (one and the same at this point) meet the Pyramid Lake Trail. The 3 trails are numbered 3, 8 and 2 respectively and can be identified as such by numbered, yellow, triangular trail markers along the way.

Follow the left-hand trail as it climbs the steep bluff above town and enters the dense lowland forest. At about 0.5 km, pass a subsidiary trail on the left; 30 m beyond, the Saturday Night Lake Loop branches to the left. Proceed along the Mina Lake Trail, turning north and intersecting the Cabin Lake Fire Road at about 1 km from the trailhead. Cross the road and continue straight ahead for 30 m, where the trail then swings abruptly to the left.

The next kilometre travels through peaceful woods, passing a large beaver pond just before arriving at Mina Lake. Though the shoreline is quite marshy, it is bordered by dry, solid ground beneath the surrounding forest—perfect for picnicking and taking in the view of the Front Ranges to the north. Find a fire box

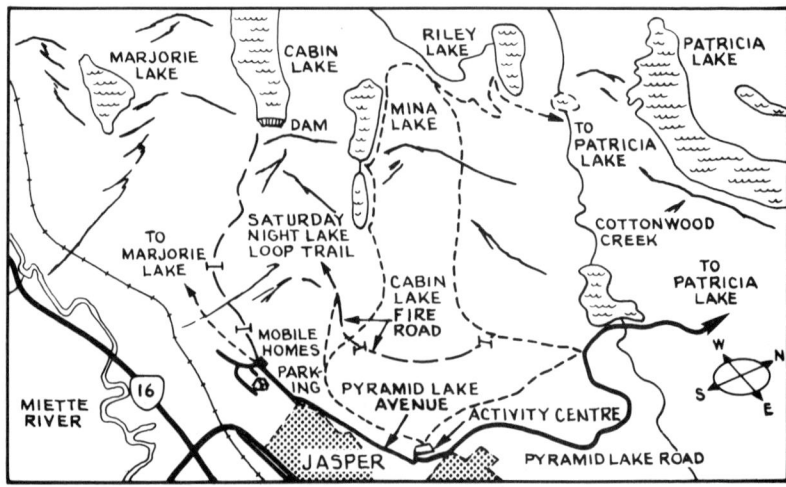

for cooking, or enjoy an afternoon of boating. (Make prior arrangements for rental boats through sporting goods stores in Jasper.) Some hikers may wish to make this their turnaround point, for a round trip of just over 4 km. Or, complete the loop by continuing along the lakeshore, then through more forest for 1.5 km to the Riley Lake spur trail. This side path descends 80 m of elevation in 1.5 km to the forested shores of Riley Lake (1180 m). While there is no defined picnic area, there are several boats and reputedly good fishing.

The main loop trail continues through forest again to another intersection with the Cabin Lake Fire Road. Turn right to reach the original intersection in about 1 km. Or, go left for an alternative return route, intersecting the Pyramid Lake Trail and following it to the right, back to the trailhead.

Mina Lake

Patricia Lake

JASPER

72 Patricia Lake Trail

Distance: 4.8 km/3 mi one way
Hiking time: 2 hours
Elevation gain: 60 m/197 ft
High point: 1210 m/3970 ft
Type: nature hike
Best time: May through mid-November
Map: Jasper 83 D/l6

Tread a path through gentle terrain, with its delightful mix of forest and marshland—an area rich with wildlife and scenic charm. Though the hike is relatively short and undemanding, views embrace mountain lakes and snowy peaks. Picnic spots abound along the loop, but carry your own water.

See Hike 71 for directions to the activity centre parking lot, then continue north to Pyramid Lake Road, which leads up and away from town. Follow this road 3.5 km to the riding stables and parking lot on the right.

The trail begins just opposite the parking lot, on the west side of Pyramid Lake Road. Start here and soon pass close to a motel. The broad trail then climbs over a small knoll to descend to the lush vegetation of the lakeshore. Views here are of colorful Pyramid Mountain (2763 m) with its crowning microwave tower.

At 2.4 km, pass a large beaver pond before reaching the Riley Lake Loop intersection. Though this trail tends to be a bit muddy from heavy horse use, hikers who take the time to investigate 0.5 km or so along this path will be rewarded with the opportunity to see some excellent examples of beaver craftsmanship.

Back on the main route, continue east, following Cottonwood Creek for about a kilometre before swinging north again to return to the road.

A good hike for the early riser or after-dinner stroller as these are the best times to view the abundant wildlife of the area.

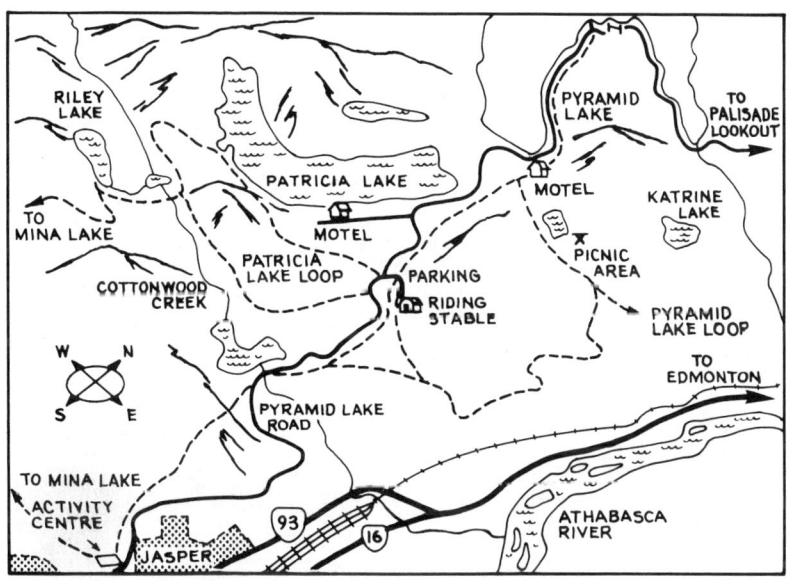

JASPER

73 Pyramid Lake Trails

Distance: 14 km/8.7 mi round trip
Hiking time: 3.5 hours
Elevation gain: 265 m/869 ft
High point: 1325 m/4346 ft
Type: day hike
Best time: May through October
Map: Jasper 83 D/16

Variety and contrast define this relatively small area where interconnecting trails create numerous possibilities for a short hike or a full day of exploration. Ramble up ridges for views of lakes and river valleys. Meander through grassy meadows and stop for lunch, relaxing among wildflowers. Or, stroll along lakeshores to picnic on the beach, fish or observe the waterfowl. Popular with equestrians and hikers alike, the wide trails are gentle and well maintained, offering excellent, easy wandering, which can be started at any of several access points. In addition, the low elevation and easy access from Jasper townsite make them popular trips throughout the year with superb ski-touring possibilities.

To begin at Jasper, see Hike 71, Mina and Riley Lakes Loop, for driving instructions to the activity centre parking lot. Find the trailhead near the rear of the parking lot. Follow the trail marked 2 heading to the right, and angle up the bluff into forest of pine, aspen and cottonwood. At 1.3 km reach the junction with Pyramid Lake Road near Cottonwood Creek. The parking lot here is a 2.3-km drive from the activity centre and provides an alternative starting point for the trail. Other access points exist along the Pyramid Lake Road at 3.5 km near the riding stables and at the Pyramid Lake Island picnic area at the end of the road (6.4 km).

From Cottonwood Creek parking area, walk along the road to cross the creek. Then pick up the trail on the other side of the road and continue through gently rolling lodgepole forest. At about 0.7 km from the road, a trail that comes from

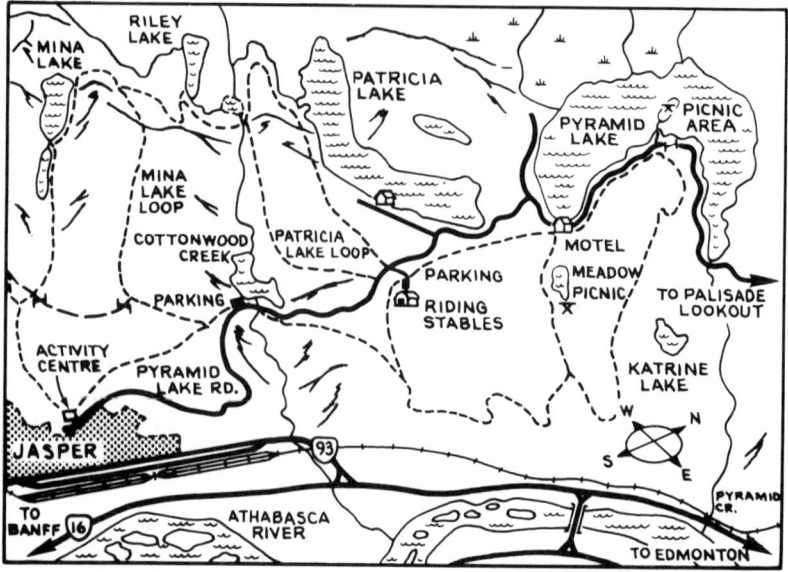

Park Ranges and Patricia Lake

the stables merges on the left. As the trail continues to ascend the ridge, the forest becomes thinner and drier and then opens up to views of the Athabasca River Valley and the Maligne Range. Upon reaching the end of the ridge, the trail doubles back into the forest, then branches right to form an alternative route (marked 2A). The left branch plunges into the forest to the west, passing a lovely picnic spot on the edge of a grassy meadow, before emerging near the motel on the shores of Pyramid Lake. About 1 km north of the motel is the Pyramid Lake Island picnic area.

The alternative route (2A) follows a shallow, green gully for about 0.5 km, then swings sharply to the left to ascend a moderately steep ridge, gaining about 250 m of elevation in 1 km. From this side of the ridge, the sparse, open forest provides unobstructed views to Patricia and Pyramid lakes below and west to the Victoria Cross Range. Then, experience a dramatic contrast while descending the steep west slope, as the forest changes from a pure lodgepole stand to a mixture of pine and aspen. The increased moisture on this side supports a lush garden of shade-loving shrubs and wildflowers, but can also make the steep trail muddy and slippery. On reaching the lake, the trail curves southward along the shore passing the Pyramid Island picnic area and the motel before entering the forest again. From here, trails loop back to the starting point by either skirting the shore of Patricia Lake or by passing near the stables. Several minor, unmarked trails intersect the main routes throughout the area and may resemble a confusing maze, but the main trails are well signed. Returning visitors to the area may even appreciate the variety offered by these other trails.

JASPER

74 Palisade Lookout

Distance: 21 km/13 mi round trip
Hiking time: 8 hours
Elevation gain: 821 m/2693 ft
High point: 2000 m/6562 ft
Type: day hike
Best time: mid-June through October
Map: Jasper 83 D/16

Sweeping views of silvery peaks and kilometres of open meadows to delight both cloud-watchers and wildflower aficionados. The expansive panorama and dramatic landscape make the Palisade Lookout Trail the most scenic of the hikes in the immediate Jasper townsite area. Although the route follows a hard, well-kept fire road (tough on plodding feet) and is often without views to break the monotony, it is indeed worth the effort to discover this vista.

See Mina and Riley Lakes Loop, Hike 71, for driving directions to the activity centre parking lot. Proceed north on Pyramid Lake Avenue about 1 block to the intersection with Pyramid Lake Road. Turn left and follow the road to its end (6.4 km) at the Pyramid Island picnic area (1180 m).

Begin the hike just beyond the gate on the fire road, which contours around the eastern end of Pyramid Lake. Notice the distinctively colored Pyramid Mountain (2763 m), which will remain in view for much of the hike.

At 1 km, cross Pyramid Creek and begin climbing the road. At 3 km, pass a small marsh-bound lake and make a short descent before beginning the serious climb to the lookout.

An energetic stream, busily carving its own small gorge at 5.5 km, supplies the only reliable source of water until you return to the lake. Just beyond are the first good views of the Colin Range and the island-studded Athabasca River. At 7.5 km,

Ptarmigan in summer plumage

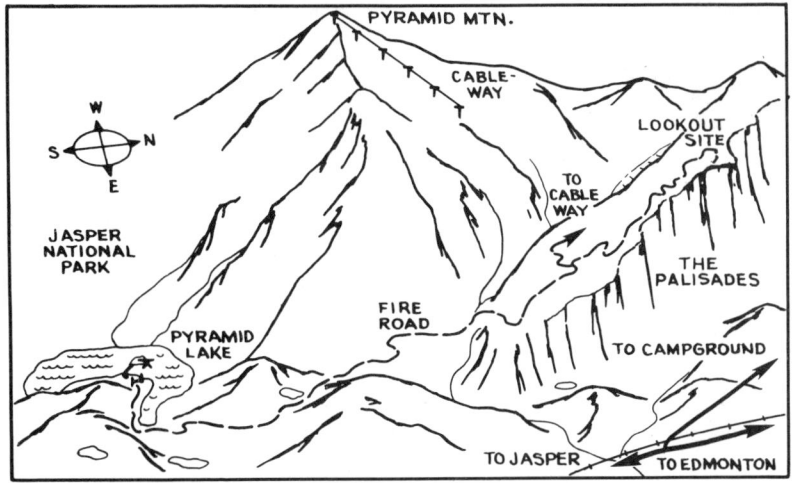

the lookout road branches to the right, leaving the well-tended microwave service road to wind its way up towards Pyramid Mountain on the left.

Near the lookout the forest opens to grass and meadowlands. Views to the northeast are of the silvery sawtooth peaks of the Colin Range, now fully visible. To the northwest lies the equally beautiful De Smet Range, separated from the Colin Range by the Athabasca River.

At 10.5 km reach the site of the former lookout cabin, now burned down. If time and energy permit, stroll to the top of the small knoll behind the cabin site for more views of Pyramid Mountain and the Victoria Cross Range and south to Mt. Edith Cavell.

Pyramid Mountain

JASPER

75 Old Fort Point

Distance: 4 km/2.5 mi round trip
Hiking time: 1 hour
Elevation gain: 130 m/426 ft
High point: 1160 m/3806 ft
Type: short hike
Best time: May through October
Map: Jasper 83 D/16

A refreshing hike through aspen groves, wooded hillsides and grassy meadows to rocky knolls and outcrops for scenic viewpoints. Old Fort Point rises just 80 m above Jasper townsite, but commands impressively wide views. Jasper townsite lies to the west and beyond stands the reddish peak of Pyramid Mountain. To the southwest are the splendid peaks of Mts. Edith Cavell and Christie. And to the north are Beauvert ("pretty green") Lake, Jasper Park Lodge and the Athabasca River, stretching to the jagged, silvery peaks of the Colin Range.

Although this site is the approximate location of a post built by William Henry in 1812, the name Old Fort Point is probably a corruption of "Old Ford Point" since this was the fording location on the river.

From the intersection of Highways 93 and 16, drive south on Highway 93 for 2 km to the Highway 93A cutoff on the east side of the road. Turn right onto Beauvert Lake Road after 1.6 km. At 0.8 km, just after crossing the Athabasca River, turn into the first parking area on the right side of the road.

The parking lot lies directly below the Old Fort Point. But save the best for last, and start the hike at the left or north side of the parking lot on the trail designated by the park as 1A. While contouring around the base of the point, the trail passes out of the thick forest into a willow and aspen grove along a dry riverbed.

The climbing starts abruptly at 1.5 km and, for a brief distance, is quite steep as it winds its way around a rocky outcrop in the ridge. A grove of aspen and an intersection mark the top and the far end of the loop. To the left, the trail continues to the Valley of the Five Lakes (Hike 38), Wabasso Lake (Hike 37) and Wabasso Lake to Big Shovel Pass (Hike 39).

The Old Fort Point Trail stays to the right preparing for its ascent to the false summit. As the trail enters the first meadows, the views start to appear. Breezy knolls and grassy slopes invite hikers to linger.

The true summit lies a bit farther to the west. Climb all the way to the rocky top and plan to spend some time identifying the numerous peaks and watching the trains roll through town below. Descend the knoll by retracing your steps to avoid tramp-

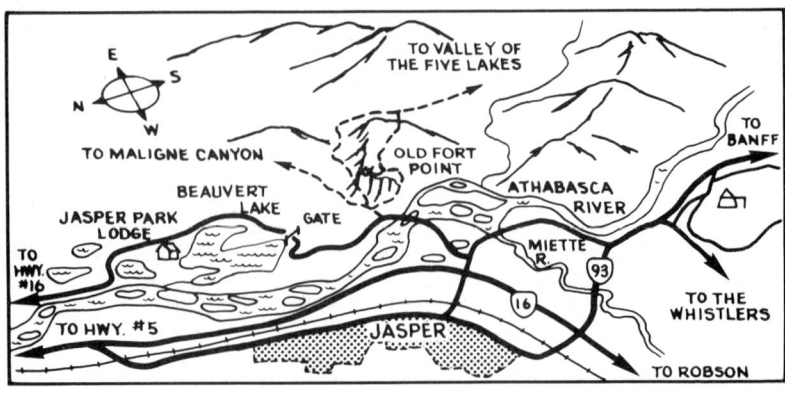

ling fragile plants. Then, follow the trail, skirting the rock buttress, and approach a broad, open slope strewn with boulders. The trail briefly disappears on the grassy hillside, but walk straight across and the trail will be encountered once again on the opposite side.

Near the end of the trail, visit a monument to David Thompson, explorer of Athabasca Pass and famous map maker. Then descend the flight of stairs to return to the trailhead.

Mt. Christie from Old Fort Point

Christine Lake

JASPER

76 Virl, Dorothy and Christine Lakes

Distance: 5 km/3.1 mi round trip to Christine Lake
Hiking time: 2.5 hours
Elevation gain: 240 m/787 ft
High point: 1340 m/4395 ft
Type: half-day hike, picnic
Best time: June through October
Map: Jasper 83 D/16

A tranquil setting for picnics, fishing or just peaceful contemplation. This cluster of woodland lakes, enclosed in stands of mixed forest, provides an excellent early season hike when higher alpine regions are still slumbering, snowbound.

The relatively low elevation here not only makes this area more accessible, but also provides the setting for early season gardens of wild rose, Indian paintbrush, Canada dogwood (bunchberry), harebells and the occasional orchid, which line the edges of this well-defined path.

Travelling east from the Jasper National Park west entrance, proceed along Highway 16 (Yellowhead Highway) for 13.7 km to a dirt road on the left, just before the Meadow Creek bridge. Or, travel west along 16 from the intersection of Highways 16 and 93 (Icefields Parkway) for 10.8 km to the bridge at Meadow Creek. Just beyond the bridge, turn right onto a dirt road and follow it for about 300 m to a small spur road and parking area on the right.

Walk west from the parking area, continuing along the dirt road to cross the railroad tracks. Then, follow the trail to the right and cross the Miette River on a wide bridge. Just beyond the bridge, note the trailhead sign and continue west along an old road that soon becomes a wide path leading gently up and away from the river. At about 0.5 km the trail switchbacks and climbs more steeply up the hillside, then becomes a gently meandering course that tops the knoll and descends slightly on the other side. Pass a marsh and small lake on the left shortly before crossing Minaga Creek on a small log bridge. Ascending gradually, the trail proceeds through pine forest and passes a trail branching to the left at about 1 km beyond Minaga Creek. It then continues another kilometre or so to the junction of a short spur trail leading to the right. A short 0.5 km along this path will lead to the grassy shores of Virl Lake. This, the smallest of the 3 lakes, offers a peaceful picnic spot with views to the south.

Backtrack to the main trail and continue for another 0.4 km, climbing a moderate grade to reach Dorothy Lake. Though much larger and deeper than Virl Lake, Dorothy Lake has a forested shoreline that lends a similar feeling of secluded calm at this favorite fishing spot. Then follow the main trail for a short jaunt over a small rise to discover the surprisingly different Christine Lake. The unexpectedly rocky shoreline provides excellent spots for relaxing or fishing from promontories and outcrops.

Though views are marginal, the lakes offer unlimited opportunities for additional roaming or exploring lakeshore ecology. There are picnic spots at all 3 lakes and rental boats are available at Dorothy and Christine lakes (make prior arrangements at sporting goods stores in Jasper). Overnight stays are not permitted.

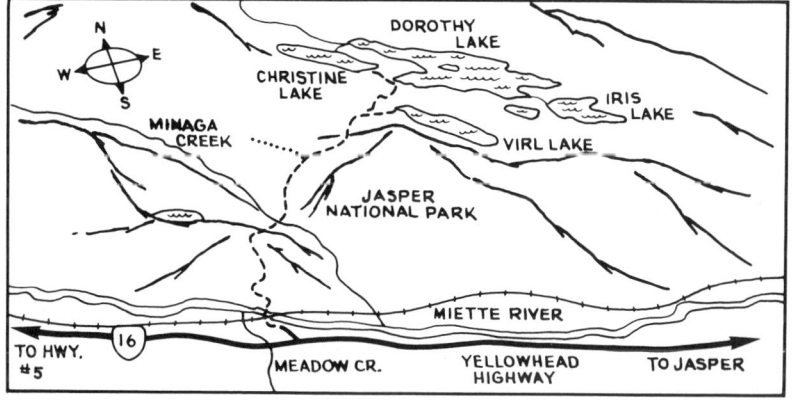

JASPER

77 Miette River Trail

Distance: 51 km/32 mi round trip
Hiking time: 4 days
Elevation gain: 914 m/3000 ft
High point: 2045 m/6711 ft
Type: backpack
Best time: July through mid-October
Maps: Jasper 83 D/16, Rainbow 83 D/15 E, Resplendent Creek 83 E/2 E

A long and lonesome route through a little-travelled section of Jasper's most untrammelled parkland, the Miette River Trail has a feeling of isolation and wilderness rarely found in a national park these days. There are long stretches of dense, mature forest, untouched except for the narrow corridor carved for the trail. Glimpses of peaks through the treetops promise exciting vistas to come while the trail persists on a gentle, easy grade for most of the trek. Here, the hikers' main companions are true inhabitants of the wild.

Two approaches to the trailhead are possible: the first, a bit longer, though more reliable; the second, requiring a difficult ford of the Miette River. Both begin near the west entrance to Jasper National Park.

For the first approach, turn north off Highway 16 (Yellowhead Highway) at 0.2 km east of the (western) Jasper Park entrance booth. Following signs to the Decoigne Warden's Station, drive the dirt road, crossing the railroad tracks and continuing until the road ends. Turn left and drive to the gate. Just to the left is the warden's station—a good place to get current trail information. This route adds 9.6 km (round trip) to the trail, but avoids fording the river. Walk along the road 4.8 km to the point where the trail branches to the right.

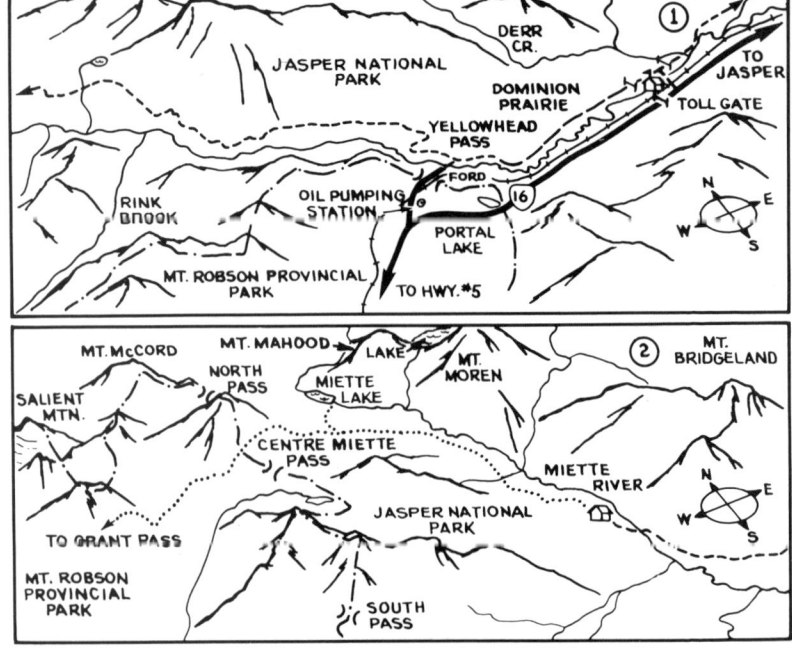

Boardwalk along Miette River Trail

The second option should be considered only in August or later to minimize the dangers of the river ford. From Yellowhead Pass (British Columbia border and entrance to Mt. Robson Park), drive west on Highway 16 for 2 km to a dirt road on the right (north) side of the highway. Follow this road for 12.8 km to its end, passing the oil pumping station, crossing the railroad tracks and finally reaching a washed-out bridge.

Park here and make the ford, then regain the road on the other side. The Miette River Trail begins about 60 m east of the washed-out bridge. The white sign is partially hidden in the trees, so hikers must watch closely to spot it.

The trail starts with a moderate climb through dense forest for 1.5 km, gaining 120 m of elevation. Scant views from the ridge allow the hiker to pick out Mt. Fitzwilliam in Robson Park and the Vista Glacier beyond. More peaks appear briefly as elevation is slowly gained, but most of the first 18 km (from the gated road) holds marginal interest due to dense forest and lack of scenic variety. At 18.5 km, reach a bridged river crossing and the warden's line cabin. At timberline, enjoy seldom-seen views of the mountainous divide between Jasper and Mt. Robson.

Stay to the left (west) of the Miette River here in the upper meadows where the trail often becomes indistinct. Centre Pass is the obvious low divide in the rolling alpine parkland. Wander to the east of the pass, towards the headwaters of the Miette River to find Miette Lake. Farther east, in a secluded little valley between Mts. Moren and Mahood, is a larger lake worth seeking out. Though no actual trail exists, the route is fairly obvious to seasoned veterans of the wild, and the way is not difficult.

The Miette River Trail is in generally good condition, receiving yearly maintenance on the lower section, though almost none farther up. It officially ends at Miette Pass, the park and province boundary. Experienced explorers with mountaineering skills and equipment may wish to continue the remote and little-travelled route into Mt. Robson Park, which eventually joins with the Moose River route to Berg Lake. It is not maintained by either Jasper or Robson Park and receives little use, so those wishing to proceed beyond the pass should be prepared to use cross-country navigational skills and might wish to register with Jasper Park wardens.

MT. ROBSON PROVINCIAL PARK

To the west of Jasper is Mt. Robson Provincial Park (2172 square kilometres), set in an exceptionally scenic, western mountain environment. Unlike the drier climate on the eastern side of the Divide, the humid climate here produces forests of immense red cedars and graceful hemlocks. From high peaks draped in snow and ice, meltwaters cascade down to lush valleys below.

The high point of a trip to Robson Park is the Mt. Robson/Berg Lake vicinity where the dynamic display of glacial forces draws visitors all season, in spite of the dubious weather. In addition to the Berg Lake route, there are several trails to remote and less travelled areas.

Being a provincial park, Robson has notable differences in operating procedures. Overnight stays in Robson's backcountry campsites do not require a permit or registration as in Jasper and Yoho. However, hikers planning to enter Jasper Park by trail must register at the warden's office in Jasper.

Mt. Robson Park Headquarters are located at Red Pass just west of Moose Lake on Highway 16 (Yellowhead Highway). Additional information and facilities are available at the visitor centre near the western park entrance at Robson Meadows. Contact park staff at either of these locations for current trail information, as many trails—other than the heavily travelled Berg Lake Trail—are maintained much less frequently and may present serious hazards.

Left: *Mt. Robson from Berg Lake Trail.*
Above: *Overlander Falls*

MT. ROBSON

78 Mt. Fitzwilliam Trail

Distance: 22 km/13.6 mi round trip
  to upper lakes
Hiking time: 5-6 hours
Elevation gain: 849 m/2785 ft
High point: 2000 m/ 6560 ft
Type: day hike or backpack
Best time: July through September
Maps: Rainbow 83 D/15 E, Jasper 83 D/16

Seekers of solitude and away-from-the-crowds campsites will find an interesting variety of peaceful settings along this trail. Pass through forest to flat, open meadows and cross streams to wander through fields of Labrador tea and willow. The trail finally terminates in an isolated parkland of meadows and small lakes from which steep, rocky hillsides rise to a terraced plain. Inveterate explorers may scale the talus slope to the upper basin, which holds a cluster of tarns, encircled on 3 sides by the upsweeping flanks of Holloway Rock, Frontier Peak, Mt. Clairvaux and a string of border peaks.

The large trailhead sign is located on the south side of Highway 16 (Yellowhead Highway) at 11.7 km from the eastern park boundary (Yellowhead Pass) or about 53 km from the western park boundary. Parking is available along the old highway, a dirt road that parallels the main road on the north and is accessible from the Lucerne road about 100 m south of the sign.

From the trailhead, the trail immediately enters dense lodgepole forest and climbs swiftly to gain 300 m of elevation in the first 2 km. It then levels somewhat and runs gently for the next 3 km to the campsite at Rockingham Creek. Beyond this point, views of Mt. Fitzwilliam dominate the skyline to the right as the trail skirts its base. By now the forest has become a grand old fir stand, which gradually gives way to broad alpine meadows. Crossing the creek on a sturdy

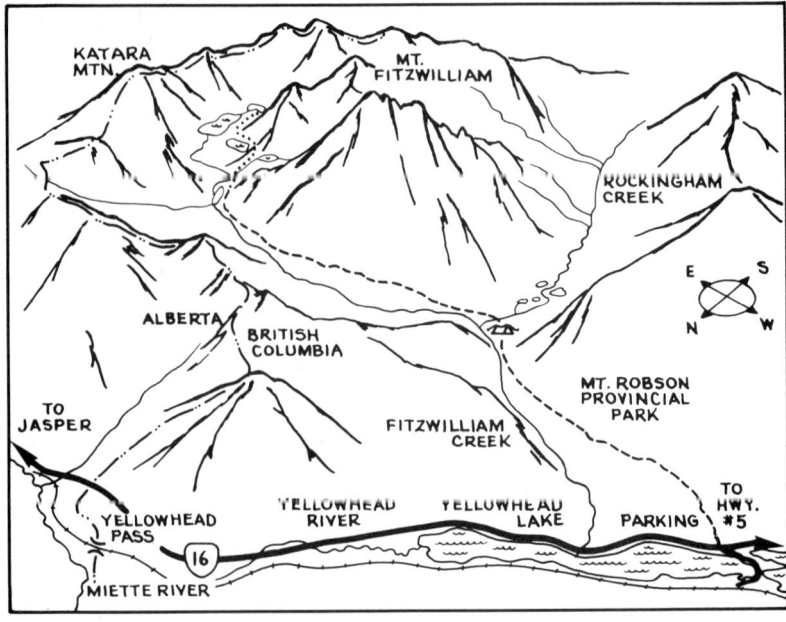

Crossing Rockingham Creek below Mt. Fitzwilliam

bridge, continue east on the gentle slope to Fitzwilliam Creek. Then cross a large boulder field before reaching the meadows at the end of the valley.

The trail is well marked to the 10-km point. Beyond here, the trail markings become more obscure and the trail seems to disappear in the meadow below the eastern flank of Mt. Fitzwilliam. The route, however, does continue, following Fitzwilliam Creek up the steep talus slope to the wide cirque at the base of Mt. Clairvaux. Here are numerous little lakes to explore for those who have come with time to spare.

The Mt. Fitzwilliam Trail is not maintained on a regular basis, so prospective visitors should check with park officials for current trail conditions.

MT. ROBSON

79 Yellowhead Mountain Trail

Distance: 9.8 km/6 mi round trip
Hiking time: 4 hours
Elevation gain: 747 m/2450 ft
High point: 1859 m/6100 ft
Type: half day hike
Best time: June through October
Map: Rainbow 83 D/15 E

A refreshing journey along a woodsy trail to overlooks and open fields, back into dense forest and finally out again to a beautiful hillside meadow of many, diverse wildflowers, set upon the lower slopes of Tête Roche on Yellowhead Mountain. From this pleasant destination are views to the southeast and Mt. Fitzwilliam. Beyond Fitzwilliam, to the right, the jagged summit of Vista Peak and the snowy expanse of the Vista Glacier are visible along Glacis Ridge. Still farther to the right are the 3 summits of Waddington Peak. This is a good trip for the early riser as the steep slopes near the beginning of the trail can be quite hot with full sun.

Mt. Fitzwilliam and Glacis Ridge from Yellowhead Mountain meadows

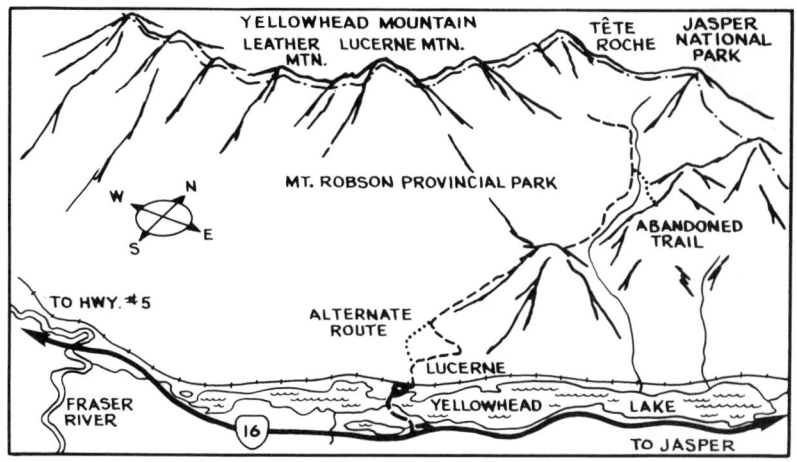

Drive Highway 16 (Yellowhead Highway) 11.7 km from Yellowhead Pass or 53 km from the western park boundary to the Lucerne access road on the north side of the highway. From the intersection of the Lucerne access road and Highway 16, drive 1 km on the dirt road to the point where it forks and makes a loop near the railroad tracks. Park on the loop near the tracks or along the dirt road. The trailhead sign is directly across the tracks from the loop.

Begin the trail with a steep climb into a fresh and airy woodland of aspen and birch. At about 0.75 km the trail forks; the right is strongly recommended here, for although it may take a few minutes longer, it has a definite scenic advantage and a much gentler grade. Running out along the ridge to a point from which views across the valley are possible, it then swings left to join the main trail again just before entering a small open meadow.

Cross the meadow and enter the burn-spawned lodgepole forest on the opposite side, continuing through semi-open forest for about 1 km. Enter another, larger meadow area at about 2.5 km, where the massive form of Yellowhead Mountain overshadows the scene. This makes a pleasant destination for those lacking time to go on, though the ultimate reward of this trip lies beyond.

Continue through dense old fir forest, passing an abandoned trail on the right and ending in a meadow at 4.9 km. Those so inclined may scramble higher to sit upon rocky outcrops amid the flowers and absorb the scenery. Technical climbing skills are required beyond this point.

MT. ROBSON

80 Moose River

Distance: 88 km/55 mi round trip
 to Moose Pass
Hiking time: 4 days
Elevation gain: 982 m/3221 ft
High point: 2027 m/6650 ft
Type: backpack
Best time: mid-July through September
Maps: Rainbow 83 D/15 W, Resplendent
 Creek 83 E/2 W, Mount Robson 83 E/3

The perfect trail for a long and lonesome sojourn, with plenty of opportunity for contemplation. So why not contemplate those early climbers making the first attempts on towering Mt. Robson, as you retrace their steps through this rugged river valley and across the Great Divide.

Since the construction of the wide-track, heavily travelled Berg Lake Trail (Hike 82), the Moose River route gets little use in comparison and is no longer regularly maintained. Still, a number of intrepid explorers seek out this route for the challenge and escape from the crowds at Berg Lake, as well as for an alternative route to or from the Mt. Robson scene. Other possibilities exist, including a connection with the North Boundary Trail (Hike 56) via the Smoky River, or a loop trip crossing 2 high passes (Grant Pass and Miette Pass), which has plenty of remote and unmaintained high-country and exits via the Miette River Trail (Hike 77).

The trailhead is located just across the railroad tracks on the north side of Highway 16, approximately 37 km from the west boundary of Mt. Robson Provincial Park or 30 km from the Robson/Jasper boundary.

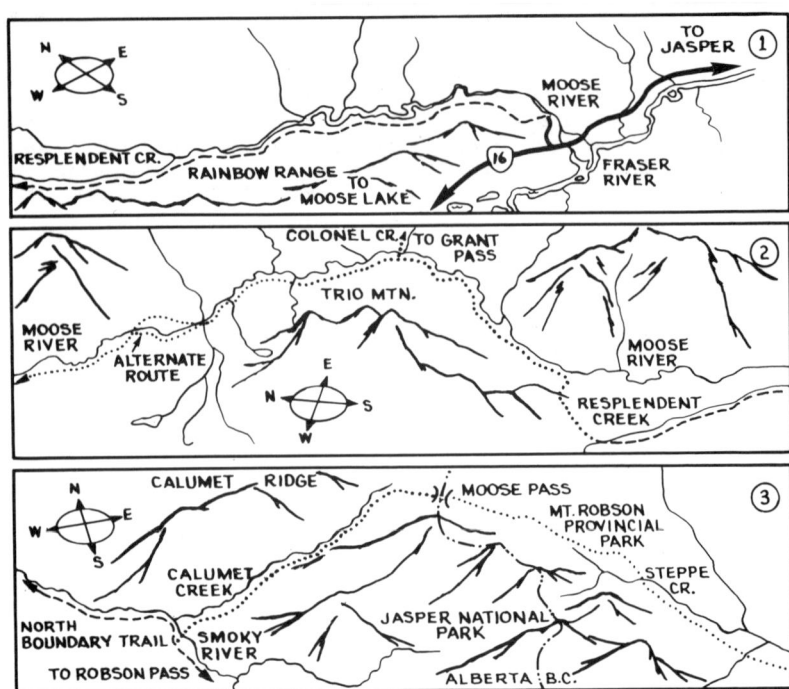

Moose River

The first 6 km of trail, to a wide bend in Moose River, are frequently hiked as a day trip. Here the trail is well defined and in reasonably good condition. It rambles through quiet forests of lodgepole and aspen interspersed with dry, rock-garden scenery. The edge of the wide river is a popular objective for photographers and picnickers or anyone just wishing to get away from the usual tourist-hiker haunts.

Beyond the bend, the trail travels north at the foot of the Rainbow Range, following the river to its junction with Resplendent Creek (10 km) and then continuing up Resplendent to a widely braided section (about 6 more kilometres) where fording is easiest. Pick up the route on the other side and continue in a northeasterly direction, reaching Moose River at about 17 km and following its left bank.

At 20 km, meet the junction with Colonel Creek and the trail to Grant and Miette passes (see Hike 77). Head north now along the river, through avalanche shrubbery, rocky slides and forest.

The route becomes a sharp contrast to the well-groomed Berg Lake Trail, especially at stream crossings. Fords of Moose River and Resplendent Creek range from hazardous to impossible during high water, which can occur at any time throughout the season. For this reason anyone planning to use this trail is advised to check at park headquarters for current trail and river conditions. With a little bushwhacking and some extra time, it is possible to make the entire trip without fording the Moose River.

The trail gains elevation rather slowly during the initial 34 km. After crossing Steppe Creek, it climbs more steeply, above the water to treeline, where the grade moderates again as the trail approaches the pass. At elevation 2027 m, Moose Pass is finally reached. Open and alpine, the area is bordered by rugged peaks and icefields of the Continental Divide—impressive scenery for brush-weary travellers.

To continue to Robson Pass or Berg Lake, drop quickly from the pass into the Calumet Creek system and follow it, mostly through forest, for 8.6 km to its confluence with the Smoky River. Turn left here and follow the river up its rocky course to Adolphus Lake and the pass. Just beyond are broad meadows and the outwash plain of Robson's remarkable glaciers.

MT. ROBSON

81 Overlander Falls

Distance: 4.5 km/2.8 mi round trip to Nature House
Hiking time: 45 minutes to falls; 1.5 hours to Nature House
Elevation loss: 61 m/200 ft
High point: 930 m/3050 ft
Type: short hike or nature walk
Best time: July and August
Map: Robson 83 E/3

Scenic and pleasant no matter what the weather, Overlander Falls offers an easily accessible bit of the wild Fraser River for close-up inspection. Witness this powerful aquatic excavator still carving at the narrow gorge through which enormous volumes of silty water rush. Rainy periods bestow an even more awesome mood to the gorge as the waters are swollen with excess volume. Since this little pocket of the Rockies receives a generous share of precipitation, come prepared and enjoy the verdant forests and impressive waterworks.

From the west entrance to Robson Provincial Park, drive east for 3.7 km on Highway 16 (Yellowhead Highway) to reach the Overlander Falls parking lot on the right. From the east entrance (Yellowhead Pass), drive west for 57.8 km to the parking area.

Stroll on this excellent trail down a minor grade to the gorge, where clouds of mist float up from the flood of green below. The falls are quickly reached from the highway and make an excellent destination point for a short leg-stretcher, the round trip being only 0.8 km.

Though the falls offer the most spectacular scenery, the rest of the trail provides a pleasant hike through dense forest of Douglas fir and spruce. Continue on from the falls, climbing slowly out of the gorge to ramble along above the north riverbank. Interesting features along the way include old log cabin sites and views of the river.

At approximately 2.6 km, descend slightly to the road and, crossing it, pick up the trail about 30 m north on the other side, a short distance from the Nature House. Rest rooms and benches are provided along the trail.

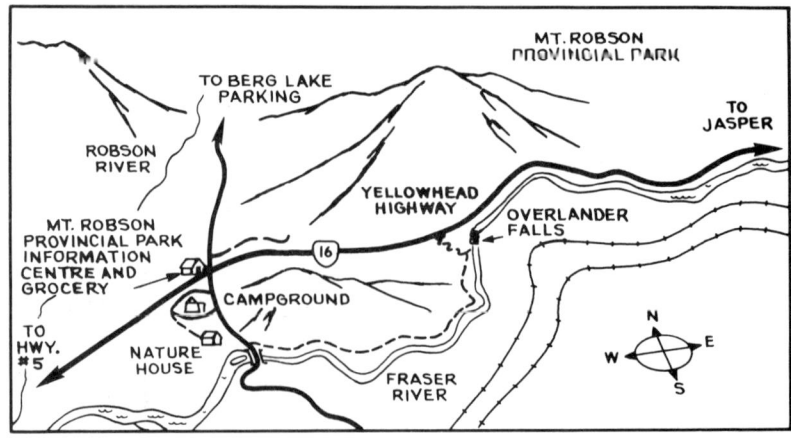

Fraser River

MT. ROBSON

82 Berg Lake

Distance: 35 km/22 mi round trip to
 Berg Lake Campground
Hiking time: 1-2 days
Elevation gain: 792 m/2600 ft
High point: 1646 m/5400 ft
Type: backpack
Best time: late June through mid-October
Map: Mount Robson 83 E/3

Whether bathed in sunlight or shrouded in fog, the "Monarch of the Canadian Rockies" is a mountain of intriguing moods and beauty. Clouds drift in and out of the valley, swirling around Robson's pyramid top and playing on seracs, while glaciers creak and groan and heave off great burdens of ice to the milky waters of Berg Lake below.

One need not travel far on this beautiful trail to understand why it is one of the most popular and heavily used trails in the Canadian mountain parks. Walk a short distance into the majestic lowland forest with its graceful western hemlocks and giant red cedars, or backpack to the ice-bound lakes at the base of Mt. Robson.

Drive east on Highway 16 from the west boundary of Mt. Robson Provincial Park.

Emperor Falls

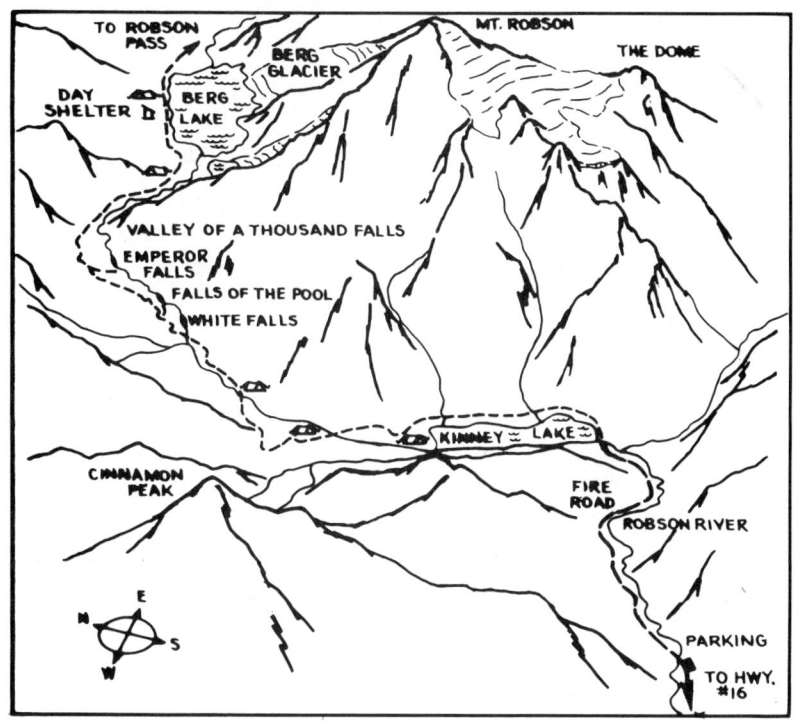

At the Robson Viewpoint and Service Centre (2.4 km), turn left (north) on a paved park road and continue 2.3 km to the Berg Lake parking area and trailhead. From Jasper, drive 59 km west of Yellowhead Pass on Highway 16 to the Robson Service Centre and continue as above.

From the parking lot at Robson River, cross the bridge to the trailhead and walk north along an old dirt road that follows the riverbank. The trail begins in a damp and earthy forest of dense shrubs and wildflowers below a cathedral-like canopy, a surprising contrast to the typically drier lodgepole and spruce forests of the Rockies.

The 4.4 km to Kinney Lake are easy walking and make an excellent half-day hike to picnic or camp along the shores of this icy green gem. Follow interpretive signs along the trail to the gravel plain at the north end of the lake where numerous bridges and foot logs cross the wildly braided inlet streams. Then begins the serious climbing as the way enters the legendary Valley of a Thousand Falls. All around are streamers of lacy, white water, tumbling and blowing from valley walls. Up on the canyon rim, glaciers crowd the precipice, letting go huge chunks of ice and snow to crash to ledges and outcrops.

The upper end of the valley steepens again, sending the waters of the Robson River cascading into several spectacular falls, creating excellent cool, scenic rest stops along this arduous ascent. The last stretch of the climb places you at the mouth of the Berg Lake basin, though about 2 km of walking remain before the lake becomes visible.

At the lake are campsites and ranger's quarters and a comfortable day-lodge where interpretive programs can be enjoyed. The area has opportunities for several days of hiking on side trails to various vantage points.

Mt. Robson

MT. ROBSON

83 Toboggan Falls

Distance: 4.8 km/3 mi round trip from Berg Lake to meadows
Hiking time: 3 hours
Elevation gain: 404 m/1325 ft
High point: 2042 m/6700 ft
Type: day hike
Best time: July through September
Map: Mount Robson 83 E/3 (trail not shown), or Mount Robson Park PS-R2

Freshly released from the frozen clutches of nearby glaciers, the waters of Toboggan Falls descend to Berg Lake in a series of cascades. Climb beside these sprightly waters on a trail that is short and steep, but offers destinations ranging from the top of the falls to the upper meadows. On sunny days this area has the special attraction of being the best place from which to photograph Mt. Robson and Berg Lake together, using a normal focal-length lens.

The Toboggan Falls Trail starts at the Berg Lake Campground (see Hike 82) just across the bridge from the day shelter. Go uphill following the stream. The trail parallels the picturesque falls for its first 1.2 km. It then leaves the forest for the subalpine zone, where muskeg blends with a colorful mix of grasses, paintbrush and mountain death camas.

The trail narrows abruptly at 1.5 km, becoming a simple boot track. Head uphill and then left, to contour towards the head of the cirque. When the trail ends at about 2.4 km, let inspiration be your guide in roaming the meadows beneath the hanging glaciers of Mt. Phillips (3249 m) and Mumm Peak (2962 m).

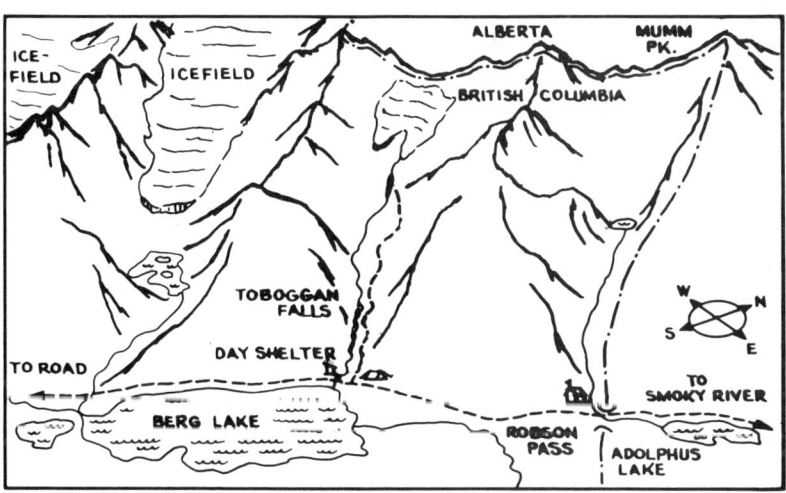

MT. ROBSON

84 Snowbird Pass

Distance: 21 km/13 mi round trip
Hiking time: 8 hours
Elevation gain: 770 m/2525 ft
High point: 2408 m/7900 ft
Type: day hike
Best time: mid-July through September
Map: Mount Robson 83 E/3
(trail not shown)

Arriving at Berg Lake, many people make the mistake of thinking they have reached the most beautiful place in the Rockies. Awesome as it is, don't be dissuaded from exploring this high pass on the northeast side of Mt. Robson. Surrounded by the numerous glaciers of the Robson Cirque, Snowbird Pass stands rocky and desolate above colorful meadows to the west. To the northeast is the vast expanse of white and blue ice known as the Reef Icefield. Throughout the hike are unsurpassed views of Mt. Robson, encircled by a court of lesser summits.

The first 7.2 km follow the Mt. Robson climbers' trail. The trail is steep and difficult and all but disappears in the meadows. Be sure to carry a map.

Strike out from Berg Lake (see Hike 82) and follow the trail around the lake to the north. At the far end of the lake descend to the gravel flats (brightly colored with yellow paintbrush and purple fireweed in late July). At 2.4 km, near the ranger's cabin, the trail divides and the main trail continues northward to follow the North Boundary Trail through Jasper National Park, while the well-defined right fork heads southeast towards the Robson Glacier.

Take the right fork, pass a small lake at 3.2 km and begin to climb through loose rock (glacial rubble) alongside the Robson Glacier. Several routes have been marked with cairns. Aim for the middle route as all paths come together eventually. At 7.2 km the trail abruptly leaves the moraine and, departing from the climbers' trail, ascends a steep embankment through low brush for a 150-m elevation gain. At the top, a

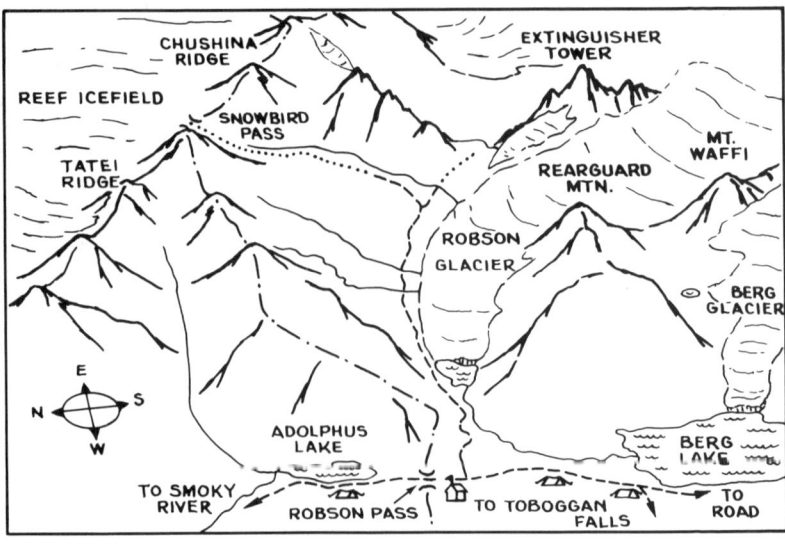

198

Robson Glacier

valley rolls out with a colorful carpet of flowers and grass: a sharp contrast to the bleak surroundings of ice and rock. The trail loses clarity among the vegetation, so use the stream as a guide, staying on the left side and aiming for the low dip that marks the pass. The climb is persistent; the last push is over rough talus. But reach the pass with its excellent views and forget the demanding ascent. Do not venture farther onto the glacier without appropriate glacier-travel equipment and experience.

WILLMORE WILDERNESS PROVINCIAL PARK

Willmore Wilderness Park lies north of Jasper Park. Perhaps less dramatic, though no less wild, the 4597 square kilometres span the Berland, Hoff and Persimmon ranges. There are rugged peaks in the western areas; to the east and north are long, open valleys and broad expanses of rolling tundra.

In the past, the primary mode of travel here, as in other Rocky Mountain parks, was by horseback, and the area is well suited to horse travel. Hikers, however, have begun to discover the exceptional opportunities for solitude, cross-country travel and ski-touring in this park. The trails described herein are some of those most easily travelled on foot, without the aid of horses. There are many other routes that penetrate deep into the wilderness, but they require extensive preparation and time and are extremely dependent upon streamflow and weather conditions for progress on foot. The routes we have included here are easily accessible for most of the hiking season.

Trails and facilities in Willmore Park are not maintained except by users. Don't expect elaborate trails, signs, camps or bridges, but be prepared to enjoy a land rich with wildlife and colorful meadows, where rolling valleys and soft-hued foothills make a sharp contrast to the rugged peaks.

Maps are recommended for hikers travelling in the Willmore. They should be obtained prior to arrival at the park as local distribution centres may not be convenient or have the required maps on hand. (See section on maps for ordering details.)

Left: *The Hoff Range from Adams Lookout*
Above: *Ground squirrel*

Private cabin at Thoreau Creek

WILLMORE

85 Wildhay River Trail

Distance: 32 km/20 mi round trip to Eagles Nest cutoff
Hiking time: 2 days
High point: 1935 m/6350 ft
Elevation gain: 427 m/1400 ft
Type: backpack
Best time: June through September
Maps: Rock Lake 83 E/8 E & W, Adams Lookout 83 E/10 E, Moberly Creek 83 E/9

Lots of opportunity for scenic wandering in this wide, rolling valley. No route-finding problem here as the trail traces portions of the historic Mountain and Indian trails. Although walking this old cart track can prove a bone-tiring ordeal, there are plenty of good campsites and scenic rest spots to help break up the journey. Indeed, possibilities for scenic day trips from the Wildhay Valley exist all along the way, including the Rock Lake Lookout, Eagles Nest Pass, Thoreau Pass and the Indian Trail.

Drive north on Highway 40 from its intersection with Highway 16 (Yellowhead

Highway) 4 km southwest of Hinton. At 39 km, turn left at Rock Lake Road (a sign here reads Rock Lake 32 km). Just after crossing Moberly Creek, make a left turn at the intersection, 2 km from the beginning of Rock Lake Road (subsequent distances are accumulative from the beginning of Rock Lake Road). Continue to the next intersection at 6 km. Follow the sign to the right; proceed to km 12 and another intersection, and make another right turn (sign here reads Rock Lake 12 miles). At 16 km, pass an unmarked side road on the right. Bear right for 2 more unmarked intersections and pass the campground turnoff at 18.6 km. Continue, passing the boat launch access road, and reach the trailhead parking lot at 33 km.

The trailhead is at the gate across the road just beyond the parking lot. Walk around the gate and continue along the road. At 1.5 km pass the Willow Creek Trail (Hike 86) on the left, then continue on to reach the Rock Lake Lookout Trail (Hike 87) and the first campsite at 4.5 km. At this point the trail crosses the Wildhay River—risky business during high water, and it may require a bit of searching to find an appropriate foot-log.

Once you are across, however, the subsequent fords you will encounter along the way (Seep, Fortyone Mile, Carson and Fault creeks) are of minor concern. Good campsites are located at several spots in the valley, especially among the trees before the junction of the Pope-Thoreau Trail at 15.5 km. Beyond this point the trail travels primarily through open grassland and valley bottom with few trees for shelter. At 16 km, the trail to Eagles Nest Pass takes off through the valley to the left. This is actually the continuation of the old Mountain Trail that eventually extends up the Rock Creek and Sulphur River valleys.

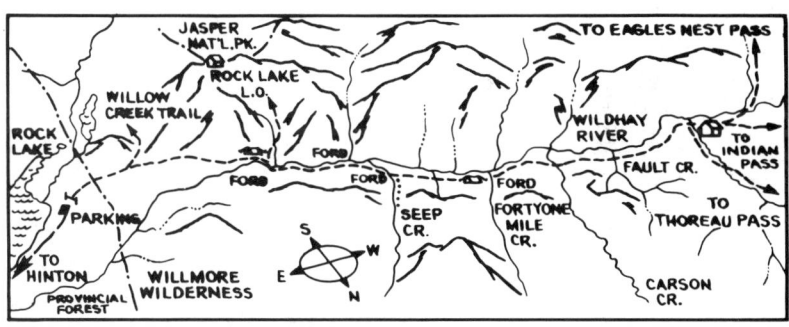

WILLMORE

86 Willow Creek Trail

Distance: 28 km/17 mi round trip
  to North Boundary Trail
Hiking time: 8 hours
Elevation gain: 91 m/300 ft in;
  152 m/500 ft out
High point: 1524 m/5000 ft
Type: day hike or backpack
Best time: June through October
Map: Rock Lake 83 E/8

The Willow Creek Trail provides the backcountry access to the North Boundary Trail (Hike 56) of Jasper National Park. A good trail with moderate grade, the Willow Creek Trail allows hikers of the 185-km North Boundary Trail to circumvent 32 km of hard-packed fire road. Hiked for its own merit, it is a pleasant, if not unique or spectacular, walk through lodgepole pines and valley-bottom willows. The semi-open forests allow minimal scenic variety, but the occasional views are good and a comfortable campsite awaits the weary traveller at trail's end.

Begin at the Rock Lake access to the Willmore Wilderness (see Hike 85) and continue along the old fire road for about 1.5 km. The Willow Creek Trail is the first major fork to the left. Do not expect to see a sign, though, as they are almost as rare as bridges in the Willmore Wilderness Park.

The next stretch of about 3 km is a slow descent (easy grade) through an old burn. The trail then comes to an abrupt bluff overlooking beaver ponds and the Snake Indian River Valley. Beyond the valley lie the mountainous reaches of Jasper National Park.

Make a short but steeper descent now to Rock Creek (6.5 km). The bridge that

Willow Creek Trail passes through lodgepole forest, DeSmet Range in distance

Grizzly bear

normally exists here was washed out in 1981. As yet, it has not been replaced, but sure-footed hikers have been improvising with logs. Nevertheless, high waters or dubious footing have caused more than a few to turn back.

At 9 km, the trail from Moosehorn Lakes (see Hike 57) merges from the east and the 2 continue through open, boggy meadowlands in a maze of criss-crossing paths. Though the path may be obscure, the general direction is not. Proceed along the Willow Creek Valley to the Rock Creek Warden's Cabin which marks the 11.5-km point. The North Boundary Trail is 2 km beyond. Turn right and go another 0.5 km to find the Willow Creek campsite.

From here, the options seem almost unlimited as hikers may choose routes along the Snake Indian River, Rock Creek or Deer Creek for days of unhurried exploration into the rugged valleys and mountains of the Jasper/Willmore boundary.

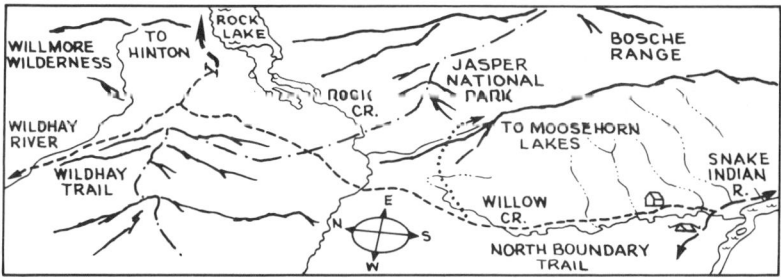

WILLMORE

87 Rock Lake Lookout

Distance: 5.2 km/3.2 mi round trip
Hiking time: 3-4 hours
Elevation gain: 579 m/1900 ft
High point: 2088 m/6850 ft
Type: day trip or side trip from Hike 85
Best time: June through mid-October
Map: Rock Lake 83 E/8 W

A lofty ridgetop sprinkled with alpine blossoms and overlooking the expansive Wildhay River and Rock Creek valleys. A place for solitude and quiet musing, this abandoned lookout station has been all but forgotten. The lack of use has left the trail in poor condition with numerous deadfalls to negotiate, but the exhilarating views are worth the effort of making the steep climb. Fortunately the trail is relatively short—only 2.6 km from valley bottom to summit.

See Hike 85, Wildhay River Trail, for driving directions, then follow the Wildhay Trail for 4.5 km to the point where it crosses the Wildhay River. As the trail turns right to ford the river, an unmarked trail takes off to the left, closely skirting a campsite. Follow this unsigned trail past the camp and continue along the creekbed, climbing moderately and steadily for about 1 km. No water is available after you leave the stream, so be sure to fill canteens here before the strenuous climb.

Moving away from the creek, climb a steep grade as the trail switchbacks through the dense forest. Nearing the ridgecrest, the trail almost disappears in the sparsely vegetated, rocky soil. Follow the crest (left) to the service road, and walk the last 0.5 km on the road. The road has not been maintained for some time; it is washed out in places and difficult to locate at the southern end.

Rising above dense forested foothills, the ridge is situated at the southeast end of the rugged Persimmon Range, providing an excellent end-long view of the entire range.

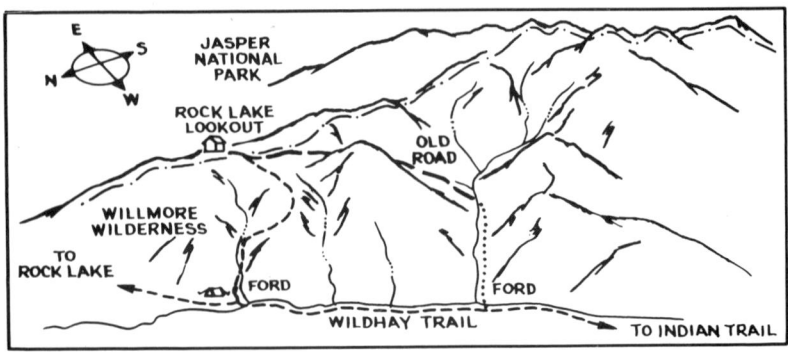

Rock Lake Lookout

WILLMORE

88 Pope-Thoreau Trail

To Thoreau Pass
Distance: 9.8 km/6 mi round trip
  from Wildhay River Trail
Hiking time: 3 hours
Elevation gain: 366 m/1200 ft
High point: 2057 m/6750 ft
Type: day hike or backpack
Best time: July through September
Maps: Moberly Creek 83 E/9,
  Adams Lookout 83 E/10 E

To South Berland River
Distance: 27.6 km/17 mi round trip
  from Wildhay River Trail
Hiking time: 2 days

Walk through fields of soft grasses and downy willows, flecked with wildflowers and rustic reminders of long-defunct coal mining activity. Spend a morning absorbing the countryside, where the color and texture of the lush meadows soften the hills. Or, spend a whole day exploring creeks and scrambling to viewpoints atop the treeless foothills. From Thoreau Pass, enjoy views to the valley below, and beyond to snow-dusted peaks in the Persimmon Range.

These 4.5 km to the pass contain the prime features in both scenic charm and overall trail conditions and are recommended here as an excellent day trip from the Wildhay Valley. Beyond the pass, the trail soon deteriorates into muddy trenches, numerous creek fords and long stretches of dense muskeg—a long, arduous trail with few rewards.

See Hike 85, Wildhay River Trail, for driving directions. The trail begins at the 15.5-km point along the Wildhay River Trail, turning north at Thoreau Creek. Follow the creek for 1.5 km, where it reaches a cluster of old cabins. Just beyond, on a knoll to the right, is an outfitters' camp. The trail continues to wind along the creek, making 2 fords (easy) before angling away from the creek and climbing towards the pass. Leave the meadow area and climb through sparse scrub forest on dry hillsides, gaining about 300 m in 2 km and reaching the pass at 4.9 km.

Beyond the pass, the trail gradually descends to the Pope Creek headwaters (about 0.5 km), then follows the stream to its junction with the South Berland River, an 8.9-km trek in which numerous and increasingly difficult stream fords mark the trail's progress. When not travelling in or along the creekbed, the trail must pass through dense muskeg, which is torturous on bare legs and often

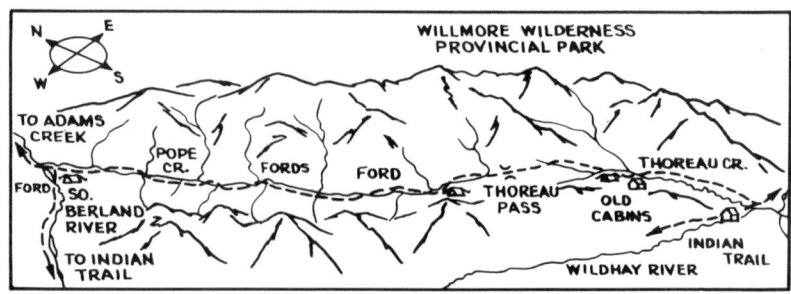

Mining relics on Thoreau Creek

shoulder high. During early season and rainy periods, the muskeg flats become a boggy mire and the trail is churned to a muddy rut by horses' hooves. Still worse, the mosquitoes are close to unbearable. Very few, if any, directional signs will be encountered on this trail and there are no bridges across the icy waters. Views are limited, though there is some possibility of spotting mountain goats in the rocky draws near the valley's end. A deep, irregular chasm also exists near the valley's end, displaying some interesting geology, though one must leave the main trail to see it. Unless you are travelling on horseback or plan to do a loop trip connecting with the Berland Trail, there is little to recommend this portion of the trail.

WILLMORE

89 Eagles Nest Pass

Distance: 12.8 km/8 mi round trip from Wildhay River Trail to pass
Hiking time: 3 hours
Elevation gain: 183 m/600 ft
High point: 1905 m/6250 ft
Type: day hike or backpack
Best time: June through mid-October
Maps: Adams Lookout 83 E/10 E, Blue Creek 83 E/7 E

Evoking images of eagles soaring high above the valley on mountain air currents, their aeries nestled among the lofty crags that line the pass, these gigantic rock slabs and towering pinnacles of silvery limestone and dolomite dominate this short, scenic route. Though we make no promises as to the probability of spotting an eagle, it is likely that mountain goats and sheep will be seen in these rocky environs.

The pass makes an excellent day hike from any of the nearby camps in the

Eagles Nest Pass

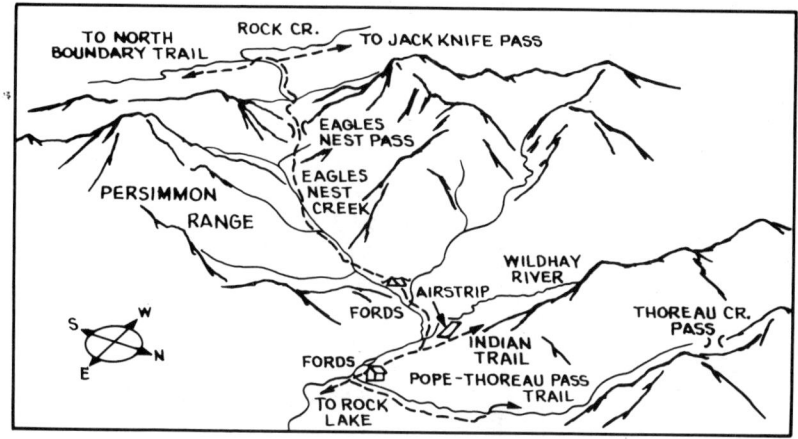

Wildhay River Valley. Or, plan to camp near the pass and spend more time exploring the rugged high-country. The trail also makes a scenic access route to the Jasper North Boundary section of the Great Divide Trail on the southwest side of the Persimmon Range.

Follow driving directions for the Wildhay River Trail (Hike 85), then proceed along that trail for 16 km to the junction with the Eagles Nest Pass Trail near an old airstrip. The trail branches southwest, descending into the valley and proceeding towards the base of the Persimmon Range. A ford of the Wildhay River is often necessary in early season, though later it is usually possible to cross via rocks and logs in the riverbed. Pass at least 3 outfitters' camps while strolling across this wide, rolling valley. The camps are easy to identify by their large tents or temporary shelters and by the evidence of pack animals in the vicinity.

Upon reaching the foot of the mountains, begin the gradual ascent of the pass. The old dirt track is easy walking and slips quickly between the steep mountain walls. Pass briefly through sparse forest near the stream and find an inviting campsite here beneath the trees. Reach the pass at 6.4 km.

Beyond the pass, the trail descends gradually to typical forested valley and joins the Rock Creek Trail below at about 2.7 km.

Indian Pass

WILLMORE

90 Indian Trail

Distance: 46 km/28.5 mi round trip from Wildhay Trail to North Berland River
Hiking time: 2-4 days
Elevation gain: 274 m/900 ft
High point: 2073 m/6800 ft
Type: day hike or backpack
Best time: July through mid-October
Maps: Adams Lookout 83 E/10 E, Adams Lookout 83 E/10 W

Leave the lower river valleys for a world of far-reaching views and flowered tundra. The Indian Trail allows travellers to penetrate wilder reaches of the park, where uncrowded trails and numerous signs of wildlife lend a feeling of true wilderness. This scenic portion of the old Indian Trail traders' route rambles across broad, rolling shoulders of the Persimmon Range, offering tantalizing views of the rugged summits and secluded valleys.

Striking out from the junction of the Wildhay River Trail (Hike 85) and the Eagles Nest Pass Trail (Hike 89), continue up the Wildhay Valley. Exchange heavy forest for meadow and shrubland and enjoy excellent views of the Persimmon Range, now visible just across the valley. The trail crosses several small creeks and seeps, as it gently climbs towards the pass. Reach the meadowed pass area at about 10 km, then descend another 1.5 km to the South Berland River.

Ford the river and relocate the trail on the opposite bank. The route heads west to climb the bank and traverse above the Persimmon Creek drainage.

At 14 km, pass a campsite and the junction to the Persimmon Creek Trail. Bearing right, begin the short climb to timberline and the rolling meadow and tundra beyond. Reach Indian Pass (2073 m) at 18.7 km where you can wander southward on rolling hills for a bird's-eye view of the Persimmon Creek Valley. Watch for white-tailed ptarmigan chicks in spring and early summer. Eagles may be spotted above, playing on mountain air currents.

Beyond the pass, the trail enters forest again, descending along a creek to reach the North Berland River at 23 km. From here, there are several options besides retracing steps to the Wildhay Trail. Make an extended loop trip by following an old trail along the North Berland River to Sunset Creek. Then go east to pick up the Berland Trail, which completes the loop at the junction of the Indian and Wildhay River trails. (Trail conditions are unknown, but can be expected to be wet until late season.)

A drier option, and perhaps a more scenic one, climbs the rolling tundra to alpine views and hours of easy wandering near Jack Knife Pass and the unnamed pass between the Snow Creek and South Muskeg River headwaters. Here, nestled in these flowered hillocks are several tarns awaiting discovery.

Though some maps may show the route of the original Indian Trail as continuing along Snow Creek and the South Muskeg River to the Muskeg River Trail, it is well to remember that trails in Willmore Wilderness Park are not regularly maintained. These trails often lie in low, poorly drained areas, and with frequent rains a common occurrence, they become extremely muddy and unpleasant for hiking. In addition, mosquitoes and biting flies are rampant until things get drier.

Finally, the headwater regions of the Muskeg and Berland rivers are important summer range areas for bighorn sheep, mountain goat, grizzly bear and caribou. Heavy human use will only compromise the quality of these meadows and thus their usefulness as ranges.

For these reasons the trail, as described here to the North Berland River, is recommended as the prime section for foot travellers. However, if you should decide to visit these more remote areas, pick the driest time of the season and try to minimize impact.

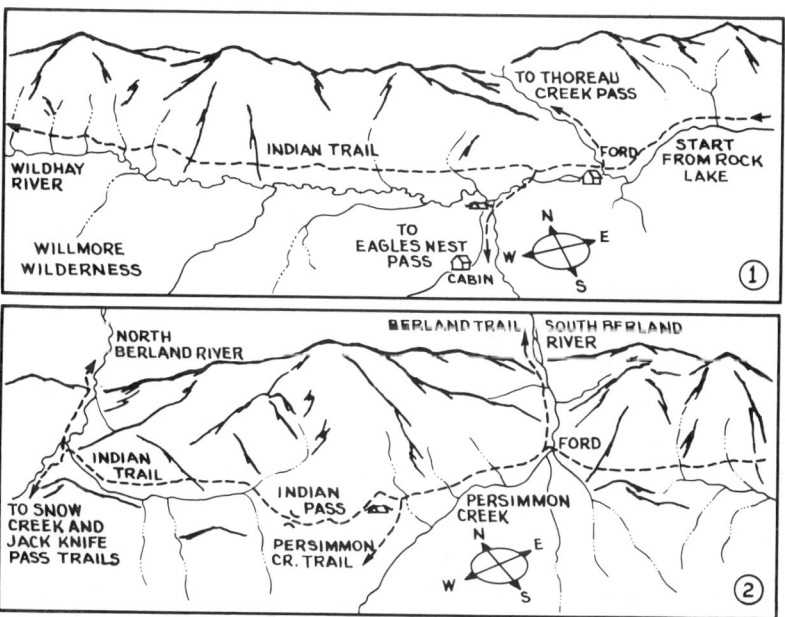

WILLMORE

91 Berland Trail

Distance: 35 km/22 mi round trip
Hiking time: 1-2 days
Elevation gain: 274 m/900 ft
High point: 1814 m/5950 ft
Type: long day hike or backpack
Best time: mid-July through September
Map: Adams Lookout 83 E/10 E

Spend a few hours or a few days exploring this river valley trail that bisects the Hoff and Berland ranges. Though it is used primarily as a connecting link in a much longer trip, this trail offers pleasant views, good camps and plenty of nearby exploring for the casual hiker.

The nearly level trail can be accessed from either the Wildhay River and Indian trails (Hikes 85 and 90) at 27.5 km from Rock Lake or by hiking 8.5 km up the Adams Creek Trail (Hike 93). The trail is actually an old road in the process of reverting to a simple hoof and boot track. It gains less than 300 m over the entire distance as it follows the course of the Berland and South Berland rivers.

Though most river fords present no serious problem (or can be avoided altogether), the Berland River at the northern end of the trail can be extremely hazardous at high water and may put an abrupt end to further progress for foot travellers. Spring meltwater, early rains and poorly drained soils all add up to extremely soggy conditions, which respond to travellers with interminable mud. Horse packers may not be troubled by this, but hikers will find conditions more pleasant and insects less bothersome in late season.

Partly open, partly forested, the river valley takes an obvious route, though signs and bridges and other hiker-oriented conveniences are conspicuously absent. Cross-country enthusiasts will find many opportunities to wander up nearby hills and ridges of the Hoff and Berland ranges.

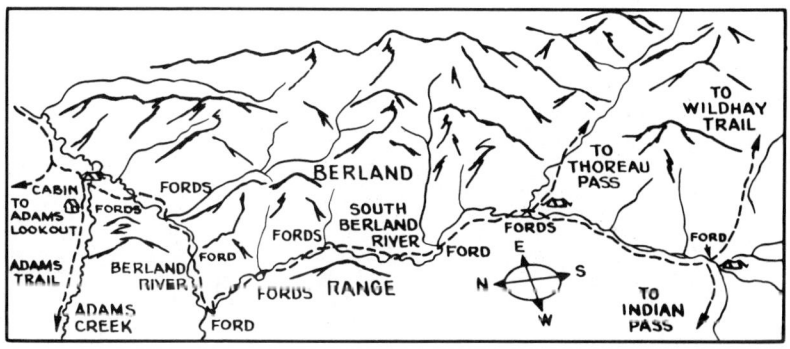

Left: *Northern end of Berland Trail*

WILLMORE

92 Persimmon Creek Trail

Distance: 14 km/8.6 mi round trip from South Berland River
Hiking time: 4 hours
Elevation gain: 152 m/500 ft
High point: 1996 m/6550 ft
Type: day hike or backpack
Best time: late July through mid-October
Map: Adams Lookout 83 E/10 E

Guarded by 2 massive limestone monoliths, the entrance to this remote wilderness valley leads to the innermost regions of the Persimmon Range. This is a perfect trail for those who seek that isolated refuge amid rugged high country where Rocky Mountain goats, bighorn sheep and caribou graze the surrounding tundra.

In the past, most visitors to this secluded valley have come on horseback,

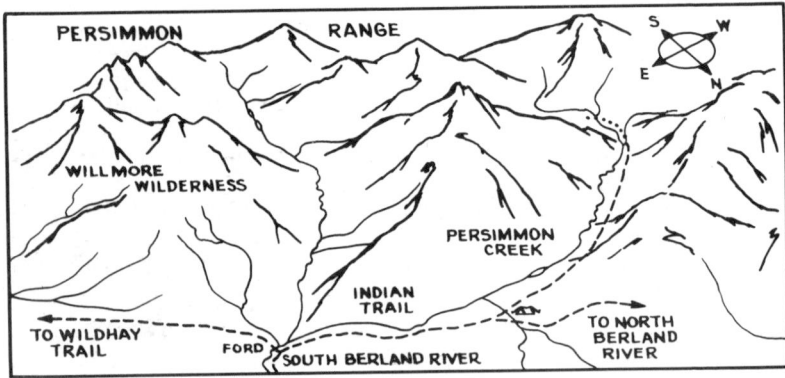

Ptarmigan in spring plumage

Persimmon Creek Valley

though more and more adventurers are making the trek on foot, waiting until mid-to-late summer to facilitate fords of the Wildhay and South Berland rivers.

See Hike 85 for driving instructions, then follow the Wildhay River Trail and then the Indian Trail (Hike 90) to the South Berland River. Make the ford and relocate the Indian Trail on the opposite bank. Follow it for 2.7 km more to the campsite and the junction with the Persimmon Creek Trail.

Travelling into the open valley below silvery, treeless peaks, the route makes a gentle descent to the creek where icy waters collect in tarns, then run off again through sparse clumps of spruce and fir. Above, rivers of scree pour down from severely sloping cliffbands—a stark contrast to the softly rounded foothills.

Continue for 4.3 km, where the valley terminates in a steep-walled basin. Near the valley end, patches of forest offer good camp spots for an extended stay in this mountainous retreat.

WILLMORE

93 Adams Creek Trail

Distance: 40 km/25 mi round trip
  to Cabin Creek Trail
Hiking time: 4 days
Elevation gain: 213 m/700 ft
High point: 1707 m/5600 ft
Type: backpack
Best time: mid-June through October
Maps: Moberly Creek 83 E/9, Adams
  Lookout 83 E/10 E

Not your typical wilderness trail, this one has cart tracks, trappers' cabins and elaborate outfitters' camps. Still, a peaceful, pastoral type of charm exists among these wide, rolling valleys and softly rounded hills of the northeastern Willmore Wilderness. Here is a refreshing alternative to highly regulated parks—an alternative that spotlights a popular scene in Alberta's pioneering history. The old trade route, once used almost exclusively by trappers and fur traders, travels through the broad and sparsely forested Berland River Valley for 8.5 km before branching to continue up the narrower Adams Creek channel.

Minimal elevation gain, gentle trails and the expansive nature of the Willmore make it ideal horse country and hikers can well expect to share these trails with local riders and outfitters. In summer the green valleys offer numerous camp and picnic spots, and fishing for Dolly Varden is a popular objective. In winter the ski-touring possibilities are unlimited and ideal.

From the intersection of Highways 16 and 40 (just west of Hinton), drive north on 40 for 74 km to the Big Berland Recreation Area. Turning left at the sign, follow the road 1 km to Big Berland Campground and continue another 0.5 km to the railroad tracks. Make a second left turn at the junction and proceed, passing an unmarked road on the right at 4 km.

The road becomes quite steep at 5.3 km and may present a problem for low-slung vehicles. But parking space is usually available here, as many horse trailers must unload at this point. Beyond the hill, the road improves somewhat. Pass another unmarked road at 6.6 km. At 7.2 km the road branches—horse traffic generally goes left, while hikers continue on to the end of the road (9.5 km), thereby avoiding a sometimes difficult ford of the Berland River.

From the parking area, walk around the gate and continue on the road, fording the few small creeks along the way. These may pose a challenge since the only bridges are crude, makeshift arrangements of rocks and foot-logs.

At 8.4 km, the trail meets with an excellent side trip to Adams Lookout (Hike 94).

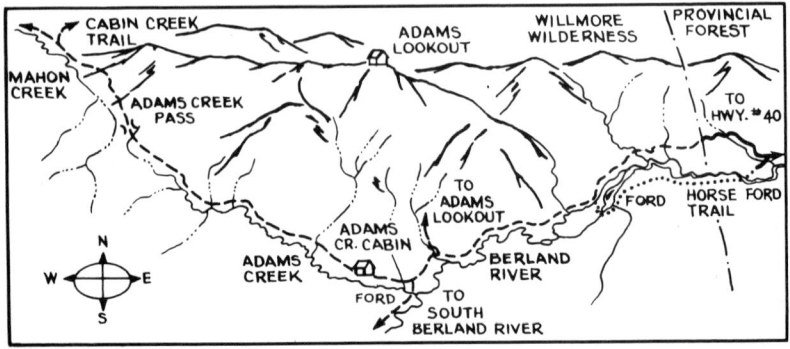

Adams Creek Valley

Just beyond, the Berland Trail (Hike 91) strays off to the left, while the main route continues on past the Adams Creek Cabin and up the Adams Creek Valley. Excellent camp spots are found in the valley flats and near the cabin for those wishing to explore the area or fish the Berland River.

For longer trips and more territory to discover, the Adams Creek Trail continues an additional 12.0 km to the Cabin Crook Trail and beyond the park boundary to the Mahon Creek Trail and the Muskeg River Trail. Gentle throughout, the trail follows a valley route below the Hoff Range to a low pass beyond the creek headwaters. Moving in and out of lodgepole forests and valley flats, the trail continues through peaceful scenery and easy terrain for the rest of the trip. This hike is especially nice for those who enjoy side-by-side wandering on wide, gentle paths, near sparkling streams that roll and tumble through meadows of wildflowers and waving grasses.

WILLMORE

94 Adams Lookout

Distance: 8.8 km/5.4 mi round
  trip from Adams Creek Trail
Hiking time: 4 hours
Elevation gain: 653 m/2143 ft
High point: 2177 m/7143 ft
Type: day hike
Best time: mid-June through September
Map: Adams Lookout 83 E/10E

A pleasant climb to the last remaining manned lookout station in Willmore Wilderness Park. Views are excellent and a visit during the summer months may include an interesting chat with the resident lookout. As a side trip from the Adams Creek Trail (Hike 93), the trip is a short (4.4 km), but steady climb from the Berland River, although it is not unreasonable to make the lookout trip from the Adams Creek trailhead parking area in 1 day. Either way, be sure to carry water on this dry and strenuous climb, as none is available after you leave the valley floor.

See Adams Creek Trail (Hike 93) for driving directions. The hike to the lookout begins at the 8.4-km point along the Adams Creek Trail and follows the old service road to the mountain top (2177 m). From the openness of the valley bottom, the trail quickly enters the pine forest and climbs determinedly, gaining 653 m in 4.4 km. As forest thins to subalpine scrub, the nearby Hoff and Berland ranges appear to the south.

The best is still to come, though. Leave the forest at 3 km and walk the remaining 1.4 km along the ridge, on a brightly flowered mat of alpine forget-me-nots, mountain avens, chickweed and many other wildflowers. These summit gardens are home for numerous marmot and squirrel families that cautiously peer at the alpine visitors and readily inspect any untended packs.

From this airy post, admire distant snow-capped peaks and rolling valleys with their intricate networks of rivers and streams. On a clear day the majestic crown of Mt. Robson is visible between 2 prominent peaks in the Persimmon Range, 80 km to the southwest.

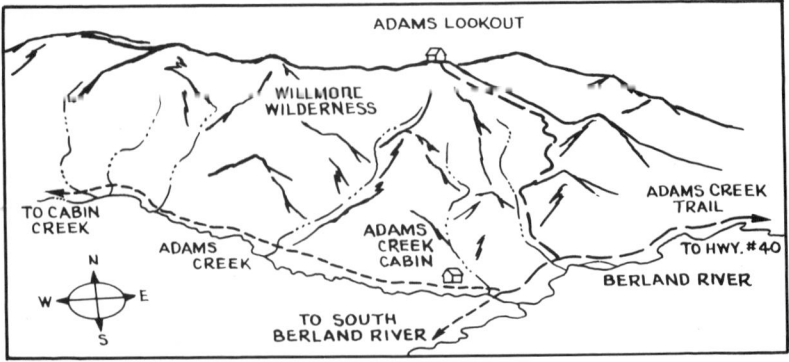

Assistant fire watcher at Adams Lookout

INDEX

Adams Creek trail   219
Adams Lookout   220
Adolphus Lake   191
All Soul's Alpine Route   69
Amethyst Lakes   113, 115, 119
Amiskwi Falls   35
Amiskwi Pass   35
Amiskwi River   34
Angel Glacier   110
Angel's Staircase Falls   48
Arrowhead Lake   117
Astoria River   112
Athabasca Pass   108
Athabasca River   94
Azure Lake   137

Bald Hills Lookout   163
Beauty Creek   78
Beaver Dam Nature Trail   24
Beaver Lake   148
Berg Lake   137, 191, 194, 197, 198
Berg Lake Trail   194
Berland Trail   209, 215
Berland River   215, 219
Big Larch Trail   60, 69
Big Shovel Pass   100, 146, 160
Brazeau Lake   82
Brazeau River   74, 85, 153
Burgess Pass   41, 44

Cabin Lakes   169
Cairn River   153
Caledonia Lake   166, 168
Calumet Creek   191
Cataract Brook   56
Cataract Pass   74
Cathedral Basin   59
Cavell Lake   112
Cavell Meadows   110
Celeste, Lake   50
Celestine Lake   133
Centre Pass   183
Chaba River   94
Christine Lake   180
Chrome Lake   117
Colonel Creek   191
Committee Punch Bowl   109
Cottonwood Creek   173, 174
Curator Lake   101, 160

Devona Lookout   132
Dorothy Lake   180
Duchesnay Basin   59
Duchesnay Creek   57

Eagles Nest Pass   210
Edith Cavell, Mt.   110
Emerald Basin   42
Emerald Lake   30, 38, 41, 42
Emerald Lake High Circuit   40
Emerald Lake Shoreline Loop   38
Emerald River   30
Eremite Valley   117
Evelyn Creek   159

Fiddle River   124, 126
Fitzwilliam, Mt.   186
Float Creek   28
Fortress Lake Trail   94
Four Point campsite   75, 85, 86
Fryatt Creek   102
Fryatt Lake   103

Geraldine Lakes   104
Geraldine Lookout   107
Giddie Creek   28
Glacier View Loop   48
Grand View Prospect   64
Great Divide Trail   28

Hamilton Falls   36
Hamilton Lake   36
Hibernia Lake   166
Hidden Lakes   46
High Lakes   169
Highline Trail   50
Hoodoo Creek   24
Hoodoos, The   24
Hungabee Lake   69
Hunter, Mt., Lookout   22

Ice River Trail   26
Indian Pass   213
Indian Trail   212

Jack Knife Pass   213
Jacques Creek   129
Jacques Lake   148, 150
John-John Creek   82
Jonas Pass Trail   86

King, Mt., Lookout   33
Kinney Lake   195

Laughing Falls   49
Linda Lake Loop   58
Little Shovel Pass   160
Little Yoho River   49
Little Yoho Valley Trail   48, 50
Lorraine Lake   159
Lower Sunwapta Falls   93

Maccarib Pass   115
Maligne Canyon   144
Maligne Lakeshore   154
Maligne Pass   88
Maligne River   88, 144
Marjorie Lake   166
Mary Lake   69
McArthur Creek   28, 62
McArthur, Lake, Circuit   60
McArthur Pass   60, 62, 65
Meadow Creek Trail   115
Medicine Tent River   152
Merlin Creek   128
Middle Whirlpool River   108
Miette Lake   183
Miette River   182
Mina Lake   170

Minaga Creek   181
Minnow Lake   168
Moat Lake   119
Mollison Creek   27
Mona Lake   159
Moose Lake   164
Moose Pass   191
Moose River   190
Moosehorn Creek   138
Moosehorn Lakes   139
Morning Glory Creek   59
Morro Creek   131
Mystery Lake   124

Nigel Pass   74
North Berland River   213
North Boundary Trail   134
Notch, The   160

O'Hara Lake   56, 58, 60, 62, 66, 68
Odaray/Grand View Prospect   64
Odaray Highline Trail   65
Oesa, Lake   66
Old Fort Point   99, 178
Opabin Lakes   68
Opal Hills Loop   157
Otterhead River   32
Ottertail River   28
Outpost Lake   116
Overlander Falls   192
Overlander Trail   131

Paget Lookout   52
Palisade Lookout   176
Patricia Lake   173
Penstock Creek   117
Persimmon Creek   217
Poboktan Creek   80
Poboktan Pass   82
Point Lace Falls   48
Poligne Creek   81, 91
Pope Creek   208
Portal Creek   115
Prairie de la Vache   101
Presidential High Route   50
Pyramid Lake Trails   174

Resplendent Creek   191
Riley Lake   170
Robson, Mt.   137, 197, 198
Rock Creek   204, 211
Rock Lake Lookout   206
Rocky River   152
Ross Lake   70

Saturday Night Lake   168
Schaffer Lake   60, 65, 69
Sherbrooke Lake   54
Signal Mountain Lookout   142
Skyline Trail   50, 143, 159
Snake Indian Falls   136
Snake Indian Pass   137
Snake Indian River   204
Snowbird Pass   198
Snowbowl   160
South Berland River   212, 215

South Boundary Trail   128, 149, 150
Southesk Pass   153
Stanley Mitchell Hut   51
Steppe Creek   191
Sulphur Skyline   122
Summit Lakes   149

Tangle Creek   76
Tekarra Lake   161
Thoreau Creek   208
Thoreau Pass   208
Toboggan Falls   197
Tocher Lookout   33
Tonquin Valley   112, 114
Twin Falls   49
Twintree Lake   137

Valley of the Five Lakes   98
Vine Creek   140
Virl Lake   180

Wabasso Lake   96
Wabasso Lakes   100
Wapta Falls   20
Watchtower Basin   146
Whaleback Trail   48
Whirlpool River   108
Whistlers, The   120
Whitehorse Pass   127
Wilcox Pass   76
Wildhay River   202, 212
Willow Creek Trail   204
Wiwaxy Alpine Route   66

Yellowhead Mountain   188
Yoho Pass   41
Yoho Lake   41, 46
Yoho Lake Loop   46
Yoho Valley Trail   48, 50